Guide to
Aegean and
Mediterranean
Turkey

by Diana Darke

Some other guides published by Michael Haag

Guide to Eastern Turkey and the Black Sea Coast
Guide to Egypt
Guide to Cairo
Guide to Greece
Guide to West Africa
Guide to East Africa
Guide to Rajasthan
Guide to North Yemen
Guide to Ethnic London

Please send for our complete list: Michael Haag Limited, PO Box 369, London
NW3 4ER, England

Guide to Aegean and Mediterranean Turkey, second edition

Cover design by Colin Elgie

Photo credits: Diana Darke, pages 103, 117, 119, 177, 189, 195, 203, 225, 235,
251; Michael Haag, pages 11, 31, 33, 35, 49, 79, 83, 88, 95, 109, 127; Turkish
Tourist Office, London, pages 59, 99, 145, 149, 151, 163, 165, 167, 217, 259, 269,
275, 281, 287; Scala/Firenze, page 207

Text © 1987 by Diana Darke

Typeset by Witwell Limited, 92 The Albany, Old Hall Street, Liverpool L3 9EJ

Printed in Great Britain by litho at the Bath Press, Lower Bristol Road, Bath
BA2 3BL

Published by Michael Haag Limited, PO Box 369, London NW3 4ER, England

ISBN 0 902743 68 6

CONTENTS

Practical Information sections follow each chapter, and there is an index at the rear.

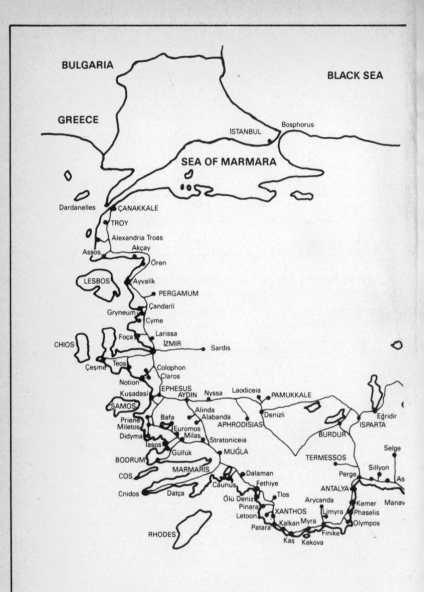

BULGARIA

BLACK SEA

GREECE

İSTANBUL   Bosphorus

SEA OF MARMARA

Dardanelles   ÇANAKKALE

TROY

Alexandria Troas

Akçay

Assos

Ören

LESBOS   Ayvalık

PERGAMUM

Gryneum   Çandarlı

Cyme

Larissa

Foça

İZMIR   Sardis

CHIOS

Çeşme   Teos

Colophon

Notion   Claros

Kuşadası   EPHESUS

AYDIN   Nyssa   Laodiceia   PAMUKKALE

SAMOS

Alinda

Priene   Bafa   Alabanda

Miletos   Euromos   APHRODISIAS   Denizli

Didyma   Milas

İasos   Stratoniceia

Güllük

BODRUM   MUĞLA

COS   MARMARİS

Cnidos   Datça

Caunus

Ölü Deniz

Pinara

Dalaman

Fethiye

Tlos

Letoon

Kalkan   Myra

Patara

Kaş   Kekova

RHODES

Denizli

BURDUR

ISPARTA

Eğridir

TERMESSOS

Selge

Perge   Sillyon

ANTALYA   As

Arycanda

Kemer   Manav

Limyra   Phaselis

Finike   Olympos

AEGEAN and
MEDITERRANEAN TURKEY
showing sites covered in this book

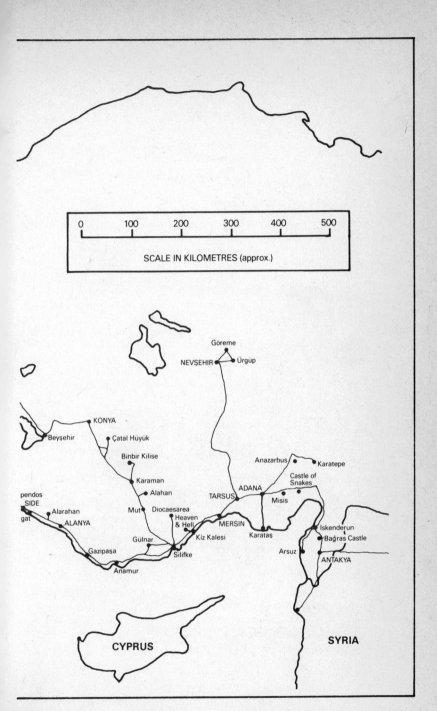

SCALE IN KILOMETRES (approx.)

0   100   200   300   400   500

Göreme
NEVŞEHIR   Ürgüp

KONYA
Beyşehir
Çatal Hüyük
Binbir Kilise
Anazarbus   Karatepe
Karaman   Castle of Snakes
Alahan   ADANA
TARSUS   Misis
pendos   Mut   Diocaesarea
SIDE   Alarahan   Heaven & Hell
gat   ALANYA   MERSIN
Gülnar   Kiz Kalesi   Karataş   Iskenderun
Gazipaşa   Silifke   Bağras Castle
Anamur   Arsuz   ANTAKYA

CYPRUS   SYRIA

5

ABOUT THIS GUIDE

The Aegean coast of Turkey has been growing quickly in popularity. It offers good beaches, outstanding archaeological sites and, like the rest of the country, is very inexpensive. The enthusiasm for the Aegean is now extending to Turkey's long Mediterranean coastline, largely undiscovered and entirely unspoilt, where the landscape is exceptionally beautiful, the ancient sites marvellously situated and the beaches among the best in the world.

This is the only guide to concentrate on these warm-water areas of Turkey. Many guide books have attempted to cover the whole of the country and have necessarily suffered from thin descriptions and entire omissions. This book corrects that by recognising that 80 percent of visitors to Turkey explore the Aegean and Mediterranean shores and require a detailed guide focusing on these coastlines.

Here you will find full descriptions of all the major sites, archaeological and natural, together with coverage of a great many smaller but equally rewarding places all too often not even mentioned in other guides. The author has discovered that many site plans published elsewhere are misleading, sometimes because continuing excavations have made them out of date, and she has made her own site sketches on the spot. Though simple, they have the virtue of being correct and immediately intelligible to the layman.

In addition to this *Guide to Aegean and Mediterranean Turkey*, the publishers have issued a *Guide to Eastern Turkey and the Black Sea Coast* by the same author. Together these provide the most comprehensive and up-to-date guides to Turkey available.

This guide is aimed principally at the independent traveller, preferably with a car, and contains *Practical Information* on accommodation, food, travel, etc, at the end of each section, as well as providing general information in the *Background* chapter. Readers are invited to contribute additional material or help update existing detail by writing to the *Area Editor for Turkey, Michael Haag Limited, PO Box 369, London NW3 4ER, England*. Thank you.

BACKGROUND

Image and reality

The usual reaction after a first visit to Turkey is surprise; surprise that a country with so much to offer should have remained so long undiscovered by tourism. Its problem has not been one of distance but of image. Turkey has long been regarded by the west as a dark, unsafe, barbaric land of guaranteed stomach upsets. Now, as more and more visitors from North America and Europe are discovering the country that image is gradually being dispelled as newcomers increasingly marvel at the wonder which is Turkey.

The best of Mediterranean climates

Turkey is a vast and varied country, six times bigger than Greece yet with 50 percent fewer inhabitants per square kilometre. It shares borders with Greece, Bulgaria, the USSR, Iran, Iraq and Syria, and this geographical position means it is neither European nor Asian, nor Middle Eastern, having traces of all three, yet distinct from them. It has the longest coastline and cleanest beaches of any Mediterranean country, and is unquestionably the richest in terms of ancient remains, reaching back to the Stone Age and the Hittites, through to its wealth of ancient Greek and Roman cities, and later its beautiful Byzantine, Seljuk and Ottoman monuments. Science, medicine, philosophy, history, geography, epic and lyric poetry and town planning all had their beginnings on Turkey's Aegean coast, while eastern Anatolia brought us such experiments with agriculture as wine and the domestication of animals. Scenically it is spectacular, ranging from green fertile hills and valleys and flat river plains, to wild rocky mountains and barren plateaux. In antiquity it was privileged in being the site of two of the seven Wonders of the World, and today it has many natural wonders, such as the rock waterfalls and springs of Pamukkale and the stone carved lunar landscapes of Cappadocia. Its coastline caters for all tastes, with long flat sandy beaches, sheltered sandy bays, tiny pebble coves, or dramatic rocky shores with cliffs rising behind. It has the best of Mediterranean climates, warmer and more reliable than Spain or Greece, but not as sweltering as Tunisia or Morocco. On top of all this it has excellent cheap food and drink and friendly people. Nothing is missing from this perfect holiday equation.

Where to Go for Information

In almost every town of any size in Turkey you will find a Tourist Information Office run by the Ministry of Culture and Tourism. These are generally stocked with maps, town plans and summarised leaflets for the regions given free of charge, and their staff will also help you with any special local information you require.

Before any trip to Turkey it is well worth visiting the Turkish Tourist Office in your own country. If it is not practicable to visit, then you can phone them and they will answer questions and gladly send you free of charge all the leaflets and maps you ask for. Particularly useful is their mini-booklet called *Turkey: Travel Guide* which, apart from listing all the state-registered hotels, also provides summarised practical information with many useful addresses.

In Britain the Turkish Tourist Office is at Egyptian House, 170 Piccadilly, London W1; Tel: 01-734 8681.

In the USA the address is 821 United Nations Plaza, New York, NY 10017; Tel: (212) 687-2194.

There are also Turkish Tourist Offices in Paris, Brussels, Amsterdam, Copenhagen, Vienna, Frankfurt, Munich Zürich, Rome, Madrid, Stockholm, Tokyo, Kuwait and Jeddah.

Getting to Turkey

By air İstanbul, Ankara, İzmir, Adana, Antalya and Dalaman are all international airports. Antalya and Dalaman are largely used in the summer months by charter flights. Turkish Airlines (Türk Hava Yollari-THY) links all the major Turkish airports with the major European cities, the Middle East and North Africa. Flying time from London to İzmir is around 3½ hours. From the USA connecting flights via Europe are plentiful.

If your local travel agent looks rather blank when you ask about travel to Turkey, visit or phone the Turkish Tourist Office and ask for their list of travel agents and tour operators specialising in Turkey. Some of these specialise in flights only, some in fly-drive, but the list will be comprehensive and detailed, so by making a few phone calls you can easily get some comparative quotes for fares.

By sea If you are driving from Europe in your own car, you can spare yourself some driving and arrive suitably rested by taking one of three car ferries:

From Venice
British Ferries Limited (20 Upper Ground, London SE1 9PF; Tel: 01-928 5550) runs a service from early May to the end of October, leaving Venice on Saturdays at 6 pm, arriving in İstanbul on Tuesdays at 9 am or in Kuşadasí on Wednesdays at 10.30 am. Prices are from £175 per passenger (including cabin, meals and port taxes) and cars from £130.

From Ancona
Turkish Maritime Lines (TML) runs a service from June to September leaving Ancona in the morning on Saturdays, arriving in İzmir in the morning on Tuesdays. Fares are similar to the Venice ferry. In Britain, contact the TML agents: Walford Lines Limited, Ibec House, 42–47 Minores, London EC3N 1AE; Tel: 01-480 5621.

From Brindisi or Piraeus

Libra Maritime, a Greek company, runs car ferries three days a week in summer connecting Brindisi, Patras, Piraeus and İzmir in 40 hours, leaving Piraeus on Mondays, Wednesdays, and Fridays at 8 pm, and leaving İzmir on Tuesdays, Thursdays and Sundays at 2 pm.

Libra in Piraeus: Plateia Loudovicou 4; Tel: (1) 411 7864.

Libra in Brindisi: 54 Corso Garibaldi; Tel: 21 935 28 004.

From the Greek islands there are ferries from Lesbos, Chios, Samos, Kos and Rhodes running to the Turkish mainland, though not much advertised. The only formality is handing in your passport 24 hours before the trip, which is then returned to you when you board. The service from Rhodes to Marmaris is daily in summer, as is the service from Samos to Kuşadasí. Boats from Lesbos to Ayvalik, Chios to Cesme, and Kos to Bodrum are not daily, but at least two or three times a week in summer. See the *Practical Information* section at the back of the relevant chapter for further details.

Turkish Maritime Lines ferries also run regularly from Turkish Cyprus to the Turkish mainland: from Taşacu near Silifke to Kyrenia three times a week, and from Mersin to Famagusta also three times a week (see the *Practical Information* section of the relevant chapter).

By train Trans-European trains to Turkey, once they reach Yugoslavia, are crowded, uncomfortable, dirty, often late, and generally not to be recommended.

By bus There are several companies offering coach runs from major French, Italian and German cities. They take two to three days each way and are very cramped. For most people the slightly lower cost does not compensate for the extra time lost in getting there.

Passports

No visa is required for any national of Western Europe, the US, Canada, Australia, New Zealand or Japan; a valid passport permits a stay of up to three months. British Visitors Passports (available from the Post Office) are valid for visitors arriving by air.

Vaccinations

No vaccinations are required.

The People

Turkish people show a genuine hospitality to visitors which is rare these days. 'The guest comes from God' is an old Turkish proverb. You will find them helpful and friendly, yet never thrusting their company on you. You will not normally be pestered and hassled to buy goods, nor will you be asked for money or baksheesh. Their friendliness is summed up by their phrase for goodbye: *Güle güle*, meaning Go with a smile.

9

Religion

Over 95 percent of Turks are Moslems, but as Turkey since the 1920s and Atatürk has been a secular state, non-Moslems are guaranteed complete freedom of worship. During Ramadan there is no problem, unlike in many of the Arab Moslem countries, with being served food and drink during the day. Life continues as always, except in the particularly holy cities like Konya. The usual rules apply for visiting mosques, where legs should be covered and women should cover their hair. Apart from the great mosques in İstanbul and other large cities, many will be found to be closed, opening only at the five times of daily prayer. Loose robes are provided in the larger, more famous mosques if you are unsuitably dressed.

Economy

Turkey is a predominantly agricultural economy, with 57 percent of its population living in the countryside. Main crops are wheat, cotton, tobacco and fruit. The main export earner is cotton, and with abundant sheep Turkey is Europe's main wool producer. Among the widespread economic reforms introduced by Prime Minister Turgut Ozal since he took office in 1983, two priorities have been privatisation of state-owned concerns and an ambitious programme of capital infrastructure construction. Both of these will serve to develop the growing tourist industry which Turkey is now keen to encourage.

The Language

Turkish derives from a Turco-Tartar language group called Ural-Altaic, a distinction it shares with Hungarian and Finnish. A language of nomadic tribesmen from Central Asia, **Nomad origins** it had a wealth of vocabulary for describing livestock and weather conditions. But this vocabulary was inadequate for coping with the complexities of civilised urban life the Turks discovered in the countries they conquered. So they borrowed the bulk of their abstract and intellectual vocabulary from Arabic (about 40 percent of the language, similar to the position of French in medieval English), and borrowed from Persian most words to do with crafts, trades and their associated objects. With the Turks' conversion to Islam and their adoption of the Arabic alphabet, their language became increasingly artificial. The Arabic alphabet was never suited to Turkish, being based on three root consonants with vowels generally left out, whereas vowels and vowel harmony are crucial to Turkish grammar.

Atatürk's reforms When Atatürk came to power in the early 1920s he set about removing foreign influences in the language, and tried to find Turkish substitutes for Arabic and Persian words. He also abandoned the Arabic alphabet and adopted the Latin alphabet in use today. Along with many other of Atatürk's

A Turkish café

reforms, the effect was to shift Turkey away from the East and towards Europe. But this led to some problems in communication between generations, where even today there are grandparents who grew up with Arabic and Persian words while their grandchildren at school are taught a new vocabulary. The language reform also had the effect of greatly simplifying the over-elaborate use of language so favoured under the Ottomans. For example, the modern Turkish civil servant will now write: 'I have been thinking about your suggestion'. His Ottoman predecessor would have written: 'Your slave has been engaged in the exercise of cogitation in respect of the proposals vouchsafed by your exalted person'.

English and German (because of the many Turkish Gastarbeiter in Germany) are widely understood.

Coping with Turkish

Pronunciation

Vowels and consonants are pronounced as in English, except for: ö = oe (Göereme); u = as in French *tu*; ı = the dotless ı which is peculiar to Turkish and is pronounced as the initial 'a' in 'away' (Topkapí = Topkapeu) — *note that in this book it has been necessary to indicate this letter with an accented í*; c = j (cami, meaning mosque = jami); ç = ch (Foça = Focha); ş = sh (Kuşadasí = kushadaseu); ğ is unpronounced, but lengthens the preceding vowel (dağ, meaning mountain = daa); h is always pronounced; e on the end of a word is always pronounced, so Pamukkale has four syllables. Stress falls evenly over the syllables in Turkish rather than being concentrated on one syllable as tends to be the case in English.

Greetings

For simple greetings in Turkey, you need only know two things: when you arrive somewhere you will be greeted by *Hoş geldeniz* (welcome), to which you reply *Hoş bulduk* (happy to be here); when you leave, those staying behind will say to you *Güle güle* (go with a smile), to which you, as the person leaving, reply *Allaha ísmarladík* (we have committed ourselves to God) — a bit of a mouthful, but worth practising as it will go down very well.

Food and drink

Other words and phrases (all given in their true Turkish spelling) you may find useful are:

breakfast	*kahvaltí*
eggs	*yumurta*
tea	*çay*
more tea	*daha çay*
coffee	*kahve*
milk	*süt*
sugar	*şeker*
bread	*ekmek*
butter	*tereyağ*
jam	*reçel*
cheese	*peynir*

soup	*çorba*
salad	*salata*
tomato	*domates*
fish	*balık*
chips	*patates*
fruit	*meyva*
ice cream	*dondurma*
cake	*pasta*
packed lunch	*piknik*
salt	*tuz*
pepper	*biber*
water	*su*
mineral water	*maden suyu*
hot water	*sıcak su*
fruit juice	*meyva suyu*
beer	*bira*
wine	*şarap*
red wine	*kırmızı şarap*
white wine	*beyaz şarap*
dry	*sek*
sweet	*tatlı*

Practical situations

hello	*merhaba*
yes	*evet*
no	*hayır*
please	*lütfen*
thank you	*teşekkur ederim*
very beautiful	*çok güzel*
how much?	*ne kadar?*
cheap	*ucuz*
expensive	*pahalı*
money	*para*
bank	*banka*
post office	*postane*
chemist	*eczane*
hospital	*hastahane*
police	*polis*
ticket office	*gişe*
toilet	*tuvalet*
gents	*baylar*
ladies	*bayanlar*

Travel

shared taxi	*dolmuş*
private car	*özel oto/araba*
good road	*iyi yol*
bad road	*bozuk yol*
road closed	*yol kapalı*
no entry	*girilmez*
attention	*dikkat*
stop	*dur*
right	*sağ*
left	*sol*
where?	*nerede?*
bus	*otobus*
ship/ferry	*vapur/feribot*

small boat	*sandal/kayík (ie caïque)*
motor boat	*motörbot*
to let/hire	*kiralík*
room	*oda*
forbidden	*yasak*
forbidden zone	*yasak bölge*

Here are also some words you will not use, but will see so often on signs at the side of the road that not knowing what they mean will drive you insane:

Road signs *Karayollarí* (+ numbers): Highways Department, ie that number department is responsible for looking after the roads at this point.

Orman: forest or wood

Dinar-il Siniri: province boundary of Dinar

Money and Currency

The unit of currency is the Turkish lira. Coins are rare, and notes come as 5, 10, 20, 50, 100, 500, 1000, 5000 and 10,000 lira.

Inflation The inflation rate in Turkey is high, between 35 and 50 percent, but the exchange rate moves to balance this so that in practice the cost of holidaying in Turkey for foreign visitors has remained fairly static over the last three years. The exchange rate within Turkey is better than outside, so apart from a small sum you may wish to change in advance, the remainder should be taken in travellers cheques and changed at banks in the normal manner. Many hotels (certainly 3-star and above, as well as many 2-star ones) also change travellers cheques and do not charge commission.

Credit cards The bigger hotels (3-star and upwards), international car hire agencies like Hertz and Avis, and the more expensive shops in cities will usually accept American Express, Diners Club, Visa, Access and Eurocard, though unless you are always staying in the top class hotels, it is best not to rely on them but rather to take them as a fall-back. They are not in general use in the more rural areas.

Shopping

Turkey is not a country where souvenir buying for friends and relations is a problem. There are of course rugs and carpets which though they may appear expensive are still considerably cheaper than the price you would have to pay at home. Bargaining is normal if the price is not marked, and as a rough guideline you should be aiming to knock a third off the first price given. To bargain successfully an air of complete indifference to the object being haggled over is essential. Once you make the fatal error of showing, either through your facial expression or the tone of your voice, that you like something, you are doomed to the losing end of the bargaining.

In some shops the prices are stuck on the items in which case you can only expect a reduction if you are buying more than one item. Alabaster in many unusual colours like green and grey for vases, ashtrays, chess pieces, etc; pottery; hand-painted tiles; ceramics; copper dishes, trays, bowls; inlaid wooden boxes; interesting cheap jewellery, both gold and silver with attractive semi-precious stones like amber, amethyst, lapis lazuli, jade and onyx; leather shoes, bags, cushions, wallets, clothes: these are just some examples of what you will find. If you buy any real antiques, beware that there are severe penalties for attempting to export them without permission.

Opening Hours
Turkey shares with Europe the Saturday and Sunday weekend.
Banks: 8.30–12.00   13.30–17.00   (closed Saturday and Sunday)
Shops: 9.00–13.00   14.00–19.00 (closed Sunday)
Museums: All close Mondays but are open on all other days. The exception is the Topkapí Palace Museum which closes on Tuesdays.

Time
GMT + 2 all the year round, ie one hour ahead when Britain is on Summer Time.

Calendar of Festivals and Public Holidays
Turkey follows the official Gregorian calendar like Europe, and so has weekends of Saturday and Sunday in the same way. However, being a predominantly Moslem country it celebrates the major Islamic festivals. The dates for these festivals are not fixed in our Gregorian calendar but are timed according to the lunar system which is 11 days shorter per year than our solar one. For example the dates for the months of *Ramadan* are approximately from 29 April to 28 May in 1987 and from 18 April to 17 May in 1988.

Lunar calendar

There are two major Islamic holidays, the approximate equivalents if you like of our Christmas and Easter. The first is the Feast of the Sacrifice (Turkish *Kurban Bayrami*) which commemorates Abraham's willingness to sacrifice his son Isaac. Each family buys an animal for sacrifice according to his means (usually a sheep, or a very rich person might buy a camel) and then it is cooked and much of the meat is given to the poor. It is a national four-day holiday, occurring in 1987 from about 4 to 7 August. Most banks close for a full week and everyone is on holiday.

The second celebrates the end of the month of fasting in Ramadan and is called in Turkish *Şeker Bayrami*. It is a three-day national holiday when much visiting of friends and family and feasting takes place to make up for the deprivation of the previous month.

During both of these major festivals, especially when they fall in the summer as they do at the moment, Turks pour out in a mass exodus from the cities to the coast, packing the resort towns all along the Aegean and Mediterranean to bursting. This is the only time you will experience difficulties in finding accommodation, and for this reason, if you are on a touring holiday, it can be wiser to plan to be inland for the duration of one of these festivals. The inland lakes like Eğridir remain surprisingly uncrowded during the festivals, so they can be an ideal spot to stay if you are keen to continue swimming.

January: Camel wrestling continues most of the month from early December onwards throughout the province of Aydín.

15–16 January: Camel wrestling festival in Selçuk Ephesus Festival of Culture and Art with folk dancing, concerts and some performances held in the Roman theatre at Ephesus.

Last week of May: Pergamum Festival. Plays and folk dancing held in the Asklepieion theatre.

First week in June: İzmir Mediterranean Festival, with folk dancing and music.

7 to 13 June: Music and Art Festival at Marmaris.

29 to 31 July: Foça, north of İzmir, folklore and watersports festival.

15 to 18 August: Çanakkale Troy Festival, folk dances, music, tours of Mt Ida and Troy.

20 August to 20 September: İzmir International Fair. Amusements fair with cultural and commercial/industrial exhibits. The city's hotels are packed during this month when İzmir is best avoided.

1 to 9 September: Bodrum Culture and Art Week, with concerts in Bodrum castle, local craft exhibits and watersports shows.

21 to 25 September: Cappadocia Festival, grape harvest celebration and folkloric festival.

15 September to 5 October: Mersin Fashion and Textile Show, with music and folklore.

1 to 9 October: Antalya Film and Art Festival, some performances in the Roman theatre at Aspendos.

29 October: Republic Day, to commemorate the proclamation of the republic by Atatürk in 1923.

6 to 8 December: St Nicholas festival in Demre.

9 to 17 December: Mevlana Festival at Konya. Hotels are packed for this, the only occasion in the year when the Whirling Dervishes can be seen performing.

December: Camel wrestling begins in December and continues till the end of January throughout the province of Aydín, especially at Germencik.

Electricity
220 volts all over Turkey, from continental 2-pin plugs.

Climate
The best time to visit Turkey is between May and September. The tourist season in the coastal regions runs from 1 April to 31 October. May, early June and September are the ideal times for touring; July and August can be a bit hot for clambering round sites in the midday sun. Average midday temperatures in degrees Fahrenheit/Celsius:

İstanbul region:

March	April	May	June	July	August
52/11	61/16	70/21	77/25	82/28	82/28
September		October		November	
74/23		66/19		60/16	

Aegean region:

March	April	May	June	July	August
61/16	65/18	75/24	82/28	88/31	90/32
September		October		November	
80/27		73/23		68/20	

Southern coast (Antalya):

March	April	May	June	July	August
64/18	68/20	75/24	84/29	89/32	93/34
September		October		November	
85/29		76/24		73/23	

To convert Fahrenheit into Celsius, subtract 32, multiply by 5, divide by 9. To convert Celsius into Fahrenheit, multiply by 9, divide by 5, add 32.

Clothing
Comfortable informal clothing should be worn and a comfortable pair of shoes for exploring ruins. Evenings cool off a lot, especially inland, even in July and August, so a pullover or warm jacket is needed. Sun hats are advisable in the hot summer months. Normal swimwear, including bikinis (but not ultra-brief), can be worn. Toplessness is not the custom on public beaches.

Watersports
Waterskiing and windsurfing facilities are available for hire in season (about June to October inclusive) in Foça, Çeşme, Kuşadsí, Bodrum, Marmaris, Ölü Deniz, Alanya and Side. Enterprising souls, often Germans or Gastarbeiter Turks, hire the equipment out at very reasonable prices on the main beaches.

Wildlife
Creepy-crawlies Mosquitoes are the main form you are likely to encounter. They are no worse than in any other Mediterranean country, but in summer from May to October it is worth going prepared with insect repellent lotion for sparing legs and

ankles while eating out of doors in the evenings. Better still, if you are staying in hotels or pensions, there will always be a two-pin socket where you can plug in the marvellous vapour mats (called *Esem*, *Sivrisinek Kovucu* in Turkish and available from most chemists in the country) with the tablets that guarantee mosquito-free nights, even with all the windows wide open.

Still on insects, butterflies are, despite abundant greenery and flowers, not very plentiful in the coastal regions. In the mountains slightly inland, however, you can see the occasional rare white admiral or even purple emperor. The abundance of pink oleander bushes means that the oleander hawk moth is quite common, but will only be seen on the wing at night.

Scorpions and snakes are not abundant but do exist, so it is worth being careful when walking with lightly-sandalled feet and bare legs through rougher land or undergrowth where not many people will have passed regularly.

... and camels

The usual domesticated sheep, cows and above all goats are everywhere as well a certain number of camels. The camels are both of the Bactrian one-humped variety, and also, in the winter, you may see the shaggier two-humped variety. Wild mountain goat, moufflon-like, can also be seen in mountain areas like Termessos, and the site guardian will delight in pointing them out at dusk high in the hills. His practised eyes can spot them at a great distance but you will have more chance with binoculars.

Useful Items to Take

Soap is not always provided at hotels, though towels are. Bring your own suntan potions, toothpaste and medicines, as you may not find the brands you want in Turkey. Bring an initial supply of toilet paper, and keep yourself stocked with it as you travel — amazing how useful it can be and how often it is not there. Bring also a flashlight, useful in exploring dark caves or the toilet when the light has blown out. It is cheaper to bring film with you, and if you want coffee, bring your own jarful, as it can be difficult to find in Turkey and is always expensive.

Toilet paper, and more toilet paper!

Accommodation

The inflation rate in Turkey is very high, recently between 35 and 50 percent, so that in the space of a few weeks prices as expressed in Turkish lira will rise right before your eyes. But the exchange rate moves to balance this: you will get more lira for your dollar or pound. In fact over the past several years the cost of holidaying in Turkey has remained unchanged for foreign visitors.

The exchange rate within Turkey is better than outside, so apart from a small sum you may wish to change abroad in advance, the remainder should be taken to Turkey as travellers cheques or cash and changed at banks or at hotels as you go along. Hotels do not charge a commission for this service.

The dollar   Because of this high rate of inflation it would be ridiculous to offer any hotel or other prices expressed as Turkish lira in this book. Instead, where prices are mentioned at all, they are given in US dollars. Sometimes the Turks will themselves express room rates (or car hire rates, etc) in dollars.

Hotel rating system and prices   The range of accommodation in Turkey is enormous, from luxury complexes down to small family-run pensions. In the Ministry of Culture and Tourism's own listings the grading of accommodation is somewhat random, and far from comprehensive as well. Many good hotels and pensions choose not to be registered: in Side, for example, only two establishments appear in the official listings whereas there are over 40 hotels and 40 pensions there. The distinction between hotels and motels is blurred as many establishments calling themselves motels are in fact perfectly normal hotels, not chalet- or bungalow-style accommodation. In view of the general confusion in the official system, this guide dispenses with Turkish classifications in favour of its own star-rating system reflecting the level of comfort and standard of facilities offered. The following prices are the average cost of a double room with breakfast included.

5-star is a luxury hotel with full facilities: $77 to $91.

4-star is a very good hotel with above-average facilities: $63 to $77.

3-star is a good tourist hotel with a moderate level of comfort, almost always with private bathroom: $35 to $63.

2-star is a simpler hotel with a moderate level of comfort, usually with private bathroom: $21 to $35.

1-star is a modest hotel or pension with simple facilities, often with no private bathroom, but clean: $14 to $21.

No-star is a very simple pension or hotel with only a small number of rooms and with shared bathroom, but clean, with willing service: $7 to $14.

Any establishments registered with the Ministry of Culture and Tourism automatically add a 10 percent tax to the bill. Price fluctuations in the 2- and 3-star category are considerable, often for no discernable reason. Some are surprisingly cheap for the facilities offered, others surprisingly expensive.

For those touring or on budget holidays, simple but clean accommodation with shared bathroom can be found cheaply at around $8.50 per night for two people including breakfast.

Hotel dining   Some of the larger registered hotels make half board (or even full board) compulsory. They are to be avoided if possible as it is invariably cheaper and more pleasant to eat out in a restaurant. Hotel food served up under demi-pension or full board arrangements tends to be mediocre and quantities are small, with minimal choice. At an outside restaurant you can order what you want (it is perfectly acceptable to go to the kitchen and point) and you will pay the same or less. There is never a shortage of restaurants, and even in the smallest villages you will often find quite a variety to choose from. This is because the Turks eat out frequently themselves.

Camping
There are few campsites in Turkey. Rough camping is legal except where notices state otherwise, but it is not generally advisable. The BP Mocamp chain has restaurants and good facilities, and some of their sites have simple chalet rooms for non-campers.

Food and Drink
Turkish cuisine has been called, even by French gourmets, one of the finest in the world. Turks are very fond of eating out themselves and so restaurants are excellent value, and even out of the way places in small villages and towns offer a considerable variety, prepared not for tourists but for the local inhabitants.

Excellent cuisine

Turkey produces all its own food, and it is fresh and of high quality. Vegetables are imaginatively used and there are, for example, over 40 ways of preparing the aubergine.

Fish if fairly expensive, as it is throughout the Mediterranean oddly, and it is generally charged by weight. River and lake fish however, as at Bafa, Manavgat and Eğridir, is particularly good value and always very fresh.

Breakfast traditionally includes white goat's cheese and black olives with bread and jam, which takes a bit of getting used to. Most travellers manage to adjust after a few days. Sweet black tea is usually served; to be certain of coffee outside of the main centres you should come equipped with your own supply of instant and just ask for hot water.

At restaurants lunch and dinner can be eaten at any time at all, no one minds when, as they are open all the time. A good meal for two with a bottle of wine costs $10.50 at the most, but more usually about $7. The pattern is to order a variety of small starters (*meze*), some cold, some hot, to put in the middle of the table for all to share, followed by the main course with salad and finally a dessert of fresh fruit. You may be offered fruit unknown in Europe, such as sharp little green cherry-like fruits, or yellow guavas with large stones, the fruit with the highest natural vitamin C content. Delicious sticky honey- and nut-covered pastries can also be eaten after a meal or at any time.

Quenching your thirst

Water is usually drinkable but often does not taste very nice as it is likely to be heavily chlorinated. Bottled mineral water is readily obtainable, cheap and usually drunk in preference. Water from a spring (çeşme) along the side of the road is drinkable and tastes good; though it may come out of a tap its origin will be from a freshwater spring. If in doubt, ask: *içilir* means drinkable, *içilmez* means not drinkable.

Ayran is the non-alcoholic national drink, a chilled unsweetened yogurt liquid, thirst-quenching and good.

Rakí (an aniseed spirit similar to ouzo) is the national alcoholic drink, usually mixed with ice and water. It goes well with Turkish food. Wines are good, both red and white. Some names to look out for are Villa Doluca, Kavaklídere, Tryka and Buzbağ. Red wine is often served chilled. Even in smaller rural places where the wine is anonymous with no label at all it can taste good. Beer is the locally produced Tuborg or Efes.

A bottle of wine in a restaurant will cost around $2, beer around 50c and soft drinks about 38c.

Pointing at dishes in the kitchen or in the refrigerated display counter is the usual way of ordering in rural areas, but in towns you may be given a menu. The following list may help.

Sample menu	*Hors-d'oeuvre: mezeler*	
	Arnavut ciğeri	: spicy fried liver with onions
	Çerkes tavuğu	: Cold chicken in walnut puree with garlic
	Çiğ köfte	: spicy raw meatballs
	Midye dolmasí	: stuffed mussels
	Tarama	: fish roe salad
	Yaprak dolmasí	: stuffed vine leaves
	Soups: çorbalar	
	Yala çorbasí	: yoghourt soup
	Düğün çorbasí	: Meat soup with egg yolks stirred in
	İşkembe çorbasí	: tripe soup
	Grills: ízgaralar	
	Bonfile	: fillet steak
	Döner kebap	: lamb grilled on a revolving spit
	Pirzola	: lamb chops
	Şiş kebap	: grilled lamb on skewers
	Şiş köfte	: grilled meatballs
	Pilafs: pilavlar	
	Sade pilav	: plain rice pilaf
	İç pilav	: rice with pine nuts, currants and onions
	Bulgur pilaví	: cracked wheat pilaf
	Cold vegetables in olive oil: zeytinyağlílar	
	İmam bayíldí	: split aubergine with tomatoes and onions
	Kabäk kízartmasí	: fried baby marrow slices served with yoghourt

| Patlícan kízartmasí | : | fried aubergine slices served with yoghourt |
| Zeytinyağlí fasulye | : | green beans in tomato sauce |

Savoury pastries: börekler

Sigara böreği	:	fried filo pastry filled with cheese
Su böreği	:	layers of filo pastry baked with cheese or meat filling
Talaş böreği	:	puff pastry filled with meat

Salads: salatalar

Cacík	:	chopped cucumber in garlic flavoured yoghourt
Çoban salatasí	:	mixed tomato, pepper, cucumber and onion salad
Patlícan salatasí	:	pureed aubergine salad
Piyaz	:	haricot bean salad

Desserts: tatlílar

Baklava	:	flaky pastry stuffed with nuts in syrup
Tel kadayíf	:	shredded wheat stuffed with nuts in syrup
Sütlaç	:	creamy cold rice pudding
Komposto	:	cold stewed fruit
Dondurma	:	Ice cream

Fruits: meyvalar

üzüm	:	Grapes
şeftali	:	Peaches
erik	:	Plums
kayísí	:	Apricots
kiraz	:	Cherries
incir	:	Figs
kavun	:	Yellow melon
karpuz	:	Water melon

Tipping

Tipping is something which Turks do not generally expect as the automatic right that it has become in the West. It is regarded rather as a gesture of appreciation for good service (as tipping originally was), and since service in Turkey is usually excellent, most Turks do in practice leave tips. In restaurants ten percent is usual, though in smaller basic restaurants, especially in rural areas, tips closer to five percent are fine. In some hotels and restaurants, notably those registered with the Ministry of Culture and Tourism, ten percent is added to your bill willy-nilly, in which case there is no need to add anything more unless you wish to express particular gratitude. Taxis are the exception worth knowing about: Turks never tip taxi drivers.

Budgeting

The cost of actually getting to Turkey will be by far the

greatest element in your holiday budget. Air fares, though getting cheapter year by year with the increase in discounted and charter flights. Car hire is the only other major expense.

Once these two expenses are settled, the cost of holidaying in Turkey is very low indeed, far lower than most Mediterranean countries. Perfectly good, well-equipped hotels can cost as little as $40 to $50 per day for two people, covering accommodation, meals, drinks, petrol and all incidental expenses.

Travel in Turkey by Public Services

By air Domestic flights are operated by Turkish Airlines (Türk Hava Yollari — THY), and these are frequent and inexpensive. İstanbul, İzmir and Ankara are linked by daily flights, and Adana and Antalya are served several times a week.

By rail Railways link only the main cities inland and are therefore not much help in visiting most of the sites described in this guide. There are no railways at all linking Bodrum, Marmaris, Fethiye and Antalya, and no line reaching the Mediterranean coast except at Mersin.

By bus Buses are a highly practical way of travelling around Turkey. There are several independent companies, varying slightly in frequency and comfort. The competition between them means that the system is efficient and cheap. Services are punctual, and on board there are pleasantnesses such as bottled drinking water and copious sprinklings of cologne provided free by the bus-boy. Stops of half an hour or so are made for breakfast, lunch and dinner, often at restaurants attached to petrol stations where the meals are basic but adequate. Buses run between almost every town in the country, leaving from the *otogar* (bus station) in the larger places or from the central square in the smaller places. Efficiency and practicality apart, the buses also provide an amusing and interesting way to travel and to meet people, and for a girl on her own are the safest way to get about the country.

Seats are reserved, so to ensure the best position on the bus you should buy your ticket a day or two in advance at the otogar office. There is also the possibility that by leaving your purchase to the last moment you will not get a seat at all. The middle seats are generally considered the best, as the ride can be bumpy towards the front or rear.

The more rural areas may not be so well served, and travel by bus in Lycia, for example, is not recommended except to those with plenty of time to spare owing to the less frequent connections. Even in areas where the service is good, as between Antalya and Side, there is still the problem of how to reach the sites from the bus stop, as most of the sites, eg Perge and Aspendos, lie a few kilometres off the main road. Walking or getting a taxi are then the only options, and so extra time and perhaps extra money must be allowed for the journey.

By taxi and dolmuş
Taxis in cities are recognisable by their chequered black and yellow bands. Although meters are usually fitted, they rarely work, so it is wise to agree on the fare first.

The dolmuş is a shared taxi which follows specific routes within larger towns and cities and is recognisable by its yellow band. The fares are fixed by the relevant municipality and each passenger pays according to the distance travelled and can get off at any of the specified stops. Much cheaper than a taxi, it is often good to get a dolmuş from the airport to the bus station or to the centre of town for example. As well as linking city centres with the suburbs, there are also some inter-city dolmuş, but these are more expensive than the bus, and often less comfortable.

By ship
Turkish Maritime Lines operates cruises starting at İstanbul, calling at İzmir, Kuşadasí, Güllük, Bodrum, Datça, Marmaris, Fethiye, Antalya, Alanya, and returning to İstanbul (duration two weeks, departing once a week in summer.) Fares are very reasonable but boats get booked up quickly in the high season.

There is also the popular TML overnight car ferry service from İstanbul to İzmir, taking 19 hours. It leaves İstanbul on Friday afternoons and leaves İzmir Sunday Afternoons all the year round, with extra trips laid on in high summer on Mondays and Wednesdays from İstanbul, and Tuesdays and Thursdays from İzmir.

Driving a Car Around Turkey

Travel by car is by far the best way of exploring Turkey. Without a car you will be able to see less, or you will need more time (adapting your plans to bus schedules, etc) to see more — and there will be some spots which will be a pain in the neck to reach without one. You can of course drive to Turkey, or you can fly and hire a car while there.

Car hire
Hertz, Avis, National/Eurocar and Dollar/InterRent have offices in Turkey, as do several local firms. Avis for example has offices at Adana, Ankara, Antalya, İstanbul, İzmir, Kuşadasí and Mersin.

Some fly-drive arrangements are cheaper than buying the flight and hiring the car separately, and it is worth shopping around. Obtain a list of tour operators from the Turkish Tourist Office and compare prices, which vary from operator to operator, destination to destination, and with time of year.

A good map is essential: that produced by the Turkish Tourist Office is better than nothing but is not the best. Try to buy one before going to Turkey.

Drivers must have a licence from their own country, and it is advisable to have an International Driving Licence, obtainable from your national automobile association.

Traffic drives on the right. In towns the speed limit is 50 km per hour, outside towns 90 km per hour. Important road signs include:

DUR: stop
DIKKAT: attention (warning you, eg, of road works)
SEHIR MERKESI: town centre

Archaeological and historical sites are indicated by yellow signs.

Some tips for the road

Driving in Turkey is no more of a problem than driving anywhere else in the Mediterranean. City traffic can be heavy, but outside the towns, especially south of Bodrum along the coast to Antalya, there is very little traffic and driving is a pleasure on near empty roads. Outside towns it is good to get into the habit of sounding your horn before overtaking. The car in front may indicate left and then turn right or vice versa, or might not indicate its intention to turn at all. Trucks can give puzzling indications, sometimes meant to inform you that it is all-clear for you to overtake, sometimes meant to inform you of the opposite. Driving at night is not recommended. Then there can be many trucks on the road, but not always with all their lights working or pointing in the right direction. In rural areas at dusk there is liable to be a great variety of agricultural vehicles, mechanised and horse-drawn, on the road, along with herds of goats returning from their pastures. It is not unusual in Lycia or Cilicia to round a corner and see a camel or a cow standing in the middle of the road looking at you as if to say 'What are you doing here?'. The dogs of goatherds sometimes decide your car is yet another creature to be rounded up and they will chase round your wheels barking furiously.

Roads are generally good and all the roads marked on the map at the beginning of this guide are well-paved. Where the road to a site is difficult, the degree of difficulty and suitability for a private car is always stated in the relevant site description in this guide.

Itineraries

To give an idea of what it is possible to do by car (those travelling by bus will have to limit their plans somewhat) some itineraries are suggested below. Places in CAPITAL letters are recommended for overnighting, and those in parentheses (the most important of which are in *italics*) can be reached by making excursions from the overnight bases or enroute while travelling from one overnight stop to the next.

Some suggested routes

From İstanbul (two weeks): İSTANBUL (four nights); BURSA; AYVALIK (*Troy*, Assos); PERGAMUM; KUSADAŞI (two nights: İzmir, *Ephesus*); ALTINKUM (*Priene, Miletos*, Didyma); BODRUM (two nights; *Bafa, Euromos*, Milas); İZMIR (Teos, Claros, Notion); PERGAMUM; İSTANBUL.

From İzmir (two weeks): İZMIR; PERGAMUM; AYVALIK (*Troy*, Assos); KUSADAŞI (two nights: *Ephesus, Priene, Miletos*, Didyma); MARMARIS (*Euromos*, Milas); FETHIYE (Caunus); KALKAN (two nights: *Xanthos, Letoon, Patara*); KAŞ (two nights: *Myra*, Andriake, *Kekova*); KEMER (*Arycanda, Olympos*); LARA (*Phaselis, Termessos*); PAMUKKALE; and back to İzmir for departure.

From İzmir (two weeks): İZMIR; KUSADAŞI (*Ephesus*); ALTINKUM (*Priene, Miletos,* Didyma); BODRUM (two nights: *Bafa, Euromos*, Milas); MARMARIS (two nights: Stratoniceia, Muğla, Cnidos); FETHIYE (Caunus); KALKAN (*Kaya, Ölü Deniz, Xanthos, Letoon*); KAŞ (*Patara*); LARA (*Myra, Phaselis*); SIDE (two nights: *Termessos, Perge, Aspendos*); PAMUKKALE; İZMIR (*Aphrodisias,* Nyssa).

From İzmir (two weeks, energetic): KUŞADASI (*Ephesus*); MARMARIS (*Priene, Miletos, Bafa, Euromos*); FETHIYE (Cnidos); KALKAN (two nights: *Kaya, Ölü Deniz, Tlos, Xanthos, Patara, Letoon*); KAŞ (two nights: *Myra*, Andriake, *Kekova boat trip*); KEMER (Limyra, *Arycanda, Olympos*); LARA (*Phaselis, Termessos*); SIDE (three nights: *Antalya museum, Perge, Aspendos, Selge, Sillyon, Manavgat*); PAMUKKALE; FOÇA (*Aphrodisias*); and back to İzmir for departure.

From İzmir (three weeks, energetic): İZMIR; ALTINKUM (*Priene, Miletos,* Didyma); BODRUM (two nights: *Bafa, Euromos,* Milas); FETHIYE (Caunus); KALKAN (*Xanthos, Letoon*); DEMRE: camping (Kaş, *Myra*); OLYMPOS: camping (*Kekova boat trip*); ANTALYA (*Olympos, Phaselis*); SIDE (two nights: *Perge, Aspendos, Manavgat*); ANAMUR (*Alanya*); SILIFKE (Kízkalesi); KONYA (two nights: Mut, *Alahan*); EĞRIDIR (two nights); PAMUKKALE; KUSADAŞI (*Aphrodisias,* Nyssa); SIĞACIK (*Ephesus,* Claros, Notion); İZMIR (Teos).

From Antalya (two weeks): ANTALYA (two nights: *museum, Termessos*); KAŞ (*Phaselis, Myra*); SIDE (three nights: *Perge, Aspendos, Sillyon, Manavgat*); ALANYA; ANAMUR; TAŞUCU (two nights: Kízkalesi, Diocaesarea); KONYA (two nights: Mut, *Alahan*); EĞRIDIR (two nights); ANTALYA.

From Antalya (three weeks): ANTALYA (two nights: *museum, Termessos*); KAŞ (*Phaselis, Olympos*); SIDE (four nights: *Perge, Aspendos, Sillyon, Manavgat, Selge,* Seleuceia); ANAMUR (*Alanya*); TAŞUCU (two nights: Kízakalesi, Diocaesarea); ADANA (two nights: Pompeopolis, *Karatepe*); NEVŞEHIR (three nights: *Göreme, Ürgüp*); KONYA (three nights); EĞRIDIR (two nights); ANTALYA.

And how you can vary them   The above itineraries assume that you are obliged to fly into and out of the same airport (ie İstanbul, İzmir, Antalya), or that having hired a car in one place you must return it to

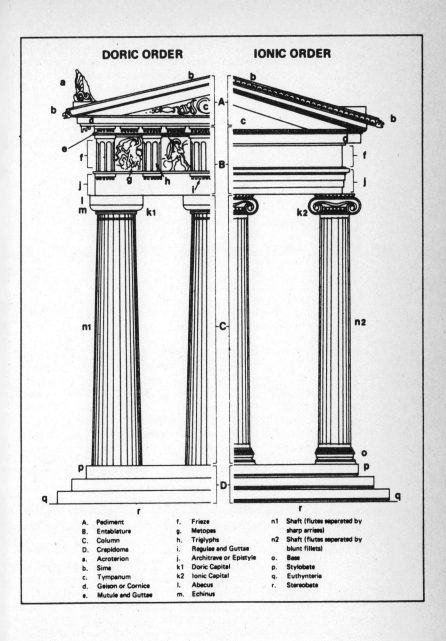

DORIC ORDER   IONIC ORDER

A.	Pediment	f.	Frieze	n1	Shaft (flutes separated by
B.	Entablature	g.	Metopes		sharp arrises)
C.	Column	h.	Triglyphs	n2	Shaft (flutes separated by
D.	Crepidoma	i.	Regulae and Guttae		blunt fillets)
a.	Acroterion	j.	Architrave or Epistyle	o.	Base
b.	Sima	k1	Doric Capital	p.	Stylobate
c.	Tympanum	k2	Ionic Capital	q.	Euthynteria
d.	Geison or Cornice	l.	Abacus	r.	Stereobate
e.	Mutule and Guttae	m.	Echinus		

27

that same place. But it is possible, say, to fly to İzmir and depart from Antalya and to hire a car one-way (though this greater flexibility will probably cost you more); and it is also possible to get a flight into Dalaman airport (between Marmaris and Fethiye), perhaps placing you more conveniently for both the Aegean and Mediterranean coasts. At any rate, these itineraries suggest what is possible and you can vary, abbreviate or extend them to suit your circumstances.

ÇANAKKALE TO İZMIR (THE TROAD AND ANCIENT AEOLIA)

Çanakkale

Troy

Alexandria Troas

Assos

Ayvalík

Pergamum

Foça

Practical Information

ASIAN LANDFALL

Symbolic
crossing

In its situation on the Asiatic bank of the Dardanelles (the ancient Hellespont) at its narrowest point, Çanakkale marks the northernmost edge of the Turkish Aegean coast. Car ferries run every hour from Eceabat on the European bank, making the crossing in 30 minutes. When Alexander the Great made this same crossing 23 centuries ago just before launching his campaign to recapture the Persian Empire, it no doubt took him a little longer. Alexander's aim in this preliminary visit was to offer sacrifice at the tomb of Protosilaus, the first Greek warrior to fall in the Trojan War, wishing, we are told by his biographer, Arrian, 'to ensure for himself better luck than Protosilaus'. It was here therefore that Alexander first set foot on 'the soil of Asia', and for many travellers coming from Europe the same will be true.

Çanakkale today is not somewhere most people choose to linger as their thoughts are usually fixed on Troy, 32 km to the south. It can be interesting however to break your journey for a cup of Turkish tea or coffee in one of the cafés or restaurants lining the seafront from where you can watch the endless coming and going of boats in the straits or to stroll round the port area with its attractive but decaying **Ottoman houses**, and its fine 15th C Turkish fortress. There is also the small **Archaeological Museum** housed in a disused church.

Troy: City of Legend and Fact
The road south from Çanakkale begins by following the Dardanelles shoreline before winding uphill through a pine forest. From the crest of the hill, the Trojan plain comes into view for the first time. The city itself, known as Truva in Turkish, stands on a hill called Hisarlik.

Pilgrimage to
a legend

Reactions on a first visit to **Troy** will vary depending on the level of expectations. Undoubtedly those who come with visions of Homer's great fortified city are in for a disappointment as the site today appears to the untrained eye like a series of shapeless mounds and ditches with occasional outcrops of wall and foundation. For others, the fact that a city so powerfully linked with legend exists at all is enough. There can be no one, however, for whom the name of Troy does not conjure up some associations, and a visit therefore takes on the quality of a pilgrimage to the place perhaps of childhood fantasies of battles over Helen of Troy, or perhaps to the place where Western literature had its beginnings.

Excavating a Dream
As the mighty city of Ilion in the *Iliad* and the *Odyssey*, Homer's accounts of the vicissitudes of the city and of the

Alexander the Great

Trojan War were thought for centuries to be pure legend. It was, as so often in archaeology and the search for the past, the romantic obsession of one man, the German businessman and amateur archaeologist Heinrich Schliemann, which first uncovered that in this case legend had its basis in fact. He obtained permission from the Ottoman government to excavate here in 1870 at his own expense, from money he had amassed in the California goldrush, and devoted the next 20 years of his life to pursuing his dream. He was rewarded with the discovery of four Troys, one on top of the other, and the so-called 'Jewels of Helen'.

Continuing the work Schliemann began, subsequent excavations have now uncovered nine major layers of habitation, many of them with further substrata. The latest University of Cincinnati excavations claim to have identified a total of 47 strata. A modern Trojan war is currently raging over which of these levels was Homer's Troy. Many Turkish archaeologists insist that Troy VI (tentatively dated c1275 BC) was Priam's city, as it was a prosperous settlement, endowed with a palace, well-built monuments and enclosed by powerful walls which seemed as if they could have resisted the Greeks' attacks throughout the ten years of the seige. The American professor Carl Blegen of Cincinnati University however, excavating from 1932–38, maintained that Homer's Troy was Troy VIIa (which he dates c1275–1240 BC), apparently destroyed by an earthquake in about 1260 BC, and coinciding, not only with the fall of Troy, but also with that of Mycenae, Tiryns, Pylos and other Mycenean cities which Homer mentions in the *Iliad* as having fought alongside Agamemnon at the siege of Troy. The uncertainty remains, but the evidence points increasingly to Troy VI.

The collected archaeological work shows evidence of habitation starting here in the early Bronze Age (3000–18000 BC), and Troy I to V belong to this period. As you walk round the site these layers are all clearly labelled, but the whole nevertheless comes across as very confusing. Each town was built on the rubble of the last and the identifiable reasons for each one's destruction are fires, earthquakes or sacking by invading armies. Add to this the equivalent of 28 years of continuous and often amateurish digging by archaeologists and you begin to understand why the place is such a maze.

The town of Troy VI lasted through the Middle and Late Bronze Ages (c1800–1275 BC), with the subsequent town of Troy VII spanning c1275–1240 BC. There was then a period of dark ages with no evidence of habitation for four centuries, till immigrants from Greece came and settled here in the 8th C BC. The town they founded was Troy VIII, the city which would have come under Persian rule and then been liberated by Alexander in 334 BC at the start of his campaign

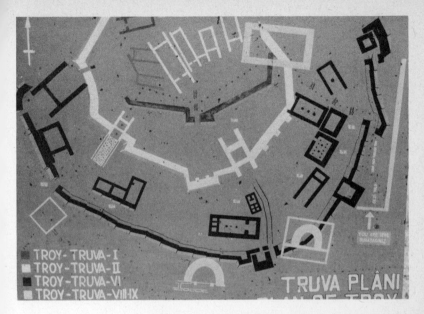

The site plan at Troy helps you through the confusion of the many-layered city

to recapture Asia from the Persians. After Alexander's death one of his generals, Lysimachus, rebuilt here the town which was called Ilium Novum throughout Hellenistic and Roman times, and now labelled Troy IX. The town gradually declined and was abandoned in the 6th C AD.

Approaching the Site

The power of a poem

The site today is surprisingly small for a place which has held such a place in peoples' imaginations over the centuries. Charles Maclaren, the first person to identify the mound of Hisarlik with the site of ancient Troy, writing in 1863, sums up the power of Troy as follows: 'Ilium was for a considerable period to the Heathen world, what Jerusalem is now to the Christian, a "sacred" city which attracted pilgrims by the fame of its wars and its woes, and by the shadow of ancient sanctity reposing upon it. Without abusing language, we may say that a voice speaking from this hill, three thousand years ago sent its utterances over the whole ancient world, as its echoes still reverberate over the modern'.

In fact of course, without Homer's epic poems Troy and its war would no doubt have long ago fallen into the oubliettes of history, and no one would make the pilgrimage to these scanty ruins.

Wooden gimmick

On approaching the site you must suppress your incredulity at the sight of an enormous reconstruction of the famous

33

Wooden Horse. This extraordinary structure is made the more absurd by the presence on the horse's back of an unexplained garden shed. One journalist, suitably pragmatic on his first visit, concluded this must be where the site guardian keeps his lawn mower. The authorities, by building this horse, evidently felt it necessary to compensate in some way for the insignificant remains on the site. Children can amuse themselves by climbing up inside and reliving the legendary climax of the siege of Troy when the Greeks tricked their way inside the city walls.

In search of Homer's Troy

The search for fact behind these colourful Homeric tales has ever fascinated historians and non-historians alike. The most recent quest has been that of Michael Wood, who in his book and television series *In Search of the Trojan War* goes on his own Odyssey to seek corroboration for the war and its heroes, notably through the Hittite tablets deciphered earlier this century. He reaches some exciting and, by his own admission, sometimes tenuous conclusions: Troy, its war, Agamemnon, Paris and Helen all have their suggested parallels. The Wooden Horse, however, remains a mystery, with speculation ranging from it being a wooden ram for knocking down the walls to it being a cult idol of Poseidon, god of earthquakes (often worshipped in the shape of a horse), left by the Greeks as a thank-offering to the god for sending an earthquake to help them complete the sack of Troy. The myth certainly goes back before Homer's time, as evidenced by the pictures of the horse with warriors inside it, drawn on an 8th C BC vase found on Mykonos.

A small **museum** stands near the entrance to the site containing various Greek pottery fragments from the 6th and 5th C BC.

Entering the Walls of Troy

Following the arrowed circuit of the site, you first reach a section of the **rampart of Troy VI** in well-built limestone blocks, with a rectangular tower still clearly discernable jutting out from the wall. If this powerfully built tower were the *Great Tower of Ilium*, it would be the setting for one of the most memorable passages in the *Iliad* in which Priam and his elders sit at the top of the tower looking out over the plain of Troy where the Trojan armies under Paris and the Achaeans under Menelaus prepare to do battle. Helen, hearing of the impending fight, rushes down towards the gate:

Great Tower of Ilium

'Old age had brought their fighting days to an end, but they were excellent speakers, these Trojan elders, sitting there on the tower like cicadas perched in the woods chirping delightfully. When they saw Helen approach, they lowered their voices. "Who on earth," they asked one another, "could blame the Trojan and the Achaean men-at-arms for suffering so long for such a woman's sake? Indeed she is the very image

Greek trick becomes modern gimmick

of an immortal goddess. All the same, and lovely as she is, let her sail home and not stay here to vex us and our children after us." King Priam was more charitable and calling Helen to sit and watch the battle with him said: "Dear child . . . I bear you no ill-will at all. I blame the gods; it is they who brought this terrible Achaean war upon me."'

Walking alongside the rampart you enter Troy VI through its **east gate**, and inside, the *foundations of houses* are still visible. To the left are the remains of a *storeroom* of Troy VII with a few buried Mycenean earthenware jars, and opposite, in Troy VI, a few column bases of what was originally a 12-columned *hypostyle house* of such colossal proportions for that period that some have speculated this could be Priam's palace.

The windy plain

Retracing your steps, you now climb up to a small **terrace** from where there is a good view towards the Dardanelles over the windy plain of Troy, scene of so many battles between the Trojans and the Achaeans. Troy today is 5 km from the sea, as it was in Homer's account, and ships can still be seen passing to and fro in the straits. From here Helen might even have watched the thousand Greek ships arriving to recapture their kidnapped queen.

As you descend walking along the *enclosure wall of Troy I*, you see first on the right a few scanty remains of the Doric **Temple of Athena Ilia** raised on the rampart of Troy II, and virtually annihilated by Schliemann in his search for Priam's treasure. In this temple Xerxes the Great sacrificed a thousand oxen before launching his attack on Greece in 480 BC, and Alexander the Great too made sacrifice here before moving on southwards down the Aegean coast.

Traces remain of the wall of Troy I, fortified even then, though it was only a fishing settlement. To the right in a depression *foundations of houses* from this early Bronze Age period have been unearthed.

Jewels of Helen

You now come to the **ramp** which gave access to Troy II. This structure is one of the most spectacular to be seen in pre-Roman Troy, still preserving its pavement of limestone by which carriages and other vehicles would have entered the city. This Bronze Age settlement was a wealthy one, exacting taxes on merchandise that passed through the straits. Traces of a royal palace were found here and various megaron-style houses. It was in one of these, under a mass of fire debris, that Schliemann found what he believed to be Priam's treasure, 'the jewels of Helen'. His Greek wife was photographed wearing these jewels in Athens, and after keeping them for 20 years he finally bequeathed the jewels to the (now East) Berlin Museum. There they stayed till 1945 when the Russians confiscated the jewels and carried them off to the USSR. Schliemann had long craved acceptance by the academic world as a serious scholar and archaeologist: his diggings at

Troy had been universally scorned, and he hoped that this find would be his vindication. In fact, so mistrustful were the academics of what they saw as this 'jumped-up tradesman' that they accused him of forging the jewels, or buying them on the black market and planting them on the site. These accusations are now largely withdrawn, but Schliemann is still criticised for his messy digging, and either way the Turkish authorities were left furious that he had smuggled the treasure out of the country. Undaunted, Schliemann went on to find more treasure at Mycenae. The fortification walls of Troy II still carry signs of the fire which ravaged the city towards 2300 BC, and which Schliemann took to be the fire of the final sack of Homer's Troy.

The arrowed circuit continues past more labelled walls and levels, passing a few **mosaics of a Roman Bath**, the poor remains of a **theatre**, and a **buleuterion** (council chamber), the most complete structure to be seen in Troy today. The small size of the theatre, built to accommodate only 6000 people, again raises the question of the smallness of the city. From Homer's descriptions the mind is quick to imagine a fabulous mighty city, but Troy was only ever a royal citadel on a little hill with a population of perhaps 1500. Even in its heyday it was never an extensive site but more like a walled palace.

THE TROAD

From Troy the scenic road leads south to the town of Ezine, centre of the region known in ancient times as the Troad. From here, you can make a short detour to the coast about 20 km to the west, and combine a trip to a rarely visited ancient site with a swim. The road reaches the sea at the fishing village of Odun Iskelesi opposite the Turkish island of Bozcaada (Tenedos in Greek).

A short drive south from the village brings you to **Alexandria Troas**, whose extensive ruins are to be seen either side of the road as you approach the sea. The most prominent structure is the colossal **Roman baths**. The city was founded in the 4th C BC by the One-Eyed King of Thrace, Antigonus. Lysimachus, King of Macedonia after Alexander's death, later killed Antigonus, took possession of the Troad and renamed the city Alexandria Troas. Throughout Hellenistic times this city, as a result of its excellent strategic position near the entrance to the Hellespont, grew rich and powerful by controlling the passing sea trade. Its importance waned when Constantinople was chosen as the capital of the Roman Empire, and during Ottoman times its buildings were plundered for stone blocks to build the Yeni Cami and Sultan Ahmet (the Blue) Mosque in Istanbul. On the beach a few colossal blocks are still lying where they fell during loading onto the ships bound for Istanbul.

Today the island of **Bozcaada** is still a military zone, an advance guard to the entrance to the Dardanelles. It also produces a good light white wine sometimes to be found in the restaurants of İzmir.

Aeolia's assets Returning to the main road, you now continue down through the Troad to **Ayvacík**. Throughout this region and southward, the landscapes grow increasingly different to the bleaker landscapes of Thrace: the soil becomes richer with wooded hills, wheat fields, orchards and verdant pastures. The Greek Aeolians, who were the first of the successive waves of migrants to leave Greece after the Doric invasion from the north, arrived here in the 10th C BC, settling on Lesbos and the surrounding Aegean coast. As a result, the region south of the Troad came to be called Aeolia, and a total of 12 cities were founded along this stretch of the northern Aegean. Having been farmers in their Greek homeland, the Aeolians contented themselves with tilling the fertile soils of Aeolia, and left politics and cultural achievement to their brilliant Ionian neighbours to the south. These, as seafarers and merchants, were far more ambitious and outgoing from the start. Herodotus wrote: 'The soil of Aeolia is better than that of Ionia, but the weather is not as good'. Cicero was equally impressed with Aeolia's natural assets when he said in one of his speeches: 'In the richness of its soil, the variety of its products, in the extent of its pastures, and in the number of its products, it surpasses all other lands'.

Ancient Assos

The northernmost of the Aeolian cities is **Assos**, 73 km south of Troy, and now called Behram Kale. The road forks off to the coast from Ayvacík, and then makes an impressive 18 km approach to the headland site ancient Assos with the Turkish village clinging to the ridge that was once the acropolis.

Shortly after a hump-backed 14th C **Ottoman bridge**, the road winds round near the Greek and Roman **necropolis**, with several sarcophagi scattered were they were left by grave-robbers. Sarcophagi (whose literal meaning is 'body-eaters') were the chief export of Assos and are to be found all over Asia Minor.

Spectacular setting The site today is worth visiting for its striking setting on a promontory directly opposite the Greek island of Lesbos. The 3 km long **Hellenistic fortification walls** of Assos are impressive, and further up the hill are the **Byzantine ramparts** with their round towers. Right at the summit of the acropolis are the remains of the **Temple of Athena**, as excavated by the American Archaeological Institute in 1881–83. First constructed c530 BC, this is the oldest Doric temple to have survived in Asia Minor. Pillaged by the Byzantines at the time of the Emperor Theodosius' edict outlawing pagan cults, and then by the Turks, very little remains of the once famous temple except its stylobate or platform and a few column capitals and the remnants of a black and white mosaic of the 4th C BC. The view from the acropolis out over the Aegean, Lesbos and the Gulf of Edremit is magnificent.

On the slope going down towards the cliff, the sites of the Hellenistic **agora**, a **buleuterion** and a **theatre** can be discerned. Further to the right are the remains of a **gymnasium** near the main **gate** of the city in the Hellenistic walls. The well-preserved gate still has its flanking towers.

Aristotle's visit Assos was founded by Aeolian settlers from Lesbos in 10th C BC. It never played any important political role, but reached its highpoint when it played host to Aristotle from 347 to 344 BC who continued his studies here in zoology, botany and biology under the patronage of the eunuch ruler of the Troad and Lesbos at the time, called Hermeias. Later, in AD 56, St Paul also called here in the course of his third apostolic voyage. Assos was known for its visitors, not its native inhabitants.

North of the acropolis are the ruins of an **Ottoman mosque** built after the Turks captured the city in 1306. From the cross and Greek inscription over the door it was evidently constructed from the blocks of an earlier Byzantine church which in turn may have been built from the ruins of the Temple of Athena.

From Behram Kale a road switches 2 km down to a small **harbour and beach** where there are restaurants by the water, a couple of small hotels and in summer far too many Germans. It can be a cheerful outpost; before it became known it was one of the sleepiest and most beautiful places around the Mediterranean. Now it is spoilt.

From Ayvacík, the road winds off towards the coast and then drops down to the Gulf of Edremit. The views here are quite beautiful, and all along the shoreline are fine sandy beaches between wooded promontories, with the hills of Mt Ida rising to the left. This stretch is well endowed with hotels and campsites, and has several resorts, notably Alkçay and Ören, fast becoming the most popular areas of the northern Aegean.

Along the Coast

Continuing southwest round the other side of the Gulf of Edremit, you come at the tip to the fishing town of **Ayvalík**, where a whole series of beaches and many good hotels and restaurants make it a good base for a trip Pergamum (modern Bergama), 63 km to the south. The scenery here is lovely, the sea set with a series of islets and the larger island of Lesbos in the background. Boats run from here to Lesbos five times a week in the summer (May to September), or just weekly in winter. Smaller boats run across to the closest island of **Ali Bey** (also linked to the mainland by a causeway) where a pleasant lunch can be taken in one of the seaside restaurants.

The drive to Pergamum from Ayvalík takes less than an hour and is clearly signposted. About half way there you pass **Dikili**, a small fishing town with a few small hotels and restaurants. It has recently built a wharf to accommodate Aegean cruise ships which now call here for their passengers to make the short coach trip to Pergamum.

PERGAMUM

Far and away the grandest of the northern Aegean sites, the ruins of Pergamum are extensive and require a full day to visit. One of the best ways is to arrive at **Bergama** (as the present-day town is called) in the afternoon, having swum and lunched at Ayvalík, see the acropolis before sunset, stay the night, and then see the rest of the site in the morning before continuing north to Troy or south to İzmir.

In contrast with its more famous northern neighbour Troy, **Pergamum** cannot fail to impress instantly by virtue of its superb setting. The sight of the steep acropolis on approaching from the south is not easily forgotten. On either side of the hill run two streams, and the type of hill, precipitous on all sides but one, was much favoured in antiquity, calling to mind the Acropolis at Athens. Yet this city was not a Greek foundation, and so it is an anomaly among the ancient cities of the Aegean. Lying back some 30 km from the sea, the site was too far inland to be settled by the early Aeolian Greeks. Remains of potsherds found here indicate that the hill was inhabited as early as the 8th C BC by indigenous Anatolians, but its distance from the coast meant that it did not feature at all in the naval campaigns of the Greeks against the Persians or in the Athenian maritime confederacy of the 5th C BC.

History of the Attalid City

Pergamum's first entry on to the political stage did not in fact come until after Alexander's death when his general Lysimachus held control over western Asia Minor. From the spoils of his conquests Lysimachus had amassed a vast treasure which he chose to deposit at Pergamum, appointing a certain Philetaerus from Paphlogonia on the Black Sea coast to rule the city and guard the treasure. When in 281 BC Lysimachus was killed by the Syrian Seleucids, Philetaerus remained in control of Pergamum and found himself the beneficiary of the treasure. Since Lysimachus had not appointed an heir, Philetaerus can hardly be blamed for keeping the treasure and indeed his claim to it was better than most. Rather than squandering it, as many who come suddenly into a large fortune do, he used it to incur the favour of his neighbouring cities by means of generous gifts and dedications, while at the same time initiating the building of many fine structures in his own city.

Philetaerus, a eunuch, was succeeded by his adopted son Eumenes, who came to be known as the first king of Pergamum, though neither he nor Philetaerus ever took that title. Eumenes was succeeded by his adopted son Attalus in

Heir to treasure

241 BC, most of whose reign was taken up in battles against the Gauls and the Seleucids. These Gauls, a wild and warlike race, had been invited into Asia from southern Europe as mercenaries by the king of Bithynia on the southern shores of the Sea of Marmara, and subsequently settled in the district which became known as Galatia, west of Ankara. They then proceeded to hassle all their neighbours, but their non-interference could be bought for suitable sums of money. While his predecessors had opted to pay, Attalus refused, so the Gauls decided to come and collect the money themselves. Attalus defeated them, aided, according to a legend, by a good omen of a sacrificial victim's entrails spelling out the words 'Victory for the King'. It transpired later that Attalus had written the words backwards on his own hand in ink and then discreetly transferred them onto the victim's liver while appearing to examine its entrails.

Heir to empire

Following this remarkable achievement, Attalus proclaimed himself King and Saviour and proceeded to fight for the remainder of his rule, gaining at one stage the largest kingdom in the east but then losing it all towards the end of his reign. What he did achieve however was the favour of the Romans, by helping them in their first entanglements in Asia Minor with the Syrian Seleucids. It was Attalus' successor Eumenes II who benefitted from this favour, for when the Romans defeated the Seleucids and Antiochus the Great at the battle of Magnesia furhter south in Ionia in 190 BC, the Romans, unwilling at that stage to take on Antiochus' conquered territories, handed them over instead to the control of Eumenes. Thus, for the second time, Pergamum rose to greatness as a result of an acquisition it had not sought, now finding itself in possession of the whole Aegean coast south to the Maeander river and as far east as the central Anatolian town of Konya.

Cultural peak

It was Eumenes who initiated the adornment of his royal capital with its most beautiful buildings. He extended the city from the upper parts of the hill downward, a move which entailed the construction of vast artificial terraces. He had the lower agora and great gymnasium built, and at the top of the acropolis added Pergamum's famous library and the Altar of Zeus. Pergamum at this time rivalled Alexandria as a centre of learning and science. All the rulers of Pergamum had been devoted patrons of the arts and sciences, and the city reached the pinnacle of its achievement and prosperity at this time, influencing contemporary Roman artists. Under Eumenes' successor and brother Attalus II, the wars continued and he founded the city of Attaleia (modern Antalya) on the south coast. He also retained the strong links with Rome.

Roman Province of Asia

The last king of Pergamum, Attalus III, was utterly unlike his predecessors. He was introverted, suspicious and cruel, and was feared by his subjects. He chose to remain for large periods in his palace studying such esoteric matters as the cultivation of medicinal and poisonous plants which he tested out on condemned criminals. He wrote a book on agriculture cited by Roman writers as the authoritative work in its field. His final act of eccentricity, when he died after only five years of rule in 133 BC, was his will in which he bequeathed the entire Pergamene kingdom to Rome. This extraordinary and unprecedented act had the effect of hastening the Roman influence, already growing, in Asia Minor. The Roman inheritors dismembered the outlying regions of the Attalid kingdom and created from the central core, with Pergamum as its capital, the Roman Province of Asia. This province consisted of the Aegean coastal regions as far south as Lake Köyceğiz near Caunus, that is the regions (north-south) of Mysia (inland from Troy), Lydia (Sardis), Ionia, part of Phrygia (inland from Ionia) and Caria. Throughout the Roman period Pergamum continued as a rich and powerful city but never achieved the cultural heights it had under the patronage of the Attalid kings.

Reconstructed view of Pergamum as it would have appeared from the west

The Acropolis of Pergamum: to the Library

Panorama

Although none of the magnificent buildings of the Attalids are standing to their full height today, there is enough left, especially after the efforts of the German reconstructors, to imagine how the city laid out on its sumptuous terraces would have looked. It is best first to head straight for the acropolis, from where you can get your bearings and develop a feel for the situation. The road to the acropolis winds round the side of the hill for several kilometres till it arrives at a car park with a ticket kiosk and soft drinks stands on a terrace just below the summit. From here it is a short walk up through a gateway in the walls into the **acropolis citadel**, the oldest part of the Attalid capital. The views from the uppermost terrace down over the valley and the rivers are spectacular: across the valley to the west, near a military zone, is the Asklepieion, the famous ancient medical complex, and in the town centre the vast Red Courtyard building looms, both to be visited later.

The citadel gateway leads through to a street running along the ridge of the acropolis, on the right of which are the remains of the various **kings' palaces**, a total of five in all. On the left side of the street at the southern end stands the famous **Library** of Eumenes II, now being restored by the German excavators. It adjoins, appropriately enough, the **Temple of Athena**, patroness of learning. Of the five rooms of the library only one, the easternmost, is recognisable as having contained books. This room has a stone bench about 1 metre high and wide running round three sides, though it is now almost flush with the ground. The excavators explain the purpose of this bench as being to keep the public away from the books while enabling the librarians to reach them.

Books at this time consisted of long strips of continuous papyrus rolled round sticks. The Attalid kings were avid collectors of books, scouring the kingdom for works old or new. The famous physician Galen, himself from Pergamum, says that books were even forged to satisfy the king's appetite. At its peak the Pergamene library was said to contain 200,000 volumes, though it is hard to see how these could have fit into a building of this size.

Rivalry of libraries

Ptolemy, creator of the mighty Alexandrian library, grew increasingly jealous of the Pergamene challenge to his cultural centre in an attempt to thwart its growth banned the export of papyrus from Egypt. Till then all books had been written on papyrus for which Egypt had the virtual monopoly. Undaunted, the king of Pergamum initiated the use of skins for writing on, which came to be known as 'pergamum paper', whence our word parchment. Skins, being so much thicker and heavier than papyrus, were not really suitable for scrolls, so they were cut for the first time into paged books. Though more expensive, they were generally preferred to the papyrus scrolls as they were so much easier to

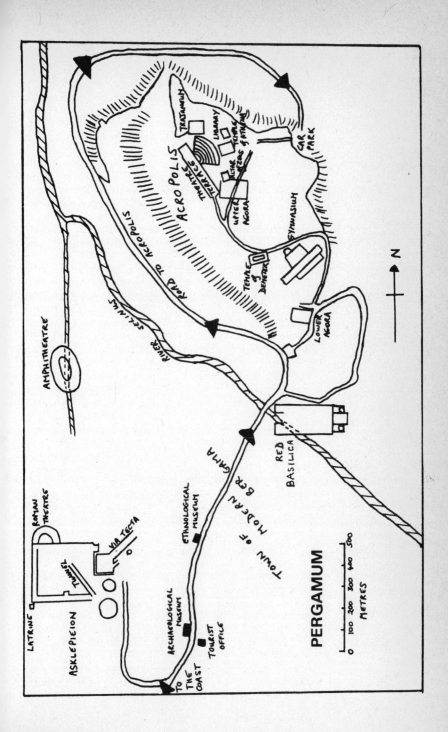

PERGAMUM

0 100 200 300 400 500
METRES

use. Finding your place again if you were interrupted reading a scroll was laborious, and the kings of Pergamum were the first to overcome this by the introduction of page numbering. But the Egyptians were to have their revenge when Mark Antony, to please Cleopatra, presented the entire Pergamene library to Alexandria.

Around the Acropolis Theatre

To the north of the Temple of Athena, on the highest point of the acropolis, stand the monumental remains of the **Trajaneum**, the largest temple in Pergamum, in honour of the Emperor Trajan (AD 98–117) who was worshipped here as a god as were the Roman emperors throughout the Imperial Age.

Triumph of engineering

You come next to what is the most spectacular and impressive structure at Pergamum today, the **theatre**, built into an exceptionally steep hillside. A remarkable piece of engineering, unrivalled by anything similar in the whole of Asia Minor, the theatre epitomises the Pergamene architectural achievement. The desire to preserve precious building space atop the acropolis meant that it had to be built on this steep slope, but the nature of the site made it impossible to round the cavea in the normal way so it was heightened instead. It has 78 rows of seats and two diazomas (horizontal walkways round the cavea), while most Hellenistic theatres in large cities had no more than about 48 rows. The orchestra extends out on to a long narrow terrace once bordered with stoas. At the northern end of the terrace are the massive remains of an **Ionic temple**, probably to Dionysus, patron of the theatre, with a flight of steps still leading up in front.

Gods versus giants

From the southern end of the theatre terrace you walk back to the idyllic setting in evergreen trees of what was once the great **Altar of Zeus**. Eumenes II constructed this altar at the peak of his prosperity but all that remains on site now are the foundations. The great frieze which once adorned its sides represented the culmination of Pergamene art, depicting battle scenes between gods and giants. Sculpture was the most favoured of Pergamum's arts, but all the surviving pieces of this magnificent frieze were transported to the Pergamum Museum in (now East) Berlin by the German excavators in 1878, where they have been reconstructed. The conflict between the gods and the giants is thought to symbolise the defence of civilisation by the Pergamene kings against the barbaric onslaughts of the Gauls. In the opinion of some, these friezes represent the culmination, not only of Pergamene art, but also of all Hellenistic art.

Just below the altar of Zeus is a terrace which was the **upper agora** of Pergamum. This marks the edge of the upper city and was the principal gathering place where those from the citadel mixed with those from the lower city. Leading out of this agora, a winding paved street leads down to the lower parts of the city. The distances involved here are quite considerable, and unless you are very hardy indeed and can contemplate the prospect of descending to the lowest part of the city and then climbing all the way back to the car park at the summit, it is best to visit the lower terraces by returning to the upper car park and driving back down the hill to the lower car park, from where the exploration of the lower terraces, though still involving a climb, is far less daunting.

The Lower Terraces

From this lower car park a footpath leads first into the **lower agora** from where the path proceeds through the Hellenistic gateway to the enormous complex of the **Gymnasium**. This impressive structure was built on three separate terraces in the 3rd C BC and extensively rebuilt in the Roman period.

Comprehensive schooling

The **uppermost terrace** and largest was for the young men (from 19 up to about 30), and consists of an open courtyard or *palaestra* for outdoor exercise, and a group of three rooms, one of which is a small *lecture theatre*. Both body and mind were trained in the gymnasia of the ancient world, and they were really more like schools and universities. It was common to invite guest speakers from other cities and the thousand-person theatre would easily be packed for such a lecture. The other two rooms were a *ceremonial hall* for official functions and prize-givings and a *chapel* for the worship of the emperor in Roman times. On the other side of the palaestra is an extensive *baths* boasting an elaborate piping system installed under Eumenes II in the 2nd C BC with water brought from the mountains and forced upwards under pressure. This is the outstanding system of its kind before the great aqueducts of the Roman period and was presumably designed by some of the king's brilliant scientists in residence at Pergamum.

The **middle terrace** of the gymnasium was for the teenage youths and has the remnants of a *temple* and a covered *stadium*. The **lowest terrace** is the smallest and is merely an open triangular playground for the youngest boys. A well-preserved *covered stairway* connects the middle and lower terraces. The three terraces together can be likened in concept to the comprehensive lower, middle and upper schools, except that as there is no trace of classrooms on the middle or lower terraces the teenagers and boys presumably came to the upper school for their lessons.

A route to heaven?

Slightly above the gymnasium you reach the **Temple of Demeter**, the oldest sanctuary in Pergamum, dating back to the beginning of the Attalid dynasty. Along the northern side of the sanctuary runs a *long building* with nine rows of seats affording space for about a thousand people. These seats were evidently for watching the celebration of the Eleusian

Mysteries which formed an important element in the cult of Demeter and Persephone, the goddesses of the underworld. These mysterious ceremonies seem to have held a particular attraction for the women of Pergamum and were essentially concerned with ritual acts of purification in an attempt to guarantee a better afterlife than was portrayed in the cold and cheerless tales of Hades and the underworld.

From the Temple of Demeter, the path, winding on towards the upper agora, has been largely cleared by the German excavators, and *chariot ruts* can still be seen in the paving. Lining the north of the street the remains of various *Hellenistic houses* have been uncovered, overlaid with *Roman shops*.

The Great Basilica

Cult building

The lowest part of the city at the very bottom of the acropolis hill is now largely covered by the town of Bergama. The town is quite attractive with an old Turkish quarter and with the river running through the centre, passing through two tunnels directly under the colossal Roman **Red Basilica** (Kízíl Avlu), built from red bricks. This unique structure began life in the 2nd C AD as a temple to Serapis, a Graeco-Egyptian god; you can see the secret passage emerging at the altar where ancient priests made noises in the pretence that theirs was the voice of the god. It was then converted to a church by the Byzantines who added the apse — you notice how newer brick has been added to the older walls.

Excavations took place here from 1934 to 1938 yet much of the building remains mysterious in its original purpose. The vast forecourt was presumably for ceremonial processions, while on either side stands a well-preserved round tower with a court in front containing a long narrow bathing pool fed by hot and cold water pipes. Beneath the two towers were extensive underground chambers which presumably played a part in the cult of Serapis who was closely linked with the underworld. The two pools themselves may have symbolised the sacred river Nile which was of ritual significance in the worship of Serapis. Beyond these is the great hall or temple itself, originally in three storeys and still standing almost complete. Nearby, a fine **Roman three-arched bridge** spans the river.

To the Asklepieion

Continuing out of the town on the same road as you entered, you pass on your right the **Archaeological Museum** (9–12, 13.30–17, closed Mondays). Here are displayed the majority of the sculptures and other antiquities discovered in the course of excavations but not carried off to East Berlin. This was the first local museum in Turkey to exhibit the finds of its site, and is still one of the more attractive small museums in

The interior of the vast nave of the Red Basilica

the country. Shortly before this you can also stop off at the **Ethnographic Museum** (same opening hours as above) to see the display of Bergama carpets and local costumes.

An ancient Lourdes   A little after the Archaeological Museum a road forks off the main road to the right to the **Asklepieion**. The cult of Asklepios, god of Healing, began originally in Epidauros and was introduced here at Pergamum early in the 4th C BC. However, on the fame and reputation of Galen, the greatest physician and medical writer of late antiquity, who was born in Pergamum in AD 129, the Asklepieion here outshone that at Epidauros and became the greatest medical shrine and centre of the ancient world. Galen's writings formed the basis of medical science till as late as the Renaissance, and earned for him the title of 'Prince of Physicians' by which he was known in the Middle Ages.

The type of medicine practised here was a mixture of psychological and practical treatment. On the psychological side it consisted of analysis of dreams, while the practical side consisted of diet, hot and cold baths and exercise. Thus, for example, a dyspeptic man from Mylasa was put on a diet of bread and cheese with parsley and lettuce, and milk mixed with honey, told to go barefoot and to take a run each day, to coat himself with mud and to anoint himself with wine before entering a hot bath. A grateful inscription tells us his treatment was successful.

The Asklepieion was extraordinarily popular with its inmates, possibly because it afforded a rare chance to gain a sense of intimate contact with the god and his priests. Some patients are known to have stayed here for over a year, which would help to explain the theatre and the library provided for entertainment. In practice, however, boredom was not likely to be something the patients suffered from, with the constant coming and going of patients, physicians, priests and visitors. As George Bean comments: 'In a slave-owning society leisure was abundant and the Greeks knew how to use it; no Greek was ever bored so long as he had someone to argue with'. Interestingly, the whole concept of boredom is a relatively modern one, with the word bore only entering the English language as late as 1766.

Touring the Health Cult Site

You enter the Asklepieion through the forecourt of the monumental gateway, and just to the right on entering is the **library**, a single square room with niches for the books. To the left of the entrance is the circular **Temple of Zeus Asklepios**, the main temple, and behind this is a second round but much better preserved building, thought to have been the main **hospital**. Originally in two storeys, the surviving structure is the lower floor which has some stone basins for washing or bathing. The staircases to the upper floor are still standing. To supply the water to these basins a long tunnel connects them with the *Sacred Well* in the centre of the main courtyard. The waters of this well were believed to have spiritual healing powers, and a recent analysis has shown them to be mildly radioactive.

The main **courtyard** of the Asklepieion was surrounded on three sides with stoas or porticos, only surviving in part in the north now. These walkways afforded shelter from the sun in summer and from the rain in winter. Behind the western stoa is a fine if small Roman **theatre** capable of seating 3500 people. It has been totally renovated and is now used in May at the time of the local festival. There cannot have been 3500 patients at the centre at any one time, so the townspeople must have attended the performances as well.

In the southwest corner of the courtyard opposite the theatre is a sumptuous example of a **latrine**. The larger room for the men had 30 splendid marble seats. In the ceiling, which was supported by four fine Corinthian columns, was an opening for light and ventilation. The ladies' room was smaller and far less grand.

Among the carvings to be found on blocks around the site you may notice those of a snake, the symbol of Asklepios. As the snake shed its skin to gain a new life, so the patients were supposed to shed their illnesses and emerge healthy.

On the flat open ground between the acropolis hill and the

Asklepieion are the very scanty remains of an amphitheatre where in Roman times gladiators fought with wild animals for the entertainment of the crowd. On some occasions the arena was flooded and sea battles or crocodile fights were enacted, and the nearby stream would obviously have come in useful for this. Much blood was shed at these ferocious spectacles, and Galen, as the chief resident physician, would have had a ready supply of wounded on whom to test his skills.

FROM PERGAMUM TO İZMIR

Ruins of Aeolia

Returning to the main road and continuing south towards İzmir you pass the sites of a succession of ancient Aeolian cities. Compared to the splendours of Pergamum these sites are totally insignificant as very little of them remains. For the traveller fortunate enough to have the leisure, however, visits to these ruined cities can be pleasantly combined with a picnic or a swim, as many are on promontories by the sea.

A Choice of Picnic Sites

The first of these Aeolian cities is at the modern town of Çandarli, 10 km off the main road, a simple fishing village on a spit dominated by a well-preserved Venetian fortress of the 14th C with five towers. Virtually nothing remains of the Aeolian city of **Pitane** which once stood here.

A few kilometres further south on the main coast road, you pass the promontory of Temaşalik Burnu, the attractive site of **Gryneum**, set in olive groves with abundant pink oleander bushes. All that remains are a few scattered column drums of its temple of Apollo. In antiquity Gryneum was famous for its oysters and mussels.

The next site is Aeolian **Myrina**, founded according to Strabo by Queen Myrina of the Amazons, but the site is difficult to reach today by a bad track, and little remains beyond a few sarcophagi around the acropolis hill.

Shortly after passing the lovely bay of Ali Ağa 6 km drive off the road to the hamlet of Namurtköy brings you to the scanty remains of **Cyme**, once 'the largest and best of the Aeolian cities' so Strabo tells us. At the time of the Delian Confederacy, Cyme paid a contribution of not only more than all the other Aeolian cities, but also more than the great Ionian cities of Ephesus and Miletos. The absence of impressive remains to reflect this importance can be partly attributed, as with so many sites on the coast, to the removal of blocks by the Byzantines and Ottomans for new buildings in İstanbul, İzmir and other cities. Increasing industrial development in the gulf of Cyme is also taking its toll.

A True Turkish Resort

About 10 km south of Cyme a road forks off west to Foça, passing through pleasantly undulating and peaceful countryside as it heads towards the sea. About 8 km before the town a prominent and unusual monument can be seen just to the right of the road, known by the Turks as *Taş Kule* (Rock Tower). Cut entirely from the rock, it is thought to be an early Phrygian tomb from around the time of King Midas in the 8th C BC (see Sardis). It is a square block with a doorway and stepped roof to a square tower.

Lively resort   Ignoring the turn off to Yeni Foça, you now continue on to the small but lively resort of **Foça** itself. This is a good place to spend the first or last night of a holiday, being only a 40-minute drive from İzmir airport. Pergamum is also within easy striking distance to the north. Foça has an active fishing port, and the Turkish Navy too is much in evidence. In the 1960s the whole area was in fact a military zone closed to the public. Now frequented mainly by Turks, it has the atmosphere of a Turkish resort, untainted by large hotels and coach tours. The locals bemoan the nearby Club Mediterranée holiday village 4 km away, saying it sends prices crazy during the season.

With cobbled streets and a twin bay divided by the wall of a **Genoese fortress**, the town itself is pretty. The seaside promenade is very pleasant with many attractive fish restaurants lining the front. The handful of hotels and pensions are almost all situated on the seafront, while the swimming beaches lie beyond the harbour just south of the town.

Surfeit of   Foça will doubtless be developed by tourism in years to
sites   come, but for the moment the locals are happy to maintain their peaceful existence. Excavations carried out in 1913 and 1953 confirmed that the current town stands on the site of a considerable Hellenistic city, *ancient Phocaea*. Recent building work has again come across remnants of the ancient city. When the bulldozers hit marble, everyone took a quick look, groaned, and then covered it over again. The upheaval of excavations under existing buildings is more than can be faced, and the locals take the view that the authorities already have more archaeological sites than they can cope with. The easiest place to see the remnants of this ancient city is, paradoxically, in the forecourt of the Petrol Ofisi station just on the edge of the town. A few yards beyond the pumps, down a dip, carved marble blocks can be seen together with the foundation stones of a large building. Ancient Phocaea, though situated in Aeolia, was in fact always an Ionian city, and as one of the best natural harbours on this coast was an obvious choice for the seafaring Ionians.

After returning to the main road from Foça, you come after another 2 km to the small village of Buruncuk on the left of the road at the foot of a steep rocky hill. The ruins on the top of this hill are thought to be those of ancient **Larisa**, the southernmost of the Aeolian cities, and consisting today of 4th C BC defence walls, the foundations of two temples and a palace. The site was excavated by German archaeologists in 1902 and again in 1932–34, but little of significance was found.

Just south of Larisa you cross the Gediz Çayí, the Greek river Hermus, taken in ancient times as the boundary between

Aeolia and Ionia. From here a drive of 10 km or so brings you to the turn-off to Ciğli, İzmir's international airport, and almost immediately after the suburbs of İzmir begin.

PRACTICAL INFORMATION

ÇANAKKALE

Tusan-Truva Motel (2-star) open March through September, 64 rooms, 15 km on the road to Troy. In a lovely setting in a pine forest overlooking the Dardanelles. Beach. Bakír (1-star), 35 rooms, near the Clock Tower.

Ferries to Eceabat run every hour on the hour and take 30 minutes. Ferries also run regularly between Gelibolu (Gallipoli) and Lapseki to the north of Çanakkale. Both are for cars as well as passengers.

Troy Festival, 15–18 August. Folk dancing and concerts, and trips to Mt Ida above the town. Hotels are liable to be fully booked at this time. An elected Helen of Troy acts as hostess.

AKÇAY

Akçam Motel (1-star) at Altínoluk, 34 rooms. Beach.
Doğan Motel (1-star) open mid-June to mid-September, 37 rooms. Beach.
Motel Aşiyan (1-star) open June to mid-September, 45 rooms. Beach.

AYVALIK

Aytaş Motel (1-star) open May through September. 46 rooms. Beach.
Büyük Berk (1-star) open March through October, 97 rooms. Pool, beach.

Many fish **restaurants and cafés** lining the front.

Boats run 5 days a week to the Greek island of Lesbos.

Annual 'panayir' in late April, a **market fair and carnival**. Gypsies come from all around, together with the colourful nomads

from the slopes of Mt Ida, called 'yürük' or wanderers.

DIKILI

Antur Motel (1-star) open June through July, 48 rooms. Beach.

BERGAMA

Tusan Motel (2-star), open March–November, 42 rooms. All rooms have private bathrooms. A small but rather fun Roman spa pool, where you can wallow and take the waters. 8 km from the site, at the junction with the main Çanakkale–İzmir road.

Afacan Motel (1-star), open mid-May to mid-October, at Incirlik, 30 km south. 17 rooms. Beach.

Annual **festival** in May held in the Asklepieion theatre, with cultural, folk and sporting events.

FOÇA

Club Mediterranée village (3-star), open May–September, bungalow-style. Full facilities including scuba diving and all watersports.

Hotel Palmeraie (1-star), on the harbour front. Old fashioned hotel, but with a few splendid rooms with huge balconies and private facilities.

Clusters of **restaurants** lining the front, offering fish specialities.

Beaches on outskirts of town.

Music, folklore and water sports **festival**, 29–31 July. Turkish and foreign folkdance teams and musicians perform, and various watersports competitions are also held.

İZMIR TO DIDYMA (ANCIENT IONIA)

ANCIENT IONIA

Flowering landscape and civilisation

Herodotus, famous historian and native of Asia Minor, maintained that Ionia was blessed with the best climate in the world. Today, 2500 years later, the climate is no less excellent, with a gentle breeze to temper the summer heat. The landscape too is beautiful in a gentle rather than a spectacular way, with rolling hills and fertile valleys covered in cypress and pine trees, olive groves and vineyards, and the clear blue sea never far away. Perhaps it was the beauty of these surroundings which encouraged the flowering of civilisation here in the great ancient cities of Ephesus and Miletos.

Greek Migrations

After the fall of Troy in c.1200 BC and the end of Mycanean civilisation, a race calling themselves the Dorians, thought to have been invaders from the north, took control of southern Greece. Unhappy with this dominance by a foreign element, many Greeks decided around this time to leave Greece and emigrate to Asia Minor, where they could found their own independent cities. The Aeolians were the first group to leave the Greek mainland, settling on the island of Lesbos and on Turkey's western coast between Troy and İzmir: this region henceforward became known as Aeolia. The next emigration of Greeks, starting around the 10th C BC, were the Ionians who eventually settled immediately south of Aeolia, in the region from İzmir to the Maeander river at Miletos, and hence this region became known as Ionia. Tradition has it that the Ionian migration was led by the many sons of Codrus, last king of Athens. The Greek newcomers seem by and large to have successfully absorbed the indigenous Anatolian population, and the cities they founded always regarded themselves as Greek rather than Anatolian, adopting for the most part Greek customs and institutions.

The region was favoured not only in climate and landscape, but in other ways too, for it was to become the breeding ground of many philosophers, scientists and poets, who heralded the beginnings of a brilliant civilisation, well in advance of the Greek mainland which was still emerging from the upheaval that followed the Dorian invasion. Homer himself, living before 700 BC, was, through the *Iliad* and the *Odyssey*, the most shining example of the literary tradition. On the scientific front, Thales of Miletos in 600 BC asserted that all things are water, thereby setting in motion a chain of deduction which has led eventually to nuclear theory and the atomic bomb. Thales was also one of the first to study the movements of the planets and stars.

Homer and nuclear theory

The cities were for the most part independently governed

by separate rulers, sometimes hereditary, sometimes not, but in around 800 BC the 12 major Ionian cities formed themselves into a loose league. Miletos was always the most active and successful member of the league, setting up, through its vigorous sea trade, nearly 100 colonies along the shores of the Sea of Marmara and the Black Sea.

Struggle with the Persians

This period of wealth and independence was brought to an end by the Persians, who, having defeated the Lydians at Sardis (see later section on Sardis), proceeded to take the Greek cities of the western coast. Although Persian rule turned out in practice not to be oppressive, merely involving the paying of tribute while local Greeks (called satraps) appointed by the Persians continued to govern the cities, a revolt was instigated against it.

Not surprisingly, it was Miletos which inspired and organised the revolt, dragging the other members of the Ionian League somewhat half-heartedly along with it, and so when it failed, it was Miletos which paid the price. After a decisive naval defeat in 494 BC off the island of Lade near Miletos, the city was plundered, the menfolk slaughtered and the women and children sold into slavery.

Massacre at Miletos

The Persian king, Darius, his appetite whetted by this success, now moved on to attempt the subjugation of Greece itself. This proved his undoing and the subsequent Athenian victories over the Persians at Marathon (490 BC), Salamis (480 BC) and Plataea (479 BC) gave Athens great prestige, bringing her up to an equal footing with Sparta in the leadership of Greece. The Greek cities of Asia Minor, suitably grateful for their deliverance from the Persians, were quick to put themselves under the aegis of Athens, and a league, called the Delian Confederacy with its treasury on the sacred island of Delos in the Aegean, was established to discourage Persia from any further aggression.

The Delian Confederacy disintegrated after Athens was defeated by Sparta in the Peloponnese War and Persia gradually took control once more of the Greek cities of Asia Minor.

The arrival of Alexander the Great on the scene opened a new era for everyone, but especially for Asia Minor. Alexander crossed the Hellespont in 334 BC at the head of an army of around 35,000 Macedonians and Greeks, with the express goal of liberating the Greek cities and conquering the Persian Empire. Apart from some small pockets of resistance, notably at Miletos and Halicarnassus (Bodrum), Alexander met virtually no opposition, and within 18 months had re-taken Asia Minor, and within three years had conquered the entire Persian Empire. On Alexander's premature death from a sudden fever in Babylon in 323 BC at the age of

Confusion after the death of Alexander the Great

32, his vast newly acquired empire was left with no successor. His generals proceeded to squabble among themselves for 20 years and finally three main kingdoms emerged: the Macedonians in Greece, the Seleucids in Syria and the Ptolemies in Egypt. The western coast of Asia Minor did not fall clearly into any of these three, so Antigonus, one of Alexander's generals, held it first, till he was killed and Lysimachus, another general, took control till he in his turn was killed in 281 BC.

The treasure Lysimachus had acquired in his rule was used to establish the Attalid dynasty at Pergamum, which rose to become as powerful as the other three new kingdoms. These four kingdoms proceeded to vie with one another to hold sway over western Asia Minor, with the periodic interference of yet another group, the Gauls, a group of three Celtic tribes from Europe, who came marauding down the western coast, eventually settling inland near what is now modern Ankara.

Despite these forces of confusion, one factor was common among the four main rivals, and that was their essentially Greek character. The process of Hellenisation in Asia Minor had therefore begun, with Greek becoming the official language and the adoption of Greek institutions. Egypt's Alexandria was the cultural centre of the Hellenistic world, with the vast library collected by the Ptolemies offering unique opportunities for research and learning. Many comparatively recent discoveries to do with the planetary movements, the moon and tides and the earth's rotation all had their origins in theories first postulated by Alexandrian scientists.

The Advent of Rome

Rome was at first drawn reluctantly into Asia Minor, crossing the Hellespont to crush the Seleucid King Antiochus III but having no desire to extend the empire here. The Romans therefore handed over the region they had conquered to Eumenes II of Pergamum. The last king of Pergamum, Attalus III, having no heir himself, returned the compliment in 133 BC by bequeathing his entire empire to Rome. Hence the western region of Asia Minor was organised by the Roman Republic into the Roman Province of Asia. Rome appointed a governor to the province each year, whose word was law. While some of these governors were honest rulers, others were despotic and saw in their province an easy means of amassing a fortune through extortionate taxes. By and large their interest stopped at financial matters, and they allowed the day to day running of the cities to continue under their own councils as they had done before. The period of Pax Romana which lasted for 300 years after the Roman Republic became the Roman Empire in 27 BC was the golden age of prosperity for almost all the

Roman opulence

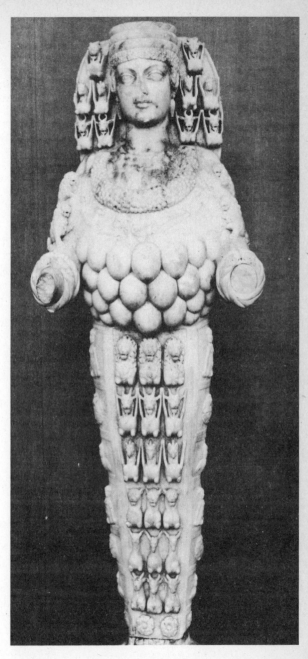

The Many-Breasted Artemis of Ephesus

cities of the province of Asia. It became one of the richest provinces in the Roman Empire, with Ephesus as its capital. Wealth increased, populations grew and standards of living were higher than at any other point till relatively recent times. The magnificent public buildings and private mansions in the cities, notably at Ephesus, testify to this period of wealth and the opulent lifestyle enjoyed.

During this time the cult of deifying the emperors began, and though the first emperor, Augustus, was initially reluctant, he relented and gave way to the tradition in the east of worshipping kings and rulers. This imperial cult in fact played an important part in holding the empire together, giving the provinces a sense of belonging and of unity with Rome. In many cities we still see temples of Hadrian and temples of Domitian alongside temples to Apollo and Artemis, as at Ephesus, for the worship of emperors in no way interfered with the worship of gods and goddesses, but was simply regarded as an adjunct to it.

Decline set in after the 3rd C AD when the emperors became increasingly incompetent and tyrannical. Endless disputes and wars sapped the strength of the empire, and further incursions by Germanic Goths from 258 till 262 weakened the province of Asia. This period coincided with the rise of Christianity and the resultant struggles between the early Christians and the Roman emperors, till Constantine himself converted to Christianity.

Christianity and Islam

The region of Ionia, especially Ephesus, was the scene of many dramatic events in the days of early Christianity, with St John and the Virgin Mary both living and dying here, and St Paul later coming here to preach. The first of the Seven Churches of the Apocalypse was founded here, and the Christian community at Ephesus became one of the most powerful in the west. The importance of its Christian relics has made Ephesus one of the major Christian shrines in the world.

Decline of Ionia Ephesus was still a rich city till the 7th C when it began to suffer from the Arab incursions (see the later section on Anemurium). In 688 it was pillaged by the Umayyad Caliph Muawiya who was returning from his abortive siege of Constantinople. Ionia, much reduced in wealth by now, largely as a result of the silting up of the harbours of Ephesus and Miletos, was then ruled by various local emirs till the Ottomans took control in 1390. In the 15th C, Aydín, further up the Maeander valley on an important junction of routes, became the chief commercial town of the region, and the previously great centres of Ephesus, Miletos and Priene, deprived of their harbours, declined to become insignificant country towns or hamlets.

İZMIR

The decline of the Ionian and other classical cities, unhappy though it was for the ancients, has been good for today's traveller, for the legacy has been to give us one of the chief pleasures of holidaying in Turkey, namely that all along the Aegean and Mediterranean coasts the places of interest and the ancient sites do not tend to lie in modern cities, but rather in small villages, on beaches, or right in the middle of the countryside. Hence you are rarely obliged to stay in a city in order to see the sights.

Arriving at İzmir

So it is with İzmir, Turkey's third largest city, a pleasant, cosmopolitan port with a turbulent past, but very little sign of it visible on the ground today. Originally described by Strabo and other historians as the most beautiful of all cities, any claims that İzmir, ancient Smyrna, has to beauty today are due almost exclusively to its striking setting around a vast bay. It is a busy commercial port as well as the Nato headquarters for the Southeastern Sector, but the harbour area in no way spoils the very attractive seafront. Its feel is of a modern, international Mediterranean city, but for those who have come on holiday to get away from a city's bustle, it would be preferable to stay in Foça to the north, or Siğacik to the south, both of which are small fishing resorts with beaches. It is not necessary to use İzmir as a base except for a visit to the ancient city of Sardis (see later section), 1½ hours' drive inland towards Ankara. If you are touring, İzmir is a good lunch stop as there is a host of excellent fish restaurants lining the seafront near the main square, Cumhuriyet Meydaní, offering such delicacies as sea bass and lobster. If you are just driving through, it is possible to use the by-pass which avoids the main town and leads between the hills of the back suburbs of İzmir, covered in extraordinary multi-coloured houses and numerous minarets. For the sake of a few extra minutes however, it is well worth following the town centre signs (şehir merkesí) as you approach from the north, as this will bring you out onto the seafront and then, at the end of the bay, take you up an extraordinary series of steep hairpin bends, giving good views back over the town and bay. This route shows İzmir in its best light to the traveller who is just passing through.

In İzmir itself, past earthquakes and the fire of 1922 have destroyed most the buildings of historic interest, leaving only the agora, the bazaars, and the flat-topped Kadifekale, the ancient acropolis, with a superb view over the town and harbour, especially at sunset. During the day, it is well-placed

Striking setting

to catch the Imbat, the breeze which blows each day from the sea in summer, dying down in the evening.

History of the City

Although originally founded by Aeolians, ancient Smyrna was soon taken over by the new wave of Ionian migrants, and was thus considered an Ionian city from about 800 BC onwards. It was not permitted, however, to enter the Ionian League, and it also suffered from its proximity to Sardis, the capital of the Lydian kings, making it an obvious early victim of Lydian attack. As a result of this, Smyrna remained no more than a small village throughout the classical Greek age, playing no role in history or politics, and not even becoming a member of the Delian Confederacy.

The goddess asks Alexander to found the city

Smyrna only in fact entered on the world stage after being singled out by Alexander the Great: while resting on Mt Pagos (the flat-topped Kadifekale) after a hunting excursion from Sardis, the goddess Nemesis appeared to him in a dream and asked him to found a city on the hill. The oracle at Claros confirmed this by pronouncing:

'Three and four times happy shall those men be thereafter Who shall dwell on Pagos beyond the sacred Meles.'

Most of the building in Smyrna on the Kadifekale in fact took place under Antigonus and Lysimachus, the two generals of Alexander who ruled the region after their leader's death. With her increased status, Smyrna was now at last allowed to join the Ionian League, and from this time on the city shared the vicissitudes of the rest of Ionia through till the Roman imperial age.

Although it was renowned for its beauty with many magnificent buildings, Smyrna's only real claim to fame was as the birthplace of Homer — a claim as dubious as everything else written about Homer. He is said to have written his epics the *Iliad* and the *Odyssey* at a cave on the banks of the river Meles. The identity of this river is not known for certain, as no less than six rivers flow into the sea near İzmir, but the most likely spot is where numerous springs from a large pool (called Halka Pínar today), anciently the **Baths of Diana**. This pretty spot surrounded by trees was a favourite haunt on hot summer evenings in the last century, but is now fenced off by the İzmir waterworks.

Revolting wine

Homer mentions in his works the famous Pramnian wine, drink of heroes, which Pliny tells us is from Smyrna. The ancients were said to like their wine sweet and mixed with honey, chalk and powdered marble. As if this were not bad enough, they also diluted it heavily, usually five parts water to two parts wine. A half-and-half mixture was considered too strong, and to drink wine neat was thought quite barbaric. Another revolting practice was to mix it with sea water, which

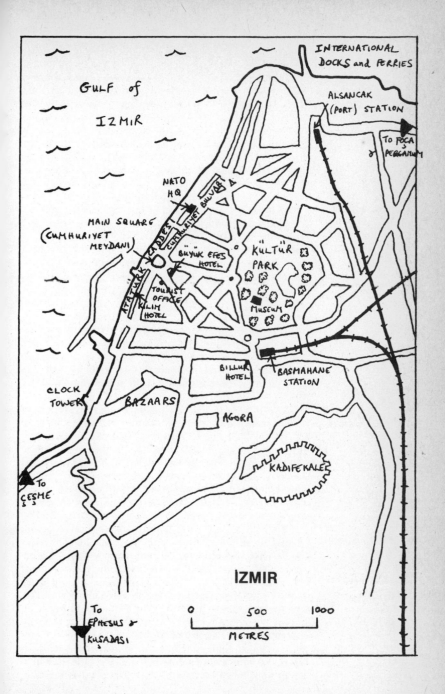

GULF of IZMIR

INTERNATIONAL DOCKS and FERRIES

ALSANCAK (PORT) STATION

TO FOÇA & PERGAMUM

NATO HQ

MAIN SQUARE (CUMHURIYET MEYDANI)

CUMHURIYET BULVARI

BÜYÜK EFES HOTEL

KÜLTÜR PARK

TOURIST OFFICE

KILIM HOTEL

ATATÜRK CADDESI

MUSEUM

BILLUR HOTEL

BASMAHANE STATION

CLOCK TOWER

BAZAARS

AGORA

KADIFEKALE

TO ÇEŞME

İZMIR

0   500   1000
METRES

TO EPHESUS & KUŞADASI

63

was thought to make it sweeter. One can only conclude that the undiluted version must have been truly revolting to have warranted so much adulteration.

With the rise of Christianity Smyrna was an important city, becoming the site of one of the Seven Churches of the Apocalypse. It was repeatedly attacked by Arab raiders and fell to the Seljuk Turks in 1097. Throughout the Crusades (see the later section on Anamur), Smyrna was fought over by Byzantines and Seljuks, and the Knights of Rhodes built a stronghold here, abandoning it after Tamerlane, 'the scourge of the East', destroyed Smyrna in 1402, slaughtering all inhabitants in usual Mongol style (see the later section on Miletos, the mosque of Ilyas Bey). Shortly afterwards it was incorporated into the Ottoman Empire.

In the 15th C a large number of Jews came to Smyrna and in the following centuries communities of English, Dutch and French traders also established themselves, involved mainly in the tobacco trade, so that it became quite a cosmopolitan place. But Greeks were in the majority: in the early years of this century they numbered 800,000 in Smyrna and its hinterland. In the First World War the Ottoman Empire was an ally of Imperial Germany; as it collapsed, British, French and Greek troops entered Constantinople and made plans to divide much of the Ottoman domain among themselves. Greece had been promised Smyrna and in 1920 the peace treaty of Sèvres with Turkey agreed that Greece was to administer the district for five years after which by plebiscite the population could ask for incorporation within the Greek state.

The Greek disaster   Greek forces landed at Smyrna under cover of the guns of British, French and American warships. But within Turkey a new nationalist movement under Mustafa Kemal (Atatürk) was rising against the Sultan who had lost the war and signed a humiliating treaty. Kemal's guerilla forces harried the Greeks who foolishly pursued them deeper into Anatolia until in unfriendly territory at the end of stretched lines of supply the tide turned. The Greek forces were obliged to retreat to Smyrna; negotiations for a peaceful solution collapsed; in August 1922 the Turks launched an all-out offensive. The fighting took on the bitter quality of civil war and degenerated into a massacre of the Greek population. Those who could escaped in boats, but the blood stopped flowing only when a colossal fire devastated the wooden houses of the city. The new Turkish city built on the ashes took the name İzmir.

A Remarkable Paucity of Sights
Smyrna, unlike Ephesus, Miletos and Priene, did not lose its natural harbour, and so unlike these ancient cities which have lain in ruins for centuries it has been inhabited throughout.

Anything of the ancient city which survived the many earthquakes and the fire of 1922 is now buried under the modern town, leaving İzmir remarkably devoid of antique monuments. One of the most extraordinary examples of the way the new city has engulfed the old is in the **Roman theatre** above the Başmahane station. The hollow of the theatre is still discernible but is now full of recently built houses. On the western side, one of the vaulted passages to the auditorium is still quite well-preserved and actually runs under one of the new houses. The stage building has also been lost among the houses fronting the street.

The **Roman agora** (open 8.30am to 5.30pm daily) is one area which has however, been excavated, with many of the columns of the portico re-erected. It forms a surprising patch of openness in the new city, clearly visible when looking down from the **Kadifekale** (Velvet Fortress), anciently Mt Pagos, acropolis of the Hellenistic city. On its north side is a large market building beneath which are some handsome vaults. Nearby are statues of Poseidon and Demeter.

The colourful **bazaar** dates from late Ottoman times and is best reached from the Ottoman **clock tower** on the seafront. This landmark is also İzmir's bus and dolmuş centre. The road on the far side of the square from the clock tower leads you into the main street of the bazaar. Nowhere near as interesting as the bazaar of İstanbul, it is nevertheless a lively place to shop.

The **Archaeological Museum** (9am to 12 and 1.30 to 5pm except Mondays), set in the lovely **Kültür Park** with its artificial lake, is crowded with exhibits from the whole of the Aegean coast. Of particular note is a lovely 4th C BC bronze bust of Demeter found in the sea near Bodrum.

THE ROAD TO SARDIS

A visit to Sardis, wealthy capital of the Lydian empire, is
always rather difficult to incorporate into the itinerary of the
touring traveller unless he bases himself in İzmir for a
minimum of two nights. **Sardis**, 90 km east of İzmir and about
90 minutes' drive away, lies up the Kavaklídere valley (where
some of Turkey's most popular wines originate), and as such
is a major detour off the route north to Pergamum or south to
Ephesus. A visit takes the best part of a day. The look and
atmosphere of the site with its impressive Temple of Artemis
and strange rock formations in the nearby hills, is undeniably
different from that of the other sites of western Turkey, but if
you are short of time and would prefer to see more of the
Aegean coast, then you are better advised to head off from
İzmir south straight to Ephesus and Kuşadasí.

A day's detour

Midas and Croesus

The Lydian empire was bordered on the west by Ionia, and on
the east by Phrygia. In the 8th C BC it was Phrygia with its
legendary King Midas of the Golden Touch which was the
dominant force. This kingdom fell victim however to the
attacks of barbarians from the northern coast of the Black
Sea called Cimmerians, and the Lydians too suffered greatly
from the raids, but their king at that time, Ardys, finally
drove the invaders out for good, and from this point the
Cimmerians vanished from history. Their name survives in
the region we know as the Crimea.

*The Golden
Touch*

The Lydian empire's strength increased and their kings
sought to extend their control over the Greek cities on coast.
Croesus, last and greatest of the Lydian kings, succeeded in
capturing them all apart from Miletos, and under his reign
Lydia achieved the phenomenal wealth which began our
expression 'rich as Croesus'. The Lydians are in fact credited
with being the first to coin money. Earlier civilisations such as
the Hittites and ancient Egyptians sometimes used metal bars
and rings as currency, but no record of actual coins made
from precious metals has been found before. The coins carry
the lion's head, the royal emblem of Sardis, and were made
originally from a gold and silver mix, and later from either
pure gold or pure silver. The coinage custom quickly caught
on among the Greek cities of the Ionian coast, and from there,
helped no doubt by the extensive spread of Miletos' colonies,
spread all over the world. The gold for the coins was found in
a small stream (the Pactolus) which flowed through Sardis,
and the early method of collecting it was by laying out
sheepskins to catch the particles in the water. The legend of
the Golden Fleece is thought to have originated from this.

Hopeful visitors will be disappointed today, for the river ceased to offer up any gold centuries ago. It is said that King Midas, standing on the river bed while performing his ablutions upstream in his kingdom of Phrygia, was the source of the nuggets.

Croesus seems by and large to have had good relations with his Greek conquests, and records show that he made generous gifts to the sacred temples and sanctuaries of the Greeks. Lydian customs, too, according to Herodotus, were similar to Greek ones, with the curious exception that girls were expected to earn their dowries by prostitution. Clearly the Lydians did not share the commonly held view that virginity and abstinence from pre-marital sex were virtues to be preserved among young girls. The Lydians also take the credit for the invention of most of the board games in use later throughout the Greek world.

Dowries earnt by prostitution

Lydia's golden age was shortlived however, for Croesus made a fateful attempt to extend his empire to Persia. The attempt was a total failure, with Cyrus, the great Persian king, driving Croesus back into Lydia and laying seige for two weeks to Sardis and then sacking the city. From here the Persians succeeded in taking all the Ionian cities along the western coast one by one. With the end of the Lydian kingdom the Greeks are said to have considered them effeminate and fit only for use as slaves. Sardis remained the capital of the Persian satraps (local Greeks approved of and appointed by the Persians to rule).

A violent earthquake in AD 17 virtually destroyed the city, but it was rebuilt on funds from the Roman Emperor Tiberius. Christianity came early, and Sardis is mentioned in Revelations as one of the Seven Churches of Asia. In Byzantine times it was also an important bishopric, ranking sixth in those subject to the Patriarch of Constantinople. Sacked once by the Persian Sassanids in the 7th C and finally by the 'scourge of the east' Tamerlane himself in 1401, the city never recovered, and was gradually buried under the soft soil washed from the hills around.

Touring the Ruins of Sardis

The various ruins are dispersed today over quite a large area, so it is best to drive from one area to the other. The modern town of **Sart** lies closest to the new excavations, just after the bridge to the left of the road as you arrive from İzmir. Here, the American excavators from the School of Oriental Research at Harvard have gone to great lengths since 1958 in restoring the later Roman ruins of Sardis, notably a **Roman road** lined with shops, a **gymnasium** and a **synagogue**. The gymnasium complex is the most impressive, dating from the 2nd C AD with a lovely marble courtyard and a monumental two-storeyed entrance. The synagogue, originally a Roman basilica, dates from the 4th C AD and its mosaic pavements and the slender columns of its peristyle have been heavily restored.

A kilometre or so further east towards Ankara, is another vast building just left of the road, a **Roman baths**. At 300 metres south of the road as you return towards Sart, the site of the **stadium** and **theatre** is recognisable at the foot of the strangely jagged acropolis hill, but both are badly ruined. Fragments of the city **fortifications** are also visible up on the acropolis hill.

Ancient souq

The area of greatest interest to the visitor to Sardis, however, is still the Temple of Artemis, set slightly over a kilometre south of modern Sart. To reach it you turn south from the main road near the bridge over the river, the legendary Pactolus, source of the gold and wealth of Sardis. Before reaching the temple you will notice on both sides of the road, **remains of shops and workrooms**. Enclosed by a wall, this remarkable area, occupying a surprisingly large site, bears a striking resemblance to the souqs and bazaars of the Arab world today. Discovered in 1965, it has been shown to date from the early 7th C BC and is hence the earliest example yet found of this kind of market area (prosaicly called the Lydian Civic Centre by the Americans). Another discovery in this area was of the workshop where the gold from the river Pactolus was refined from the 6th C BC onwards, using many pits where the gold was melted over fires.

Further on, to the right of the road, are Byzantine buildings and a 13th C **basilica** with an impressive mosaic flooring and some fragmentary wall paintings.

Cybele and Artemis

You come now to the **Temple of Artemis**, still the most striking monument of Sardis. In the 18th C, travellers' records tell us eight columns complete with architrave were visible, but in the last 200-odd years the number has been whittled down to two. Excavation of the temple was a considerable task, first embarked on by Princeton University in 1910. It involved clearing nearly 10 metres of earth from the eastern section which had built up gradually from the soft soil washed off the hills. The original Lydian temple on this site was to Cybele, the Anatolian mother fertility goddess, but this was destroyed by the Persians at the time of the Ionian revolt in 499 BC. Its rebuilding was ordered by Alexander the Great, who was welcomed in the city with no opposition, and from that point on, it was dedicated to Artemis, the Greek version of the fertility goddess. Of the original total of 82 columns in the temple, only two are still intact, with 13 others standing to part of their height. The Ionic capitals of these columns are among the most beautiful known. The temple faces west, as opposed to the usual east, and on its western side are a flight of steps and an altar for sacrifices to Artemis. In Roman times its eastern half also served as a temple to the

Empress Faustina (see Miletos) and the whole therefore became a kind of double temple: another example of the simultaneous worship of rulers and deities.

The curious pointed hills around Sardis contain hundreds of **Lydian tombs**, some dating back to the 7th C BC. Many were cleared in 1910 but have since been covered up again by the constantly crumbling soil.

A further extensive **Lydian necropolis** lies 10km north of Sart, on the road that continues north from the Temple of Artemis and crosses the main road. The necropolis, its curious circular based tumuli visible from the Sardis road, is called Bin Tepe (a thousand hills) and runs along a ridge of hills for several kilometres. Dating from the 7th C BC, the largest of these are thought to be tombs of the Lydian kings.

Along the Way Back

If you have time on the return journey, you can make a detour about 20km before İzmir, to the town of **Kemalpaşa** where the ruins of the **Byzantine Palace of Nymphaeum** can be seen in a field at the side of the road. This was one of the imperial residences of the Lascarids who ruled the Byzantine Empire from Nicaea while Constantinople was under Latin occupation.

The Hittite Father

More interesting than this, however, is the **Hittite rock carving** which lies 8km beyond Kemalpaşa, at **Karabel**. The figure is carved on a rock about 100 metres to the left after passing under an arch. A step path leads up to it. In profile from the right, the figure is a typical stocky Hittite warrior, slightly over life size, wearing a pointed hat, dressed in a short tunic and walking in pointed boots. A bow is carried over one shoulder, while in his left hand he carries a spear. Above the spear is the outline of a bird and some worn hieroglyphic symbols. When first discovered by European scholars in 1840, the figure was thought to be an Egyptian pharaoh because of these hieroglyphs and a passage in Herodotus describing it. The Hittites were still a mystery race at this time, and were not re-discovered till the end of the 19th C. The locals call it 'Eti Baba', the Hittite Father. A second similar figure was found carved on a fallen rock about 200 metres below the first, by the left bank of the stream. At one time lost, this figure has now reappeared, and the two together are one of the very few Hittite relics in this part of Turkey, most of the major sites lying much further east (See the later section on Mersin).

SOUTH OF İZMIR

There are two major roads leaving İzmir to the south. The more major one leads due south to Ephesus and Kuşadasí, while the other leads off southwest to the resort of Çeşme at the end of a peninsula directly opposite the Greek island of Chios. This route is for those interested first and foremost in beaches, for though there are no less than five ancient Ionian cities on this peninsula, all are of very minor importance and little remains to be seen of them today. Of the five it is Teos, near the fishing village of Síğacík, which is the most attractive, set virtually on the beach; and it is also the most accessible.

The road leaving İzmir is marked Çesme and leads through heavily built-up suburbs along the coast. The first turn-off right after 10km or so is to **Incíraltí**, the closest beach resort to İzmir and consequently very overcrowded.

To the left a sign points off to the **Baths of Agamemnon**. These are hot sulphurous springs where Agamemnon, before the fall of Troy, was said to have gone with his soldiers to heal their wounds after a fierce battle. The waters are still taken today as a cure for rheumatism, sciatica, gallstones and eczema, and it is much frequented by local people. No sign of antiquity remains on the site today and it has the appearance of a normal thermal establishment.

A further 15km on you reach the town of Güzelbahçe, and it is just after this that a road forks off south to Síğacík.

Síğacík and Teos
The seaside village of **Síğacík** is a pretty spot with a fine Genoese fortress dominating its little fishing harbour. Continuing on to the headland beyond it (c.2km, signposted Akkum), are a couple of hotels with camping sites, situated in a pair of very pretty small sandy coves, making a pleasant last night stay if you are returning via İzmir airport, a total of about 1¼ hours' drive away.

Nearby on the headland, a road forks off to the site of **Teos**, with the **Temple of Dionysus** situated among the olive trees, and the whole area around scattered with fragments of columns, carved blocks and walls. A small **odeon** with 11 rows of seats can also be discerned in the undergrowth. The **theatre** is very overgrown and is set off a few hundred yards' walk from the temple across the fields.

From the temple it is just a short distance on to a huge open sandy beach for a swim. There are a few shacks selling refreshments here, but no accommodation.

Pipped to death Founded around 900 BC, the city of Teos was one of the wealthiest of the Ionian cities, and at one stage was a more

70

significant port than Smyrna. Dionysus was the principal deity at Teos, and in the 3rd C BC the city was given the honour of being chosen as the residence for a branch of the Artists of Dionysus. These artists were professional actors and musicians paid to perform in the theatres and at festivals throughout the Greek world. As artists under the patronage of Dionysus, they had special status and were exempt from taxation and guaranteed safe conduct. The artistic temperament being what it is, however, these men were notoriously difficult and many quarrels broke out between them and the townspeople. They were finally compelled to move on to Ephesus around 150 BC, where they were no more popular. This period did, however, give Teos its most notable citizen, Anacreon, one of the greatest lyric poets, who lived here all his life composing poems on wine, women and song, till at a banquet at the age of 85 he died choking on a grape pip.

Teos is described in Pliny's geographical accounts as an island, a comment which has led scholars to speculate on coastal changes, or man-made canals built by Alexander the Great. No such construction can be found, however, and it is more likely, as George Bean comments in one of his many withering asides on Pliny, 'that we have merely another of Pliny's numerous mistakes'.

Çeşme

Returning from Sığacík to the main road near Güzelbahçe, you now turn left and head due west along the peninsula towards Çeşme. A detour can be made off to the right after about 10 km near Urla to see the ancient site of **Clazomenae**, one of the Ionian cities, originally an island connected to the mainland by a causeway built by Alexander the Great. Parts of this ancient causeway are still visible, next to a modern one but the island today houses a quarantine area with a hospital for bone diseases, so visitors are not very welcome. Little remains of the ancient town now, for its closeness to the sea and ease of access by boat meant that it served early on as a quarry for the architects of Byzantine and Ottoman Constantinople, for whom it was easier to ship out ready-carved blocks than to quarry new marble and limestone.

A further 16 km on another road forks left and runs along the 60 km of spectacular coastline to **Karaburun** on the headland north of Çeşme. If you have the time to spare, driving round these little developed areas can be highly enjoyable, and whole stretches are totally uninhabited.

The main road continues on to **Çeşme** 35 km away, a well-developed resort and thermal spa with long sandy beaches, several holiday villages and the full range of water sports. On the harbour stands a handsome **Genoese fortress** built in the 14th C, and later heavily restored by the

Ottomans. On 5 July 1770 the bay of Çeşme was witness to the fierce naval battle between the Russians and the Ottomans which destroyed part of the Turkish fleet. Near the fortress are the ruins of an 18thC **caravanserai**. From the harbour a regular ferry (daily in summer) runs to the Greek island of Chios, just 14 km distant.

Abandoned
Greek homes There are several smaller resorts in the vicinity of Çeşme, all of which can be explored for those with time. One of the most interesting is off to the north on the west side of the peninsula, near the popular resort of Ilíca. North of Ilíca a road leads on to the seaside village of **Ildír**, site of ancient Erythrae, another of the Ionian cities. The setting is very attractive, though the ruins themselves are scanty, consisting largely of the city wall, an aqueduct and a theatre. Ildír itself had a largely Greek population, which explains the deserted houses abandoned in the exchange of populations in 1923.

Colophon, Claros and Notion

Leaving İzmir by the more major of the two routes, towards Selçuk and Aydín, the road eventually leaves the urban sprawl of İzmir behind, and begins to enter a pleasantly green landscape with rolling hills and lush valleys. Branching off this road after about 10 km, a detour can be made towards the sea, to visit three more Ionian cities, all closely linked. The first of these, **Colophon**, near the village of Değirmendere, is of interest only to archaeologists, as nothing remains save a few crumbling walls. In antiquity, however, Colophon was a very prosperous city, famous for its horses and cavalry supplemented by fierce dogs as vanguards. Its wealth stemmed mainly from the thousands of pilgrims who came to visit the oracle of Apollo at nearby Claros.

Archaeology
in reverse Although **Claros** was never a city, consisting only of the oracle and temple of Apollo, more is left of Claros today than of Colophon. The site of Claros is reached by continuing on past Degirmendere towards the coast, and the ruins lie about 500 metres off to the left of the road. As they are not visible from the road, being set down in an overgrown hollow of a river valley, locating them is not that straightforward. Tumbled by an earthquake and then silted up under the river mud, the site of the temple was unknown for a long time. The French finally conducted excavations in 1950 and the **Temple of Apollo** and the oracle chambers underneath were brought to light. Set below the level of the water table as it was, excavations were always difficult, and constant pumping had to be done to keep the ruins above the water. It has already fast become silted up again, and the vivid descriptions of stairways leading down to the oracle chambers which can be read in accounts written in the 1960s are unfortunately no longer accurate records of what is to be seen. It is astonishing that 20-odd years of neglect and silting can so transform a

site, so that what now remains visible in the overgrown hollow are a few large fragments of the cult statue of Apollo and some massive column drums. The enormous altar table, nearly 20 metres long, and the underground chambers from where the oracle delivered his pronouncements, have totally disappeared. In a few years time, if no excavation work is done, there will probably be nothing left to see at all. It is a remarkable case of archaeology going backwards.

A further 2 km on is a large sand beach between two headlands, with the fragmentary ruins of **Notion**, port to Colophon, scattered over the left headland as you face the sea. Exploring these makes a bracing cliff-top walk, though the ruins, among which are a temple, agora and theatre, are all very poorly preserved. On the beach are a handful of tatty restaurants offering very basic accommodation facilities and camping.

Undeveloped coastline

These three sites, though of some interest, are minor and represent a considerable detour from the main route to Ephesus: Ephesus itself is only 15 to 20 km from Notion along the coast, but the road is poor and can become very marshy, so unless you have a four-wheel drive vehicle it is advisable to retrace your steps all the way back to the main road before continuing southwards. This trio of sites are therefore really more suitable as a day trip for travellers based in İzmir than as a stop for travellers touring with limited time. An alternative beach is at **Gümüşsu**, which has a campsite and motel, reached by forking off west, a little north of Değirmendere. From Gümüşsu a drivable road forks off left (west) to **Doğanbey**, a small town in a spectacular setting on a barren plateau overlooking the sea and passing near the heavily ruined city of **Lebedos**, a minor Ionian town on the way. From Doğanbey a winding drive along a dusty but spectacular track leads along the coast to Seferihisar, from where you can stay in Síğacík and then return on to İzmir. This drive gives you an excellent feel for the beauty of the Aegean coast away from resorts like Kuşadasí.

EPHESUS

Mystery tomb

An unusual monument of interest enroute to Ephesus lies 16 km north of Selçuk, just off the main road, at the village of **Belevi**. It is reached by turning left near a petrol station and left again a little later at the entrance to the village of Belevi on the unmade-up road to Tire. Lying on a hill about 100 metres to the right of the road, you will see a magnificent and unusual **mausoleum** which has not yet been identified despite extensive excavations as no inscriptions have been found here. Thought to date from the 3rd C BC the structure was about 23 metres high, consisting of a huge core of rock 25 metres square, faced with solid marble blocks. On this was a chamber of marble, elaborately decorated with friezes. The sarcophagus, now on display in the Ephesus museum, was secreted inside the rock core and is finely carved with reliefs and the dead man himself reclining on his elbow on the lid.

It has been speculated that this magnificent mausoleum, lying roughly on the ancient route from Ephesus to Sardis was the tomb of Antiochus II of Syria, assassinated in Ephesus in 246 BC by his wife and half-sister Laodice. Some scholars however think it dates from around the 4th C BC, when the region was under Persian rule, in which case it could have been the tomb of a wealthy Persian noble.

Showpiece of the Aegean

As you continue southwards through the fertile Ionian landscape, the sight of a crenellated Byzantine fortress on a hilltop to the right of the road heralds your imminent arrival in **Selçuk**, the site of ancient **Ephesus** (Efes in Turkish).

Surreal city

Famous throughout history for its Temple of Artemis, one of the Seven Wonders of the Ancient World and the most important shrine of Asia Minor, this great and sacred city lay in ruins in southwestern Turkey largely forgotten till earlier this century. H V Morton, writing in 1936 said: 'Ephesus stands dignified and alone in its death with no sign of life but a goatherd leaning on a broken sarcophagus or a lonely peasant outlined against a mournful sunset. Few people ever visit it. Ephesus has a weird, haunted look'.

Today's visitor is most unlikely to see Ephesus under the same conditions. The poor roads which had previously made a visit of any sort difficult have now been replaced by a fast stretch of tarmac which links you with İzmir in less than an hour, and Ephesus, transformed by excavations into the showpiece site of Turkey's Aegean coast, is visited daily by thousands — in summer, anyway: a winter visit can sometimes find not another soul in sight, perhaps a darkening sky streaked with sudden sunlight lighting up the empty white

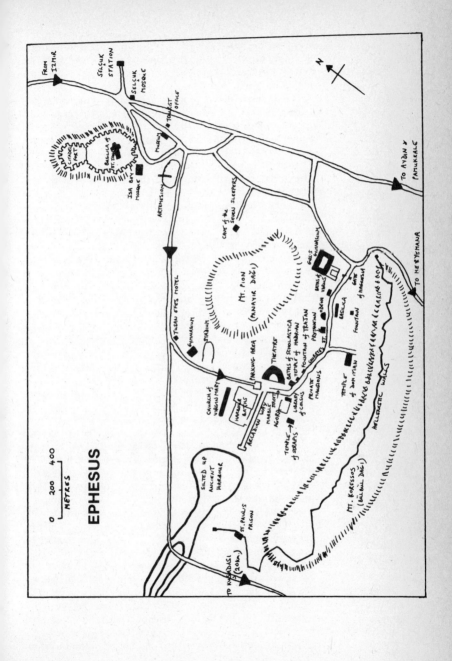

EPHESUS

0 200 400
MÈTRES

FROM IZMIR

SELÇUK STATION

SELÇUK MOSQUE

TOURIST OFFICE

MUSEUM

ISA BEY MOSQUE

BASILICA of ST. JOHN
BYZANTINE FORT

ARTEMISION

CAVE of the SEVEN SLEEPERS

TO AYDIN & PAMUKKALE

N

MT. PION (PANAYIR DAĞI)

TUSAN EFES MOTEL

GYMNASIUM

STADIUM

PARKING AREA

THEATRE

CHURCH of VIRGIN MARY

HARBOUR BATHS

ARCADIANE WAY

MARBLE STREET

AGORA

LIBRARY of CELSUS

TEMPLE of SERAPIS

BATHS of SCHOLASTICA
TEMPLE of HADRIAN
FOUNTAIN of TRAJAN

CURETES ST.

PRYTANEUM

ODEON

PRIVATE MANSIONS

BASILICA

BATHS & VARIUS

GATE of HADRIAN

GIRLS GYMNASIUM

FOUNTAIN

TEMPLE of DOMITIAN

MT. KORESSOS (BÜLBÜL DAĞI)

HELLENISTIC WALLS

SILTED UP ANCIENT HARBOUR

ST. PAUL'S PRISON

TO KUŞADASI (20 km.)

TO MERYEMANA

75

marble streets, the whole effect that of an unreal ghost city.

Ephesus is one of the largest archaeological sites in the world, and falls into three distinct areas to visit today: the Artemesion (site of the Temple of Artemis, equivalent to the Roman Diana); the old acropolis with the Byzantine fortress, St John's Basilica, the Isa Bey Mosque and the museum; and finally the main city of Ephesus itself, about 2 km further on along the road to Kuşadasí.

Many people seem not to bother with the first two areas, but head instead straight off to the main site. As a result these areas are often pleasantly deserted and can make an enjoyable stroll for a hour and a half or so before or after the main site, which needs at least three hours.

One of the Seven Wonders of the Ancient World

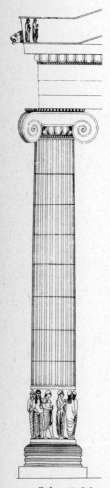

Forking right in the town of Sclçuk towards Kuşadasí, you pass first the tourist office, artisans' shops and a little museum, and then after 200 metres or so, the road passes immediately to the left of the **Artemision**, announced by yellow signs. Consisting for most of the year of one column rising out of a muddy pool, many do not even stop. The temple is, admittedly, a far cry from the spectacular Wonder of the World people may have seen in artists' reconstructions. Originally four times greater in area than the Parthenon, it had 127 columns, each nearly 20 metres high. The site of the temple was totally unknown till the late 19th C when an English engineer and architect, John T Wood, arrived on the scene. This man made it has life's ambition to discover the temple and he worked at Ephesus between 1863 and 1874 embarking on a series of largely random excavations, and spending a considerable private fortune in the process. His clue finally came in the form of an inscription found in the theatre which described how sacred images were carried from the theatre to the Magnesian Gate and along the sacred way to the temple. Wood located the Magnesian Gate (the gate facing Magnesia to the southeast of the city), but the sacred way from here was buried deep underground as a result of the gradual silting up of Ephesus' natural harbour. Thus protected, the sacred way had survived in good condition, with marble paving over 10 metres wide, and after much digging it eventually led to the temple itself, buried 5 metres below the surface. His romantic ambitions fulfilled after 11 years of painstaking effort, Wood returned to England and it was left to David Hogarth, the archaeologist and traveller, to excavate in 1904 to uncover the temple to its lowest level. There, in the foundations, he discovered a magnificent collection of gold objects and reliefs which he promptly shipped back to the British Museum. The earliest finds here have been dated to the 8th C BC.

Many people have expressed surprise at the uninspiring

Column of the Artemision

position of the temple on low flat ground outside the city. A prominent Parthenon-like position would seem more appropriate. In fact most of the major Ionic temples of Asia Minor are likewise situated, as at Sardis and Didyma, and the theory is that the tall slender Ionic columns were shown off better by flat ground, while the broader, squatter Doric columns needed a higher position to be seen to their best advantage.

Lady of All Wild Things

Artemis of the Ephesians was never a truly Greek goddess, but was rather a Greek adaptation of the earlier Anatolian earth-mother goddess, Cybele, who had a sanctuary here before the Ionian founders of Ephesus arrived in c1100 BC. Her outstanding characteristic was her fertility, and it is this which has been carried through to Artemis Ephesia, unmistakably fertile in her multi-breasted form. The two alabaster statues in the site museum show her in highly stylised form, covered from the hips down in finely carved animals, lions, bulls, sphinxes and even the mythical chimaera (see the later section on Olympos), and from the waist up in rows of breasts. While undeniably a powerful symbol of fertility, Artemis in this form bears little resemblance to the lithe virgin huntress of the Greeks. The only point of similarity is the animals, often shown at the feet of the Greek Artemis. Some have speculated that Artemis/Cybele derived from the mythical Amazons, a race of warrior maidens who cut off their right breast so that it did not impede their use of bow and arrow. They shunned men, but slept with them once a year in order to perpetuate the race. The resultant male children were made slaves and the female children were trained for fighting. Artemis was often depicted as an Amazon, left breast bare, with a drape over the right half to cover the scar. This could be seen as the link with the chastity of Artemis as the goddess of the hunt, and also seems a plausible explanation of the annual orgies held in Ephesus on the feast day of Artemis. With this in mind, Homer's description of her as 'Mistress of Beasts and Lady of All Wild Things' seems apt.

When the Romans arrived, they too embraced the worship of the goddess, identifying her with Diana, their own fertility goddess and protectress of women in childbirth. The power of the goddess was remarkable, and her widespread fame made Ephesus the object of pilgrimage for more than 1000 years, bringing great wealth to the city, and emperors conferred special privileges on her sanctuary. Anyone taking refuge in the temple was granted immediate asylum.

St Paul, St John and the Virgin Mary

The rival to her dominance came finally in the form of Christianity, which took root early in Ephesus. When St Paul came her in AD 53 he already found a small group of converts. Paul lived in the city for three years and his preaching was so successful that local businessmen whose living from selling artefacts for the temple and the goddess was being damaged, staged a riot against the Christians who they claimed were challenging the greatness of Artemis. Paul left Ephesus after this incident, later to write his letters to the Ephesians, the most profound of his Epistles. St John too, accompanied according to many by the Virgin Mary, also lived in Ephesus, between AD 37 and 48, returning to write his gospel till he died in AD 95. With the spread of Christianity Ephesus became in the 4th C the seat of a vast diocese covering several provinces. The temples of the city were abandoned at this point and served as marble quarries for new construction. The beautiful marble blocks of the Temple of Artemis were dismantled and used to build the basilica of St John in Ephesus and other buildings.

Church, Mosque and Citadel

The decline of the Roman Empire in the 3rd C coincided in Ephesus with the ever increasing problems of the silting up of the harbour. The sea had originally come in all the way to the Artemision, making a natural sheltered harbour on the mouth of the river Cayster. The silting up of the river over the years meant that the city had to be moved, shortly after Alexander's death in 323 BC, to a new site further to the west. Throughout its most prosperous times in the height of the Roman Empire, Ephesus was always struggling against the constant silting up of the harbour. Nero and Hadrian instituted measures to try to counteract it, such as diverting the course of the river, but all efforts were in vain, and the port of Ephesus is now over 5 km from the sea. Its link with the sea severed in the 6th C, Ephesus' period of greatness was over. Justinian confirmed this break by building the Basilica of St John away from the city on the hill above the present town of Selçuk, which has remained the centre of habitation to this day.

Decline, mud and fall

From the Artemision the next building, slightly to the north at the foot of the hill, is the Seljuk **Isa Bey Camii**. The double-domed mosque, dating from the 14th C, is approached through a magnificent stalactite portal leading into a picturesquely ruined courtyard with grass and bird's nests on its high walls. The court was once run round on three sides by domed arcades supported by white marble and grey granite classical columns and capitals. Within the mosque itself, restored in the 1970s, the arches are supported by large granite antique columns, grey and pink, which came originally from the Port Baths of Ephesus; the capitals are Seljuk except for one which is Roman. There is no minbar and the mihrab is concrete. The mosque was built in 1375 by isa Bey, son of Mehmet Bey, one of the emirs of Aydín; the Seljuks had captured Ephesus in 1304 and ruled over much of western Turkey before the Ottomans.

Only a single column of the Artemision remains; beyond is the basilica of St John

A climb of 200 metres up the road beside the mosque brings you to the **Gate of Persecution**, the entrance to the precinct of the crenellated fortress on the hilltop, within which lies the Basilica of St John. This **fortress**, originally built by the Byzantines but restored by the Seljuks, was the stronghold of the town, called Ayasoluk by the Turks at that time. This was the final flourish of prosperity the town enjoyed before sliding into oblivion. Part of the fortress is now a military camp into which entry is forbidden.

The **Basilica of St John**, built during the reign of Justinian in the early 6thC, is impressive partly for its fine site and view down over what used to be the harbour of Ephesus towards the sea and partly because of its vast proportions. Within a large arcaded court the basilica, 110 metres long and 40 metres wide, had a five-domed narthex, four domes running down the nave and a dome in each arm of the transept. The upper storeys of the nave and transept are supported by flying buttresses. All this is undergoing complete reconstruction: the church suffered greatly during the Byzantines' attempt to repulse the Turks in the 13thC, though the Turks in turn restored it, converting it into a mosque in 1330. But then the sanctuary was partly destroyed by an earthquake and in 1402 the church was razed when Tamerlane's Mongols sacked the town. Some floor *mosaics* and *frescoes* survive.

Approaching the site from the south you should bear left for the *narthex*, passing from there into the nave (otherwise you might find yourself arriving at almost any point of the basilica and become completely confused). The *nave* has aisles on either side, marked off by massive smooth marble columns, white streaked with grey. At the altar four columns with spiral fluting indicate the *tomb of the Apostle John* who died in Ephesus around AD 100 after returning from his exile on Patmos.

On the south side of the church, at the edge of the terrace, is a topographical block showing, as you look out over the landscape below, the shifting shoreline through the centuries and the various positions adopted by Ephesus as it chased after the receding sea.

The attractive little **museum** (9am to 12, 1.30 to 6pm, except Mondays) is well worth a visit for the two marble *statues of Artemis Ephesia* in her multi-breasted form (37 to be precise), found in the Prytaneion or town hall of Ephesus, and dating from the 1st and 2nd C AD. Some scholars have postulated that the three rows of breasts are in fact a necklase of huge eggs to symbolise her fertility, and certainly the breasts are distinctly egg-shaped. Continuing the theme of fertility, there is also the statue of Priapus, who is, as one journalist put it "balancing a basket of fruit on his instrument of plenty." The other notable exhibit is in the entrance hall, a lovely bronze statue of *Eros riding a dolphin*, dating from the 2nd C AD.

Entering the Main Ephesus Site

About 1 km beyond the Artemision, towards the sea and Kuşadasí, a road turns off left at the Tusan Efes Motel towards the site of the main city of Ephesus located between the slopes of two hills, Mt Pion and Mt Koressos (Bülbül Daği or Nightingale Mountain in Turkish). Though the position of the site cannot be claimed to be in anyway spectacular, unlike such sites as Pergamum and Priene, its unique interest lies in its completeness as a city. With its magnificently paved white marble streets flanked with colonnades, numerous civic buildings and its extensive quarter of wealthy houses, it is perhaps easier in Ephesus than in any other Graeco-Roman city to relive its past grandeurs. Austrian archaeologists have been almost exclusively responsible for the excavations of the city on and off since 1898.

The approach road takes you past the ruins of a vast **gymnasium** (2nd C AD) and a **stadium**, which you can examine at your leisure after visiting the main site. The stadium is now in a poor state of preservation because its blocks were plundered and used to rebuild the Byzantine fortress at Selçuk. The official site entrance is at the parking area a little further on, with clusters of crass souvenir shops and a few tea houses and restaurants. Tickets are bought here and parking and cameras are charged extra. The site is open daily from 8.30 to sunset.

View from the theatre

The best thing to do first is to head straight on from the entrance to the theatre at the junction of the marble road and the Arcadian Way, and climb to the top seats, from where you can get your bearings and digest the history.

The grandiose ruins of Ephesus you see before you date almost exclusively from the Roman imperial age. First founded by Ionians in around 1100 BC, the original city was located on the north slope of the theatre hill, above where the current stadium is. This area was at that time on the sea, and with its natural harbour together with its sanctuary of Artemis, Ephesus quickly prospered from sea-trade and the constant influx of pilgrims visiting the shrine. Its prosperity attracted the Lydian king. Croesus of Sardis (already 'rich as Croesus') who sought to make it his first colony. He destroyed the city but did not touch the sanctuary, instead donating column drums for its completion carved with his name (now on display in the British Museum). He moved the inhabitants to the land south of the Artemision, which is where the classical city stood until the 4th C BC. This area has never been properly excavated, and indeed excavations would be difficult because of the change in the water table since antiquity. The city stood here unwalled and militarily indefensible, but thanks to its harbour and its sanctuary, its prosperity continued throughout Lydian, then Persian rule, then under the Delian Confederacy. It remained under Persian dominion till Alexander's arrival in 334 BC. Shortly

An arsonist's bid for fame

before this, in 356 BC, Herostratus, a maniac in need of immortal fame, set fire to the Temple of Artemis and destroyed it — that his name is remembered today shows that perhaps he was not so crazy after all. On Alexander's arrival the Ephesians were still rebuilding it. So impressed was Alexander by the construction that he offered to pay all expenses, past and future, to complete the structure, if the dedicatory inscription could be in his name. The Ephesians politely declined this magnanimous gesture, saying it was not fitting for a god to make a dedication to another god. It was this version of the temple which, after finally being completed by the Ephesians' own efforts, was hailed as one of the Seven Wonders of the World and as the greatest temple in Asia Minor.

On Alexander's death Ephesus came, like the rest of Ionia, under the rule of Lysimachus, one of Alexander's generals. Seeing the increasing silting up of the harbour, Lysimachus abandoned the old city and harbour and moved the city to its current site, with the new harbour to the west (at the end of the Arcadian Way). The only construction which remains from this time are the extensive defence walls built by Lysimachus, still standing high on the hill above the theatre and running down towards the harbour and ending in a handsome tower called, for no discernible reason, St Paul's Prison. The Roman remnants of today were rebuilt over the earlier Hellenistic ones, which is why nothing remains of them.

Throughout her history Ephesus was not noted for her firm loyalties, but rather she perfected the art of bending whichever way the wind was blowing, and thus remained prosperous throughout.

She was at the height of her prosperity in the early Roman Empire, as capital city of the Roman Province of Asia and residence of the governor. Her population at this time has been estimated at around a quarter of a million, and she styled herself 'first and greatest metropolis of Asia'.

From the Theatre to the Harbour

The **theatre** itself testifies to this importance, with a seating capacity of about 25,000. Its acoustics are excellent and it is still used for performances during the Seljuk Ephesus Festival of Culture and Art in May. The original building is Hellenistic, dating from the time of Lysimachus, with the cavea slightly more than a semi-circle in the Greek style and with 12 stairways and two diazomas (horizontal walkways round the cavea). The stage building in particular was rebuilt and enlarged on several occasions during Roman rule, starting in AD 40 and taking 70 years to complete. Building was therefore still in progress when St Paul preached here in the theatre during his stay in Ephesus.

Cleopatra's grand entry

The view from the theatre along the **Arcadian Way** towards the sea and ancient harbour conjurs up visions of past grandeur. 500 metres long and 11 metres wide, paved in white marble and lined with shops and porticoes, it led straight to the ancient harbour, now silted up, but still just discernible from the different colour of the grass. It was up this thoroughfare that Cleopatra, Queen of Egypt, made her triumphal entry to the city on a visit to Mark Antony. We know from inscriptions that the street was also provided with street lighting from 400 BC onwards, a great rarity. Antioch, modern Antakya, had it from the 4th C BC but still in the 1st C BC the streets of Rome were unlit. Like all the other streets at Ephesus, it is endowed with elaborate water and sewage systems.

The northern side of the Arcadian Way is bordered by an enormous complex of *harbour baths* and a *gymnasium* with two large *palaestras* (open courtyards for exercise).

A short walk behind the harbour baths brings you to the curious long thin building called the **Church of the Virgin Mary**. It was not originally a church at all, but a long hall with

View of Ephesus from the theatre and along the Arcadian Way

an apse at each end, and a row of small rooms along each side.
It was used for lectures, discussions and seminars, and was
the closest thing to a place of higher education. It was
destroyed by fire in the 3rd C AD and the ruins of the western
half were converted into a basilica with a courtyard in front.
It was here that the violent third Ecumenical Council was
held in AD 431 where Nestorius, the Patriarch of Constantinople, who denied the virgin birth and claimed that
Jesus was God in man but not God, was charged with heresy
and thrown out of the church. A baptistry was added on the
north side of the courtyard, still quite well-preserved with a
walk-in font for immersion during baptism. Two later
churches have also been built on the site, adding to the
general confusion of the architectural plan.

To the Heart of the City

Returning to the theatre and turning right, you now enter the
Marble Street, its paving still in very good condition. From
the ruts, it was clearly not just a pedestrian precinct. The
handsome *Doric stoa* on its west side dates from the 1st C AD.

At the end of the Marble Street on the right stands the
impressive **Library of Celsus**, the best preserved structure of
its kind in the world, recently painstakingly restored by the
Austrian excavators. An interesting architectural trick in the
facade is the way the columns and capitals at the edges are

smaller than those in the middle, thus creating an illusion of greater width. It faces due east following the rule laid down by the Roman architect Vitruvius, so that it gets the morning light. Inside it was one large room, over 15 metres high, with three storeys of galleries running round on all sides. Niches for the books are visible only on the lower storey. At the back wall is the grave chamber of Celsus himself, Proconsul of Asia in AD 106, usually kept locked, with a marble sarcophagus inside. Burial inside the city like this as opposed to outside the walls in the graveyard, was a considerable honour. Both the library and tomb were built in his memory by his son.

Hecate's wrath From the courtyard in front of the library, a fine marble gateway with three arches leads through to the **agora**. A threatening graffiti scrawled on one side of the gate warns: 'Whoso relieves himself here shall suffer the wrath of Hecate'.

Behind the library to the west are the ruins of the **Temple of Serapis**. Based on the Apis full of Saggara combined with Osiris, Serapis was an invention of the Ptolemies who imposed on its Egyptian origins the features of a Greek god. Serapis became surprisingly popular with the Greeks and the Romans, and his cult flourished in many major cities of the eastern provinces. This temple is remarkable, as are so many Egyptian monuments, for its massive scale. It had eight gigantic monolithic columns, each column 1.5 metres in diameter and 15 metres high. It is all very ruinous. Several of the surviving blocks and columns show traces of the red paint with which it was originally painted. Most temples and statues were painted in antiquity, and of the two colours most commonly used, red and blue, the red was always the more durable.

Downtown Ephesus ... From the library the Curetes Street, named after an order of priests attached to the Artemision and the most impressive marble street in ancient Ephesus, climbs up between the two hills to lead eventually to the Magnesian Gate. This was downtown Ephesus, so to speak, with all the expensive private houses to the right and the various public buildings to the left.

... and the red light district At the beginning of the street on the left are the **Baths of Scholastica**, named after a Christian matron called Scholastica who renovated it in the 4th C. The complex included, besides the baths themselves, a large dining hall, a dormitory and a large well-appointed cluster of latrines in white marble. Graffiti on the walls and various lurid figurines found in this area suggest that the complex was at one stage used as a brothel.

The next building fronting on to the street is one of the most attractive buildings in Ephesus, the **Temple of Hadrian**. This small but elegant temple, with its graceful arch and facade of two centred columns and two pillars, re-erected from fragments found during the excavations, was built in the 2nd C AD by a wealthy Ephesian who dedicated the temple to the deified emperor. The elaborate reliefs which decorate its facade are plaster casts of the originals which are in the site museum in Seljuk.

Opposite the Temple of Hadrian on the other hillside is the extensive **quarter of wealthy Roman apartments**, still being excavated and many of them locked up and protected by roofing erected by the Austrian excavators. Dating from the 1st to the 6th C AD, many of these houses, more like mansions with several storeys, have remnants of well-preserved murals with colours still visible and mosaic floors. These houses, together with the three main marble streets, more than anything make Ephesus a uniquely complete city, closer today to its atmosphere of 1800 years ago than almost any other ancient city.

Continuing up the street, on the left just above the Temple of Hadrian is the elaborate **Fountain of Trajan**, another Roman emperor, and the statues which once adorned the niches are on display in the Ephesus museum. The base of the colossal statue of the emperor himself still sits here with one of his two enormous feet resting nonchalantly on a globe of the world.

Further up the street, both sides are flanked with remnants of columns, fountains, pedestals and statues, till you reach a junction branching off to the right. A little way along this fork on the right you see the enormous foundations of the **Temple of Domitian**, erected in the 1st C for the deified emperor, and beyond this a **Museum of Inscriptions**.

Artemis 'the many-breasted' protected from the Christians

Returning to the Curetes Street and continuing up the hill, you come next to the **Prytaneion**, or town hall of Ephesus, on your left. It was in this building that the two famous statues of Artemis 'polymastros' were found, for it contained an area consecrated to the goddess, as well as being the place where acts of government were passed and where magistrates and ambassadors were based. Though the building and its contents were despoiled by over-enthusiastic Christians after the 6th C, the two statues were singled out and deferentially wrapped up for protection, a testimony to the power the goddess held, even at this late stage.

Immediately next door to the Prytaneion is the **odeon**, with 23 rows of seats, used for both senate meetings and for musical performances. Built around AD 150, the auditorium could hold about 1400 people.

Opposite the odeon is the large **state agora**, ruined apart from the columns along its northern side. A double row of columns with alternate Corinthian and Ionic capitals (with bulls' heads) divided a large basilica into three naves. In a raised platform area on the west side of the agora, the foundations of a small Doric **temple** have been found.

Objects found in the area suggest it was dedicated to Isis, and nearby the head of a huge statue closely resembling Mark Antony was found. Antony was known to have visited Ephesus on various occasions between 42 and 31 BC, and given his association with Cleopatra, who in any case identified herself with Isis, the excavators have suggested that Mark Antony had the temple built to the Egyptian goddess. Its age also fits, as it dates to the second half of the 1st C BC.

On the south side of the agora is a large **fountain** at the end of the aqueduct which brought water to the city from the spring of Marmas, 6 km away to the south. Some arches of this aqueduct can still be seen on the Aydín road, 5 km from Selçuk, to the right of the road.

The final monument before the Magnesian Gate at the edge of the city is the **Baths of Varius**. Dating from the 4th or 5th C AD, the baths still have latrines and a large mosaic floor.

Through the Magnesian Gate
The **Magnesian Gate** is today largely ruined, but it was from here that the **sacred way** led round the back of Mt Pion to the Artemision, a distance of over 2 km. This gives an idea of the scale of the task that the English engineer John Wood set himself, digging it out from under several metres of earth, in his quest for the Temple of Artemis. The vast **gymnasium** to the left opened out on to the sacred way. It is sometimes called the Girls' Gymnasium, not because it was for young girls, but because of the large number of female statues found in it.

The big sleep
You can in fact leave the site by this sacred way if you are feeling energetic, through the second site entrance here, and walk back to the site of the Artemision. A little over halfway there a track forks off left to the **Cave of the Seven Sleepers** of Ephesus at the foot of Mt Pion, site of an impressive Byzantine necropolis. According to the legend, seven young men were persecuted for their Christian faith at the time of the Emperor Decius (AD 248–251) and took refuge in a cave in the vicinity of Ephesus. Here the seven men fell asleep, and on waking up, went to the city to buy bread and found that they had slept not for one night but for 200 years, and were now in the reign of Theodosius with Christianity proclaimed as the state religion. Theodosius, on being told this remarkable story, took it as confirmation of the doctrine of the bodily resurrection, a thorny issue in the Church, then as it is now. When the seven men eventually died they were buried in the cave where they had slept and a church was built next to it. The cave henceforth became an object of pilgrimage as well as a burial area. Excavations carried out here in 1927–28 revealed a small church with a rock-cut gallery beneath it, and numerous other tombs.

Meryemana: Christian Shrine

The final place to visit near Ephesus is Meryemana, **House of the Blessed Virgin**, where Mary was said to have lived her last days. The presence of this shrine has made the spot an object of pilgrimage from all over the Christian world. Reached by forking right off the main Selçuk-Bodrum road about 1 km south of Selçuk, passing by the Magnesian Gate site entrance, and then continuing for 7 km till you reach what is called today Panayia Kapulu. The house-chapel here lies in a pretty rural spot with abundant trees and terraces, a fountain, shops and a little restaurant. Irrespective of your religious beliefs, its a pleasant and peaceful spot for lunch.

The Ephesians had long insisted that when St John came to Ephesus Mary accompanied him and lived here between AD 37 and 48, and then died here. Christ had after all entrusted his mother to John on the cross. This was contrary to the canonical tradition that Mary died in Jerusalem at the age of 63. Between AD 37 and 48 there was no information as to where John was and what he was doing, and he may therefore well have been at Ephesus with Mary, far from the events recorded in Palestine. This could also explain why St Paul on arrival in Asia Minor in around AD 50 already found churches established.

A remarkable vision
This house at Panayia Kapulu was not discovered till the end of the 19th C when an invalid German woman, Catherine Emmerich, published a *Life of the Blessed Virgin Mary* based on her visions. Confined to her bed for the last 12 years of her life and never having set foot in Ephesus or Turkey, Emmerich described in her book the exact location of the Virgin's house on a hillside near Ephesus. Following this detailed description, the Father Superior of the Lazarists from İzmir led a search party in 1891 in the hills round Ephesus, and discovered this ruined house which exactly fitted the description in Emmerich's visionary book. The masonry of the house has been dated to the 6th C, but scholars have said the foundations might well go back as far as the 1st C. The Lazarists also discovered that the local Orthodox Greeks had for a long time assembled here on 15 August each year to hold a festival commemorating the death of the Virgin. On the basis of this extraordinary story, the archbishop of İzmir in 1892 authorised the celebration of mass in the building, and the house was pronounced an official place of pilgrimage. It was tastefully restored in 1951, and in 1967 Pope Paul VI made a visit here.

Numerous pilgrims have claimed to have been cured from their illnesses and afflictions here, and many still come in search of a cure. The **Virgin's tomb** itself was described in Catherine Emmerich's book as being about 1 km from the house, but all efforts to find it have so far been unsuccessful.

KUŞADASI

A pleasant drive of about 20 km west beyond Ephesus leads on to **Kuşadasí**, the major Aegean resort of Turkey. Unfortunately the town itself does not live up to the promise of the drive. Once the loveliest bay on the Aegean with a pretty fishing village, it is now one of the most developed pieces of coastline in Turkey packed with hotels and pensions, and has consequently lost most of its original charm. Even Turks express their dislike of it since it has become so built-up. The development now extends beyond the main town beach, into the next bay, called Kadínlar Plají, where hotels like the Imbat stand. In hotels like these, with disco and private beach, you could be anywhere in the Mediterranean. The converted 17th C Kervansaray hotel in the main town square at least has a Turkish flavour.

For the birds   Kuşadasí (Bird Island) is so named after the island now linked to the mainland by a concrete causeway at the far end of the bay. The **Genoese fortress** on the island with its fine vaulted keep, has good views over land and sea. There has been a harbour here since the early settlement of this coast. It was known as Ania to the Byzantines and as Scala Nuova to the Italian merchants who used it in the 15th C. It is now a

Sailing yacht at Bird Island, Kuşadasí

major port of call for Aegean cruise ships, stopping long enough to pour their passengers out into the shops and into nearby Ephesus for their dose of culture.

A Good Base

Kuşadasí does, however, have the virtue of being extremely well placed as a base for visiting the sites of Ephesus, Priene, Miletos, Didyma, Lake Bafa, Aphrodisias and Pamukkale. So if you can find a hotel you like (perhaps on B & B terms so that you can sample the many restaurants lining the front), you can combine the pleasures of sunshine and sea with occasional adventures inland. Other plus points for the town are the good public beach on its main bay, an interesting market with a fine selection of jewellery and leather clothes and a general liveliness — though in winter it is irredeniably dull.

Boats run daily in summer across to the Greek island of Samos where you can go for just the day or longer.

PRIENE

Setting off from either Kuşadasí or Selçuk, you can visit the southernmost cluster of Ionian sites, Priene, Miletos and Didyma, in a full day, ending either at Altínkum if you are touring, or else returning to Kuşadasí if this is your base. The drive south from Kuşadasí to Söke passes through some of the loveliest Ionian landscapes, and then 8 km south of Söke a yellow sign marks Priene off to the right. A further 12 km or so takes you to the village of Güllübahçe (the Rosy Garden) at the far end of which are some pleasant cafés nestling into the lee of a mountain and set among shady trees with running streams. Immediately after these, a steep road forks up to the official entrance of the site, where cars can be parked.

Among the Finest of Hellenistic Cities

Cliff ledge setting

The setting of **Priene** is unquestionably the most spectacular of any of the Ionian cities, reminiscent of Delphi in many respects, and a visit is highly recommended. Perched up in the lee of a vast outcrop of rock which towers above it, it looked out in antiquity over the sea and was a flourishing port. Its prosperity was shortlived however, for the Maeander (in Turkish, the Menderes) river living up to its name, wandered down to the Aegean depositing silt far and wide, gradually turning what used to be sea into a vast flat alluvial plain.

The other attractive feature of Priene, coming perhaps as a welcome change from Ephesus with its grandiose Roman buildings, is that most of the town we see today is modestly Greek. The absence of the later vast Roman monuments which abound in so many sites, reflects the fact that Priene was not an important town in Roman times. The scale of the town too is smaller, giving it a more intimate atmosphere in contrast to the vast grandeur of Ephesus.

Nothing of the city is visible from the ticket kiosk, and the visitor must first climb a steepish ramp leading up and round to the right to breach the city walls. This leads into one of the main arterial streets of Priene, still well-paved and provided with drainage and water systems, from which a climb of five minutes or so leads up to the centre of the city, where the Temple of Athena, the city's main monument, stands. At least two hours should be allowed for a visit, or more if you explore the upper and lower parts of the city, which involves quite a lot of steep climbing. It is best first to find somewhere to sit with a good view of the temple while you read about life in ancient Priene.

The original city was founded in the 10th C BC during the Ionian migration by one of the grandsons of Codrus, last king of Athens, and Priene, with its temple to Athena, forever

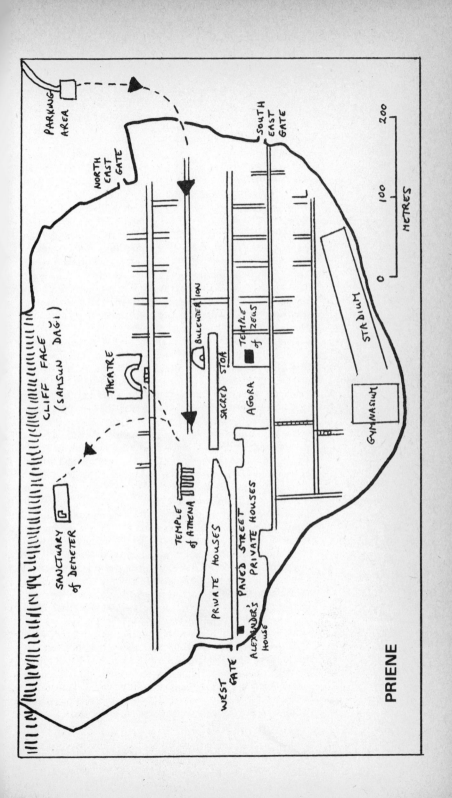

PRIENE

looked to Athens as her mother city. Always a member of the Ionian League, Priene's main claim to fame was that the Panionium, the central meeting place and sanctuary of the league, was on its territory. This original city was located down in the plain below, but the increasing silting up of the river, as at Ephesus, necessitated a move. Now buried deep under the mud, not a trace of this early city has been found except for one solitary coin. The rebuilding of the city at the new site, the site we see today, was in progress when Alexander the Great arrived in Priene in 334 BC, liberating the Ionian cities from Persian rule.

Alexander's dedication

As at Ephesus, he offered to pay all building costs of the Temple of Athena if he were permitted to make the dedication. The inhabitants of Priene, less proud and less wealthy than the Ephesians, accepted the offer. The stone carrying Alexander's dedication now sits in the British Museum, the standard practice being to ship the finds from early excavations to the excavators' homeland. The many statues originally adorning the theatre met the same fate and were carried off by the later German excavators to adorn the Berlin Museum.

Under the early days of Roman control, Priene suffered, like the other cities of the Roman Province of Asia, from the imposition of stiff taxes. Later, under the prosperous golden age of the Roman Empire, Priene, eclipsed by her more powerful neighbour Miletos, and with her harbour under threat from the silting river, was not to share in the general increase in wealth enjoyed by so many cities at this time, and hence hardly any later Roman structures were overlaid on the earlier Hellenistic buildings. While being unfortunate for Priene, this has nevertheless left for us one of the best examples in the world of a Hellenistic city.

Climbing Around Priene

On the huge rock towering above Priene (now called Samsun Daği, is the **acropolis** which used to house a permanent garrison. Nothing remains on the summit now except some remnants of the fortification wall, but if you like heights and steep climbs up rocky paths, it is still possible to make the ascent. The path passes by a little sanctuary with rock-cut reliefs and statue bases on the way up, and the view from the top is magnificent over towards the sea, now more than 15 km away.

The city was first excavated in 1868–69 by the English Dilettanti Society. The **Temple of Athena**, though plundered for building blocks by the locals and victim of an earthquake in 1955 which caused many of its columns to collapse, is nevertheless a striking building. Designed and built by the architect Pytheos, a Carian, who had also worked on the Mausoleum of Halicarnassus, it was the model used in a book

Pytheos wrote on the art of temple construction, and the temple has henceforward come to be seen as the archetypal Ionic temple. The concept of a temple was as a house for the deity, not, as with a church, a place for communal worship. Ordinary people were therefore never permitted to enter the temple, but had to remain outside, and only the priests were permitted to enter to perform ceremonies and ritual sacrifices to Athena, goddess of wisdom and the liberal arts.

An evening stroll

Looking down from the temple terrace to the city below you will notice a long well-paved street leading in from the west gate of the city, running in eventually to the **Sacred Stoa** along the northern edge of the **central agora**. This stoa and the long promenade approach to it must have been one of the loveliest features of the town and it is easy to imagine citizens of Priene having their evening stroll along it enjoying the once fine sunsets over the sea.

Bathroom shortage

On either side of this street is a **quarter of private houses**, many quite grand and built round a courtyard. The houses are similar and consist of two or three rooms, usually with two storeys. The upper storeys have not survived but traces of stairs have been found in some houses. There is no evidence of separate women's quarters and it is possible that the women lived upstairs as was sometimes the case in classical Athens. Ceilings were high, about 5 to 6 metres, suited to a hot climate, and in winter the rooms were heated by portable braziers. In the whole of the residential quarter, only one bathroom was found by the excavators, tiny, 1.8 metres by one metre, designed to accommodate one person with his feet in a basin-like hollow. Latrines have been found in only three or four houses, and no public latrines have been found in Priene at all, which raises eyebrows about public hygiene. The coins found in these houses date them to the 3rd C BC. The *largest of the houses*, near the west gate on a street corner, seems to have served as a sanctuary as well. A marble statuette was found here of Alexander, and it has been postulated that Alexander stayed in this house while at Priene during the siege of Milètos, and so the house was later sanctified. The streets are all on a regular grid pattern, the main ones running east-west and the minor ones north-south.

Retracing your steps along the main approach street, you come after about 15 metres to the little **buleuterion** or council chamber of Priene immediately to the right, very well-preserved with ten rows of seats. In the middle of the orchestra is a little altar decorated with bulls' heads and laurel leaves. The chamber would originally have had a wooden roof. Going out from its doors at the far side takes you onto the Sacred Stoa on the north side of the agora. On the eastern side of the agora is the **Temple of Zeus**, the second most important sanctuary of Priene, but little of it remains today beyond the foundations. On the western side, you can follow the stoa out through the residential area to take a closer look at the private houses. From the southwest corner of the agora, a stepped path also leads down steeply to the gymnasium and stadium, lying on the flat ground at the foot of the city.

Cold showers The Hellenistic **gymnasium** has a well-preserved courtyard and wash area, a row of basins with outlets in the form of lions' heads pouring out cold water: Greek ablutions were a spartan affair compared to the extensive hot bath complexes the Romans were so keen on. A wall in one of the lecture rooms of the gymnasium is still covered in the graffiti of the ancient students' names, over 700 in all.

A few seats only of the **stadium** remain, but on the west end the starting sill is still partially preserved. Contrary to popular belief, stadia were not used in Greek times for chariot and horse races (which were held separately in the hippodrome), but were for athletics, sprinting, upright wrestling, boxing and the pentathlon. This included discus, javelin, running, wrestling and the long jump. The ancients did not seem to go in for the high jump. At these events winning was all, and inscriptions tell us that prizes were only ever awarded to the victor, not the runners-up.

One of the finest Greek theatres in Turkey The thought of the descent to this lower part of town and climb back up may be somewhat daunting on a hot day, so if energy is in short supply it is better from the agora to return to the main east-west street and head northwards in the direction of the **theatre**. You enter this charming and well-preserved structure from the stage door onto the paved orchestra. Its setting is lovely, right in the lee of the huge rock with tall pine trees sheltering it on all sides. Also eye-catching, for those with delusions of grandeur, are the fine carved *thrones* in the front row. One of these is especially well-preserved, with its shaped back and lions' feet, and makes a surprisingly comfortable rest place. The theatre is essentially Greek, the cavea slightly more than a semi-circle, but with some Roman additions in the stage building area. The five special thrones of honour were, as in the theatre of Athens, reserved for the priests. In the middle of the fifth row of seats is a *royal box*, and in the middle of the front row is an *altar to Dionysus*, god of the theatre, to whom sacrifices were offered before each performance. Dating from the 3rd C BC, the narrow front section of the *stage building*, with its ten Doric half columns on the facade, is unusually well-preserved for a Hellenistic theatre. Some traces of red and blue paint even survive on the facade. From the smallness of the theatre it has been speculated that the population of Priene in the 4th C BC was no more than 5000, a mere fiftieth of the population of the mighty Ephesus during its heyday.

Front row seat at the Priene theatre

Surveying the City from Above

Peaceful retreat

From the left (west) of the theatre, or the right (east) of the Temple of Athena, a small path leads up towards the huge rocky outcrop, reaching after c.200 metres the **Sanctuary of Demeter and Kore**, set on a rocky shelf of the outcrop, surrounded by trees. This detour away from the main site is a good ploy to escape any coach tour which may have invaded (as Priene, being so close to Kuşadaşí, along with Miletos and Didyma, is daily visited by many people). The view down over the site and the Temple of Athena from this sanctuary is very fine indeed and the spot is beautifully peaceful and shaded. Raised up as it is with the cliff face behind, there is always a welcome breeze and the soothing rushing sound of the wind in the pines.

The sanctuary itself is heavily ruined but, dating from early Hellenistic times, is the oldest temple in Priene and was in use before Alexander's construction of the Temple of Athena. The path brings you in from the east side into the enclosed courtyard, with the temple itself at the far western end. The sacrificial pit here is most unusual, square and carefully lined with blocks, and with one of the triangular stone slabs to cover it still in place. The pit was used for pouring the blood of the sacrificial victims to the deities of the underworld, among whom Demeter and Kore (Persephone) were prominent. Persephone, goddess of spring, was picking flowers in a field when she was kidnapped by her uncle, Hades, king of the underworld, and carried away to be his queen in his underground kingdom. Her mother, Demeter, goddess of the harvest, searched everywhere, but being unable to find her daughter, forbade all trees to fruit and all grain to ripen. As life itself was threatened by extinction as a result, a compromise was reached whereby Persephone stayed the six winter months in the underworld with Hades, and returned to earth for the other six months, bringing spring and new growth with her each year. A later *Roman altar*, recognisable from its inferior masonry, can be seen on the left just as you leave the sanctuary, near the entrance to the courtyard.

MILETOS

Descending the steep road from Priene down to sea level again, you turn right and the road leads you on across the flat featureless river plain, once an inlet of the Aegean. After about 25 km, shortly before the village of Balat, a vague mound can be seen to the left, your first sight of **Miletos** (Milet in Turkish), once the greatest of the Ionian cities.

Abandoned by the Sea

As with Ephesus and Priene, Miletos too was ruined by the retreating sea and consequent loss of its trading role. The geographical changes effected by the silting up of rivers wrought havoc all along the Ionian coast, but perhaps nowhere as strikingly as at Miletos. Even as recently as the 1950s the Maeander valley used to flood each winter and Miletos could only be approached by a rough track which had to be rebuilt annually. This, and the very flatness of the area immediately around, make it easy to imagine how it must have looked in antiquity with the sea lapping against the harbour walls. Now nearly 8 km from the sea, the process has not stopped and the coastline is advancing westwards at the remarkable rate of 6 metres per year.

A tarmac road brings today's visitor right up to the site, to a parking area with a ticket kiosk and shaded refreshments hut in front of the theatre set into its mound opposite.

Although lacking the spectacular setting of Priene, the site of Miletos nevertheless has unique attractions of its own and repays close examination, notably of the areas behind the theatre hill. The site area is extensive and at least three hours should be allowed for a visit.

A great trading city In its position in antiquity at the head of the Latmian Gulf (an isolated remnant of which now forms the freshwater Lake Bafa) and heavily fortified on a peninsula with four well-sheltered harbours, the site of Miletos was always suited to a great trading city, and in early Ionian times it was indeed the greatest commercial city of the Greek world, trading in purple dyes, metals and wool. The presence of the oracle of Apollo at nearby Didyma, attracting many pilgrims, also contributed to the city's wealth.

The first settlement is thought to have been from Minoan Crete, and some of the earliest pottery finds at Miletos point to a Mycenaean settlement here between 1400 and 1200 BC. When the Ionian colonists arrived 200 years later, they found the site occupied by a mixture of Cretans and indigenous Carians. Herodotus tells us the Ionians slaughtered the entire male population and married the widows, having brought no women on their migration with them. From that day forth, the women of Miletos swore never to sit at table with the menfolk, nor to call them husband. But this did not affect the menfolks' spirit of enterprise, for by the 8th and 7th C BC Miletos had become the leading sea-trading city of the Greek world, founding nearly 100 colonies on the shores of the Hellespont, the Sea of Marmara and around the Black Sea coast.

Better a human than an animal, a man than a woman, a Greek than a Barbarian

Civilisation accompanied trade and Miletos played a major role in the Hellenisation of Asia Minor. Thales, one of the Seven Sages of antiquity, was born here in the early 6th C BC. Postulating that 'all things are water', he was arguing for the fundamental unity of the physical world beneath the apparent disorder and complexity of things. It is an assumption that the universe is capable of rational explanation and marks the transition in Greek thought from myth to science. Not that Thales was slow to make a fast buck. From his study of astronomy he knew that the following years' harvest of olives would be very good, so he cornered the olive press market and then hired out the presses at harvest time at exorbitant rates. He calculated the height of the Pyramids in Egypt by measuring their shadow at the time of day when a man's shadow is equal to his height. His most famous saying, 'Know thyself', was inscribed on the temple at Delphi. Less fashionable today, though doubtless apt at the time, Thales thanked the gods for three things: that he was human and not an animal; a man and not a woman; and a Greek and not a Barbarian.

Origins of the Persian wars

The city was also a military power. It had resisted the Lydians and had come to favourable terms with the Persians. But when the Ionian cities revolted against Persian rule in 499 BC, Miletos joined them. The decisive battle was fought in 494 BC off the island of Lade just west of Miletos; the Ionian fleet was defeated, Miletos was sacked and its population massacred, enslaved or resettled along the Persian Gulf. For Miletos, though it flourished again in later centuries, it was the end of its preeminence. But for the Greek world the defeat of the Ionians off Lade was the beginning of glory.

The strange fate of the island of Lade

The Athenians had given help to the Ionians against the Persians, and in Athens in 493 BC a poet called Phrynichos produced a tragedy called *The Fall of Miletos*. It was a sensation, but the play was banned and the poet fined for impiety in introducing a contemporary and jarring note on what was meant to be a sacred occasion. But the play was a sign of the stirrings of Athenian opinion; that same spring an archon was elected who stood for no surrender: his name was Themistokles. At this time also a refugee arrived from Miletos: his name was Miltiades. When the Persians decided to punish the Athenians for their involvement in the Ionian Revolt, it was Miltiades in 490 BC who met them at Marathon. And when the Persians decided to destroy the

A three-legged camel ruminates along the ruins of Miletos

Athenians for the humiliation at Marathon, it was Themistokles in 480 BC who met them at Salamis. The island of Lade, off which these great events were set in train, can be seen today from the hill above the theatre at Miletos: the sea has retreated as the Maeander has deposited the silt which Turkish farmers turn with their ploughs, and to the west of the ancient city, rising from a field, is Lade, an island no more.

In prosperity Miletos recovered quickly, for by the mid-5th C, the city was paying five talents a year as a member of the Delian Confederacy, a sum only marginally less than Ephesus. When Alexander arrived in 334 BC to rid Asia Minor of the Persians once and for all it would be natural to assume Miletos would welcome him with open arms, given their past suffering at the hands of the Persians. But Miletos resisted; Alexander at once laid seige to it, taking the island of Lade, and the city fell shortly afterwards to a violent assault.

In the confusion that followed Alexander's death, Miletos suffered the same succession of rulers as the rest of Ionia, coming under Antigonus and Lysimachus (generals of Alexander), the Seleucids of Syria, the Ptolemies of Egypt, the Attalids of Pergamum and finally the Romans. In the Roman golden age, Miletos, like so many other cities in the Roman Province of Asia, grew rich and prosperous again on sea trade. St Paul preached to the Jewish community here, but by the 4th C AD the silting up of the river had cost Miletos its harbour and its prosperity, and Lade too ceased to be an island. Mosquitoes became a serious problem, and the once great city slowly sank into the river mud.

Discovering Ancient Miletos

The major monument of the city today is the magnificent **theatre**, set into the hillside facing the official site entrance, though in antiquity it would have been facing a bay and been still more impressive for that. Originally Hellenistic, with a seating capacity of 5300, it was enlarged in the Roman period to a capacity of 15,000 and is perhaps the outstanding Graeco-Roman theatre in Turkey. (Turkey has more than 200 Greek or Roman theatres, the best of the former at Priene and of the latter at Aspendos; here at Miletos you see the one transformed into the other). The emperor would sit in the lowest row where a baldachin would be stretched over four columns, two of which are still *in situ*. Remarkably preserved are the vaulted passages at either side leading onto the seats which are totally preserved up to the level of the first diazoma (the horizontal walkway round the cavea), and along the third to sixth rows inscriptions are still visible reserving seats for notables.

Harbour beneath the mud Climbing out above the theatre onto the hillside you see the crumbling remains of a **Byzantine fortification**. But most strikingly you realise that below you where the hill falls away to the west and north there was in ancient times the sea. Particularly interesting from this vantage point is to study the contours of the principal harbour off to the east, now a marshy area of grass and mud between the theatre hill and the lower hill opposite. As you descend you can pick out two spots of brilliant white stone set about 150 metres apart: these are the two **marble lions** which crouched on either side of the harbour, guarding its entrance. Now the lions are sitting in muddy hollows and can be difficult to find if you search for them at ground level, which is why it is best to pinpoint them first from the height of the theatre hill. You are looking down upon the **Bay of Lions** and to its south are the remains of the **central area of the city** — not so easy for the layman to comprehend, though intermittent excavations and reconstruction are making some sense of it, and the site is labelled.

Depending on the time of year (though usually in spring), much of this area can be underwater or at least marshy. On the other hand you will probably have the area to yourself as almost all visitors to Miletos content themselves with a look at the theatre and then depart. And in May downtown Miletos can be especially lovely, when hosts of white irises abound among the ruins.

The northernmost building on the east side of the harbour is a **Roman baths and palaestra**. Its walls are still standing

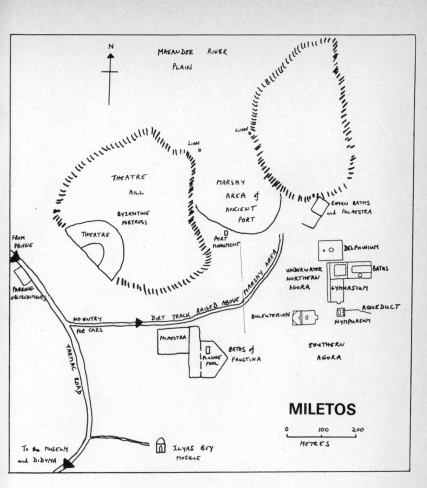

high, and locals use the shelter afforded to house their animals. Cows and sheep are often found here tied to a tree in what was once the tepidarium.

Immediately south of the harbour is the **north agora**, and to its east is the **Delphinion**, a sanctuary of Apollo which was the chief religious centre in Miletos though secondary to the Temple of Apollo at Didyma, linked to Miletos by a sacred way 20 km long. South of the Delphinion the **Ionic stoa** is being reconstructed; its shops looked out onto the main street, a broad processional road with wide pedestrian pavements. Behind the stoa at its north end were **another Roman baths**, at its south end a **gymnasium** (today, attached to the north end of the stoa, is a **Seljuk hamam**). Just beyond (south of) the gymnasium is the **Nymphaion**, a once splendid building used to distribute water to the city and fed by an aqueduct from the rear. Once three-storeys tall and richly embellished, only the ground floor remains, its carved decorations lying about.

Still further south is a large flat area that is the **south agora**, entered from the northeast by a ruinous monumental gate not dissimilar to the facade of the Library of Celsus at Ephesus. Between the north and south agoras is the **Buleuterion** or council chamber, one of the earliest surviving buildings at Miletos, built around 170 BC.

If you head northwest from the north agora to the edge of the harbour you will see a circular three-stepped base with a couple of blocks upon it carved on the south side with a half-man, half-fish triton, on the north side with marine fish. There is disagreement as to what this **harbour monument** commemorates: one explanation is that it was erected in 63 BC, probably in honour of Pompey for his successful war against the pirates; another is that it was erected for Augustus' naval victory over Antony and Cleopatra at Actium in 31 BC.

West of the south agora are the well-preserved **Baths of Faustina**, erected towards the end of the 2nd C AD by the wife of Marcus Aurelius. They are a complex of rooms with walls still over 15 metres high. In the frigidarium, the cold room with a shallow plunge pool in the centre, there is a headless but otherwise fine *reclining statue of a river god* of the Meander, and a *marble lion*. Water was fed into the pool from the base of the statue and through the lion's mouth.

There is much else in this quarter of the city, largely indeterminate or not yet even excavated; these are the principal sights at the moment and you can wander about, reading what signs there are which identify other bits and pieces of this central area of the city.

Associations with Tamerlane

Mongol memento

From the Baths of Faustina, before returning to the parking area in front of the theatre, it is well worth making a short detour to the **Ilyas Bey Camii**, its derelict domed tiled roof so overgrown with grass that from afar it looks like thatch. Romantically set by itself with a courtyard surrounded by trees, it is a charming and peaceful spot. The storks' nests on the roof are splendid and a very good view of the storks can be had if you approach with sufficient stealth. The main entrance leads into an overgrown courtyard lined with the various buildings dependent on the mosque. The marble facade of the mosque entrance itself is in a bad way and, neglected as it is, will not be standing for too much longer. From inside the mosque, a dark stairway still leads up inside the thick walls to what would have been the minaret, now missing. The whole complex was built by Ilyas Bey in 1404 to celebrate his escape from the Mongol Tamerlane, a thing worthy indeed of celebration.

Reclining in the lap of a river god at the Baths of Faustina

Tamerlane, leader of the Mongol horsemen, had swept into eastern Anatolia in 1401, having already overrun Central Asia, India, Persia, Iraq and Syria, leaving a trail of destruction behind him. Exceptionally aggressive and warlike, the Mongols specialised in slaughtering wholesale anyone they came across, virtually wiping out the populations of the cities they took, and then building pyramids of the victims' decapitated heads. They destroyed the priceless palaces and libraries of the east, while the revered mosques of Bukhara served them as stables. Any skilled craftsmen were carried away to Tamerlane's capital in Samarkand. Among the Mongols more charming habits were drinking the blood of their horses by cutting a hole in the leg and then blocking it up with mud, and having themselves buried surrounded by beautiful young maidens.

The earlier wave of Mongol hordes under Ghengis Khan in 1243 caused the downfall of the Seljuk state; they also brought an end to the Crusader kingdoms in southeast Anatolia and the Arab Abbasid Caliphate in Baghdad in 1258, a date Oxford University until recently regarded as the end of Arab history. Ghengis Khan described himself as 'the scourge of god sent to men as a punishment for their sins'.

Tamerlane (Timur the Lame), claiming descent from and modelling himself on Ghengis Khan, crushed the chief Ottoman cities of Ankara, İznik, Bursa and İzmir. He then returned to his native steppeland without consolidating his victories, but leaving behind him a devastation from which it took the Ottomans 50 years to recover, thereby temporarily halting the Ottoman advance into Europe, and giving the Byzantine Empire another 50 years' respite.

Thugs and flowers

In his avowed aim to conquer the world and establish an empire, Tamerlane failed, for bringing with him no religion or culture he could offer nothing on which to base his power except destruction. His reputation today therefore is not as a founder of a great dynasty but as the most comprehensively destructive conqueror in history. With these associations it is surprising, to say the least, that Timur is still a popular boys' name in Turkey today. Many Turkish girls' names, in contrast, are derived from flowers.

As you leave Miletos, not by the road you approached on but by the road which runs in front of the mosque, you will notice a small **museum** on the right of the road, housing the recent finds of the German site excavators.

DIDYMA AND ITS ORACLE

Continuing southwards from Miletos you shortly reach the town of Akkoy, where you follow the yellow sign straight on to Didyma (Didim in Turkish), ignoring the left turn to rejoin the main Milas/Bodrum highway. The 15 km of road on to Didyma must be retraced to this point before continuing your journey southwards, but this is a pleasurable detour as it gives you the chance to overnight at Altínkum (golden sand) where you can enjoy the lovely beach and find a comfortable hotel.

At the end of the day As the southernmost site in Ionia, the traveller inevitably arrives at **Didyma** exhausted, late in the day, having scrambled all over Priene and Miletos (and in some cases Ephesus too). The temple is at its most impressive at sunset, but you can always pass on to Altínkum and call at the temple the following morning if your energy has flagged.

Excavations

Didyma, never a city, rather a temple precinct, is impressive for the size and preservation of its Temple of Apollo. From 300 BC it took over 500 years to build, and was in fact never completely finished. It is said to have resembled the Temple of Artemis at Ephesus, the largest Ionic temple in the world, and although its dimensions are considerably smaller, it does serve as an indication of the vastness of that other temple of which only one column now remains standing. There was also a cult here to Artemis, twin sister of Apollo, and her sanctuary was discovered in 1983, but it was always minor. The name Didyma bears a striking resemblance to Greek didymi for twins, but this may just be accidental as the name is thought to be of indigenous Anatolian origin.

Abducting treasure Extensive French and German excavations have transformed the temple from its appearance as described by Sir Charles Newton in 1858: 'Two giant columns supporting a piece of architrave, and a third unfinished column are all that remain standing of the Temple of Apollo, of which the mighty ruins lie as they originally fell, piled up like shattered icebergs'. Newton did, however, see many statues dating from the 6th C BC which were lining the sacred way leading to the small nearby harbour at Panormas, the usual arrival point of pilgrims. These he duly collected up and shipped back to the British Museum, where they can be seen today, many seated in a formal posture. They were mainly of priests and priestesses of the oracle, together with a lion and a sphinx bearing inscriptions. There is no doubt that at the time, the wholesale carting off of exceptional archaeological treasures from the sites of ancient Greece and Turkey, preserved them from all manner of indignities they would otherwise have suffered at the hands of their native populations. Stories of Turks shooting off pieces of sculpture from the Acropolis in Athens abound, and throughout Greece and Turkey there is ample evidence of the plundering of ancient monuments for re-use in modern building. At the time that most of the famous monuments such as the Elgin Marbles and the Xanthos sculptures were taken away, Greece and Turkey did not have proper museums in which to protect them from abuse. Now that this is no longer so, there is certainly a case for returning them to museums in their native countries, while plaster casts could be put *in situ* to enhance the appearance of the sites.

Excavations have today exposed the temple at Didyma well down below road level, revealing not only the temple virtually complete apart from its colonnade, but also further associated buildings. To the left of the road shortly before arriving from Miletos, the German Archaeological Institute has revealed the paving of the **sacred way** built by the Roman Emperor Trajan to link the oracle with the Delphinium in the centre of Miletos. The sanctuary belonged to the territory of Miletos, and the chief priest was usually an official from the city. About 5 metres wide between two pavements, shops and houses have been found lining the way at this point. The way ends on the north edge of the temple after first crossing a depression which the excavators have speculated may have been the site of the sacred grove of laurels frequently mentioned in the accounts of ancient historians. In this area excavations in 1974 also revealed the remains of a **Roman baths**, still with some traces of white marble paving. In the area in front of the temple, remains of **Hellenistic and Roman houses** have been found, presumably the dwellings of the priestly family who tended the oracle throughout its history.

Along the southern (far side) of the temple, the **stadium** ran, with the 7 steps of the side of the temple itself actually serving as one half of the seats. The lower steps are still carved with names for reserved seats and over 200 names have been read. From the profusion of names on the lowest steps we can safely conclude that these were considered the best seats, closest to the action.

The action which took place here was the festival of the Great Didymeia, which took place every four years from as early as 200 BC. Here the usual athletic events were held, as well as contests in oratory, music and drama which were probably held in the theatre of Miletos, where the festival was partly held, in the absence of a theatre at Didyma. The starting sill for the sprint races is still visible in the ground at the east end of the stadium, consisting of nine stone blocks pierced with holes for holding posts upright.

Apollo's Oracle

We now come to the vast **Temple of Apollo** itself, resting on a colossal platform with seven high steps. This platform is not

Deceptive lines

horizontal, but raised slightly in the middle to correct the optical illusion of a straight line seeming to sag in the middle. This trick was standard practice in Greek temples, and the Parthenon has been said not to contain a single straight line. This main raised area originally had a double colonnade of 120 colossal columns in all, 103 of which today stand all round its edge. Many have decorated bases and capitals, and most are fluted while some are still plain, showing that the building was never finally completed. The columns supported an architrave bearing a frieze dating from the 1st C BC with a series of huge *heads of Medusa* (one of which is on the ground by the modern steps leading down to the temple site).

Location of the oracle

The *pronaos* or open forecourt at the top of the 13 steps at the front of the temple, has 12 columns, their bases variously decorated. The forecourt leads on to an *antechamber* with two more columns, the floor of which consists of one colossal slab of marble 8 metres by 2 metres by one metre which must have weighed at least 48 metric tons. From the back of this antechamber, a most unusual feature in this kind of temple, three doors lead out onto a flight of *monumental steps* down into the open grassy cella. Equally unusually, two sets of *stairways* lead up from either side of the antechamber to the top of the cella walls. Exceptionally large, the *cella* was never roofed, but its walls still stand to their full height of over 20 metres. Lead was apparently poured between the walls for added strength. From the front forecourt, this cella is reached by two *ramps*, one either side of the temple, another unusual arrangement. In antiquity of course, no mere mortal was permitted to enter the cella, be it via these ramps or via the monumental stairway. The upper part of the walls of the stairway are decorated with a fine *frieze of griffins and lyres* running between the mock pillars. At the end of the cella stood a small *Ionic temple* to house the cult statue of Apollo, but only the foundations remain. It was in this little temple that the *sacred spring*, inspiration of the oracle, lay and was indeed located by the excavators a few years ago.

The art of divination held strong sway over the ancients. Apollo's most famous oracle was at Delphi, but he also had oracles at Claros, Didyma, Patara and many other places. The existence of an oracle at Didyma is very long standing, and when the Ionian migrants reached here in the 10th C BC they already found a sanctuary with a sacred grove and spring. The priestesses, drawn in the earliest days of the oracle exclusively from a family claiming Delphic origins called the Branchides, were said to abstain from food for three days, then to inhale the sulphur fumes from the spring till they swooned in a state of divine inspiration. Their incoherent ramblings were then translated by the priests into hexameter verse and given to the suppliant in writing. The earliest oracular verdict we know of dates from 600 BC when it was asked if it was right for the younger generation to engage in the practice of piracy. The reply was: 'It is right to do as your fathers did'.

Gushing for Alexander

With the Persian incursion and the collapse of Miletos after the thwarted Ionian revolt, Didyma was, like Miletos, plundered and the sanctuary destroyed. Suitably offended, it remained silent throughout the 5th and 4th C BC till the day Alexander the Great was born, whereupon the sacred spring, dry throughout the period of silence, gushed forth again. At this point it made its most remarkable prophesy, namely that Alexander was a true son of Zeus and would be victorious over the Persians. The temple as it is today was built by Seleucus around 300 BC. The oracle had also singled him out for greatness, and had predicted, when he was still only an officer under Alexander, that he would become king. When Seleucus later asked the oracle whether he should return to Greece, the reply came: 'Be in no hurry to reach Europe; Asia is for you far better'. Sure enough, when Seleucus crossed into Greece in 280 BC for the first time since Alexander's men had crossed from the other direction, he was promptly stabbed to death by an enemy.

The oracle's forte

Predictions of a rise to greatness seemed to be a speciality of the oracle (although of course we do not hear of the thousands it may have singled out for greatness who never made it), and it also predicted to Trajan very early in his career that he would become emperor: hence Trajan's later generosity once the prophesy came true in building the sacred way to link with Miletos. The oracle was also favoured under Hadrian and enjoyed a period of great prosperity till the invasion of the Goths in AD 262. At that time the temple was hastily converted into a fortress for defence, and the excavators had to clear the remains of this later building from the site. The real cause of the decline of the oracle was, however, the onset of Christianity which took hold relatively early in Miletos. As epitomes of pagan ritual, oracles were naturally the target of vehement Christian attack, physical and verbal. The process was completed when in 385 the Emperor Theodosius issued his famous edict that: 'No mortal man shall have the effrontery to encourage vain hopes by the inspection of entrails, or which is worse, attempt to learn the future by the detestable consultation of oracles. The severest penalties await those who disobey'. As the final humiliation, a Christian chapel was erected in the holiest part of the temple.

Christian spoilsports

The little site **museum** houses fragments of friezes and statues found during the excavations.

Just 4 km beyond Didyma is the extensive beach of **Altínkum**, a fast developing resort offering a good selection

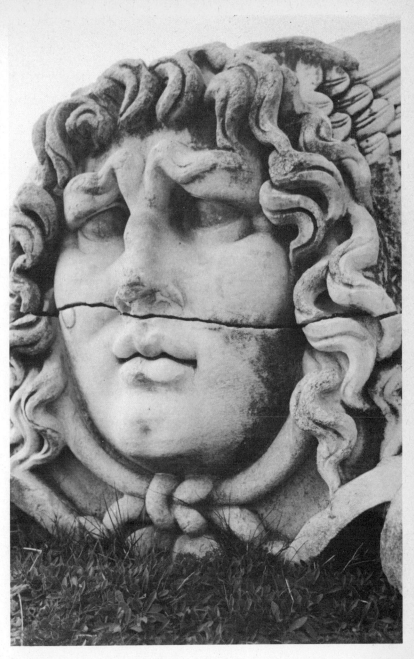

The Medusa at Didyma

of hotels and restaurants. A local speciality to try is Karagöz, literally 'black-eyed fish', better known to us as sea bream. These fish look like much larger versions of red mullet, with pink scales and quite a rounded shape, and taste delicious.

PRACTICAL INFORMATION

İZMIR

Avoid İzmir during its annual trade fair from 20 August to 29 September, held in the Kültür Park, as it becomes very difficult to find **accommodation**.

Büyük Efes (4-star), 296 rooms, on the main square, Cumhuriyet Meydaní. Rates vary depending on the view. Pool and gardens.

Etap (3-star), 128 rooms, on the main square, Cumhuriyet Meydaní.

Kísmet (3-star), 67 rooms, in a small street near the Büyük Efes.

İzmir Palas (3-star), 153 rooms, on harbour front, Atatürk Caddesi, near Cumhuriyet Meydaní.

Anba (2-star), 53 rooms, on main road, Cumhuriyet Bulvarí, a block back from the harbour front.

Kilim (2-star), 88 rooms, on harbour front, Atatürk Caddesi.

Billur Hotel (1-star), 60 rooms. Family-run, near the gardens of the Kültür Park and the Başmahane railway station. Roof restaurant.

Fa Pansiyon, a handful of rooms up a side street near Cumhuriyet Meydaní. Cheap with a generous breakfast, but dark dingy rooms with shared bathroom.

Restaurants, for fish, along the seafront near Cumhuriyet Meydaní, or in the Kültür Park on the edge of the lake.

Boats sail from the quayside to Çeşme, Chios, Kuşadasí, Samos, Bodrum, Kos, Marmaris, Rhodes, İstanbul and Piraeus.

Buses to and from the **airport**: the Büyük Efes Hotel serves as the terminus.

Hertz Rent-a-Car, 368 Atatürk Caddesi.

The nearest **beach** is 12km away at Inciraltí, on the Çeşme road, and a not very good beach at that.

ÇEŞME

A seaside resort with good **beaches** and a thermal spa, 90 minutes' drive from İzmir airport. Opposite is the Greek island of Chios, to which boats run daily in summer.

All **hotels** are on the beach.

Altínyunus (Golden Dolphin) (3-star). Holiday Village, huge complex of 514 rooms. Good sports facilities.

Çeşme (3-star), 135 rooms, Olympic pool, private beach.

Turtes Motel (2-star), open May–September, 106 bungalows.

Balin Moteli (1-star), open May–October, 52 rooms.

Motes Motel (1-star), May–September, 44 rooms.

GÜMÜŞSU

Small resort on **beach**, closest **accommodation** for Claros, Notion and Colophon:

Sultan (2-star), 110 rooms.

Paşa (2-star), 106 rooms.

SIĞACIK

Small fishing village, closest **accommodation** for Teos, 1 hour's drive from İzmir airport. Two hotels, one with camping, on bay of Akkum, just beyond Siğacík on a promontory. **Restaurants** overlooking the Genoese fortress on the route to Akkum.

EPHESUS

Tusan Efes Motel (2-star), 12 rooms, only 10 minutes' walk to the site. Excellent location if you are not interested in Kuşadasí or beaches. Small pool.

Camel wrestling festival in Selçuk, (1316 January, part of the camel wrestling that takes place throughout December and January all around Aydín. First week of May, **Selçuk Ephesus Festival of Culture and Art** with folk dancing, concerts; some performances held in the Graeco-Roman theatre.

KUŞADASI

Club Mediterranée Village (3-star), open mid-May to mid-October, 400 bungalow chalets, all sports facilities.

Kísmet (3-star), open April–October, 65 rooms, best situation in Kuşadasí, 2 km before town on its own promontory. Lovely gardens. Private beach. Most sought after hotel in Kuşadasí, usually very booked up by packages for the season.

Tusan (3-star), 63 rooms, 7 km before town. Pool, private beach.

Kervansaray (3-star), open mid-May to mid-October, 35 rooms, 300-year old Ottoman caravanserai converted in 1974, in the centre of town on the front. Good restaurant with a lush courtyard. No pool, so you use the public beach. Can be noisy. Run till recently by Club Mediterranée.

Imbat (3-star), open April–October, 139 rooms. 4 km out of town on Kadínlar Plaji. Good setting and beach. Sea water pool. Mediocre food and service, hence popular with the English.

Motel Akdeniz (2-star), 157 rooms, 8 km before town. Popular with families, pool, private beach, garden. Water sports.

Courtesy bus to Kuşadasí twice daily.

There are numerous cheaper small hotels and pensions up the hill above the town, such as the Akman (47 rooms) and the Stella, getting cheaper the further you are from the beach.

Camping: there are several campsites on or near the beaches on the road between Ephesus and Kuşadasí.

BP Mocamp, a few simple chalets for non-campers as well. On Selçuk-Kuşadasí road 10 km from Kuşadasí.

There are numerous **restaurants** all along the front. The Kervansaray offers the most sophisticated environs for an evening meal.

Boats run to Samos daily in summer, and the harbour is port of call for many cruise ships touring the Aegean.

ALTINKUM

Resort on the sea 4 km beyond Didyma, with a huge **beach** Lots of Turkish holiday **villas**, privately owned, as well as **hotels** and **campsites**.

Didim Motel (1-star), open March–November, 32 rooms.

LAKE BAFA TO MARMARIS (ANCIENT CARIA: THE COAST)

ANCIENT CARIA: THE COAST

South of the Menderes river (the ancient Maeander), as the road leaves the valley and begins climbing up into the hills, you are entering the mountainous region that was ancient Caria, always a distinct area, whose borders correspond today almost exactly with the province of Muğla, extending south as far as Lake Köyceğiz near Fethiye where what was ancient Lycia begins.

Greek Foundations

Who were the Carians?

The principal Carian cities were purely Greek in their foundation, especially those on the coast like Halicarnassus (modern Bodrum), the chief city of the region. Inland, the smaller towns have their own peculiarly Carian character, such as Mylasa and Euromos. The origin of the Carians is in some dispute, reflecting this divide, and some scholars believe they came originally from the Aegean islands or from Crete, while others believe they were an indigenous Anatolian race. In Homer's *Iliad* the Carians are referred to as allies of the Trojans, 'barbarous of speech' and, curiously, the dialect spoken around Muğla today is the harshest in western Turkey. They did in fact have their own Carian language, distinct from Greek, which is still not understood, mainly because the number of inscriptions found to date is too small to allow standard deciphering techniques to be applied.

Of the successive wave of Greek migrants, Aeolians, Ionians and Dorians who made their way across to Asia Minor after the fall of Troy, the Dorians were the last and southernmost. They occupied the islands of Rhodes and Kos and a few cities on the Carian mainland, notably Halicarnassus (Bodrum) and Cnidos, forming a league of six cities, known as the Dorian Hexapolis, which met periodically at the festival of Apollo near Cnidos.

Perisan Satrapy and Roman Rule

Ambitious Mausolus

Until the 4th C BC Caria shared essentially the same succession of rulers as Ionia, but then, with the appearance of Mausolus, Caria began to create its own history.

The extensive Persian Empire was divided into regions called satrapies, ruled by satraps or local governors. Mausolus was the son of the first satrap of Caria. An ambitious and energetic man, he took advantage of the huge distance of his satrapy from the Persian capital to set himself up as a virtually independent ruler. Mausolus established his capital initially at Mylasa, later moving to Halicarnassus (Bodrum), which he had rebuilt on a grand scale as his headquarters. Throughout Caria he built defence walls round his cities, notably at Heracleia ad Latmos and at Caunus, at the extremities of his territory.

Mausolus died fairly young in 353 BC, leaving two brothers and two sisters. He had married his elder sister, Artemisia, and as they had no children, Artemisia became Queen of Caria. This formidable woman is famous for building the Mausoleum, one of the Seven Wonders of the Ancient World, in honour of her husband, and for her naval successes against Rhodes. On her death, Mausolus' elder brother came to power and married his younger sister Ada, a not uncommon way of keeping things in the family at that time. But on his death his younger brother took charge and exiled Ada.

Alexander ...

Caria was visited in 334 BC by Alexander the Great during his campaign to overthrow the Persian Empire. He met resistance in only a few places in Asia Minor, notably at Halicarnassus. On its defeat he brought back the exiled Ada and gave her the rule of Caria before continuing his drive against the Persians.

... then Antony

Ultimately the entire Hellenistic world fell under the control of the Romans, western Asia Minor becoming the Roman province of Asia. But the province, and in particular Caria, was a victim of the greed of local governors. The unsettled period after Julius Caesar's murder in 44 BC was especially difficult for the province. The traitors Brutus and Cassius milked Asia for wealth and manpower in a vain effort to stave off the defeat and death they found at Philippi in Greece in 42 BC at the hands of Antony and Octavian. The victors divided the world between them, Antony taking the East and repeating Brutus' demand for the equivalent of ten years' worth of taxes to finance in turn his ambitions. These centred on Alexandria and his alliance with Cleopatra; but while he was in Egypt the Parthians, Rome's long-time enemies, attacked the Asian province, Caria suffering particularly severely before Antony could drive them off. The world proved not large enough to contain the ambitions of both Octavian and Antony, and in 31 BC in the sea battle of Actium off the coast of western Greece Antony and Cleopatra were beaten.

In these years of civil war the Roman Republic died, and in 29 BC the Roman Empire was founded with Octavian, now Augustus, as the first emperor. For the next two centuries the province of Asia was treated well, enjoying stability, peace and prosperity. Though nominally under the control of Rome, the province was allowed to conduct its own internal affairs without interference.

The Coming of the Turks

Caria was on the whole slow to convert to Christianity. St Paul did not visit here, and the only early churches are in Laodiceia and Colossae, right on the edge of the region. Only when the Emperor Constantine converted to Christianity did it begin to make some inroads.

From the Byzantine period onwards the region suffered greatly under attacks from the Arab armies which made annual sallies from their base in Syria. But in the 12th and 13th C, the Seljuk Turks never advanced from their capital at Konya west of the Denizli-Fethiye road, and the Carian region, mountainous and well-forested as it is, was not easily accessible to nomad camel drivers from the north and east. It remained an outpost of Byzantine resistance, as around Lake Bafa.

In the 14th C the Turkish Menteşe emirs established a local emirate in Caria from their capital, Milas, before the Ottomans siezed it in 1390. The Mongol leader Tamerlane, after defeating the Ottomans in the battle of Ankara in 1402, restored the emirate to the Menteşe emirs, who reigned for a brief time again, till in 1425 the Ottomans recaptured it.

LAKE BAFA AND THE ROAD SOUTH

Charm of
the lake

Having visited the Priene, Miletus and Didyma cluster, the road south begins to climb up out of the Maeander valley, and very soon Lake Bafa comes into view. **Lake Bafa** is a beautiful spot and time spent lingering on its shores is always enjoyable. It is a delightful detour for the touring traveller or even a day trip from Kuşadasí. The main road from Ephesus to Bodrum and Marmaris passes along the southern lake shore, where you come to a clutch of simple restaurants on the left and a campsite/motel offering basic accommodation. Lunch spent here sampling the excellent Bafa fish will be memorable, not least because of the interruptions of a mad Bafa duck, whose persistent quackings are such that you are puzzled as to whether it is on a quest for love and affection or simply for food.

Lakeside Ruins

Continuing towards Bodrum and Marmaris till you appear to have left the lake totally behind, you come to the village of Çamiçi, from where a yellow sign points off left 9 kms to the site of **Heracleia ad Latmos**, a ruined city on the northern edge of Caria. The road is dirt track, but presents no real problems to a car as it winds its way through villagers' huts and farmland back to the western lake shore, beneath the five-fingered mountain, ancient *Mt Latmos* (1500 metres).

It is the setting of the ruins on the lake shore with the mountain backdrop, rather than their state of preservation which is the chief attraction of Heracleia. The Byzantine ruins on the little islands are particularly appealing, and there is a simple restaurant on the eastern shore at the foot of the site for a meal or refreshments. Swimming in the lake is very refreshing, but care must be taken to choose a spot free from reeds.

In antiquity Heracleia stood on the Ionian coast, as Bafa was at that time an inlet of the sea, cut off over time by the silting up of the Maeander river valley, and over the centuries it has changed to become a freshwater lake. With limited land and Miletus at the head of the inlet to take most of the sea trade, Heracleia was never a prominent city. It was really just a fortified outpost of northern Caria, but to this day it is these fortifications which are the most remarkable feature of the site. The city was enclosed by the extensive and well-preserved **defence walls** dating from about 300 BC, which rise up about 500 metres from the lake along a ridge of Mt Latmos, for a total distance of 6½ km. Many of the towers, windows, gates and stairways up to the parapets are still in excellent condition.

Buffet at Bafa, Mt Latmos across the lake

The moon sleeps with Endymion

Legend has it that this is the spot where the handsome demi-god Endymion was sleeping when the moon goddess, Selene, saw him and fell in love with him. Zeus, jealous of a rumoured amour between Endymion and Hera, decreed that Endymion would sleep forever on Mt Latmos, and in his dreams Selene slept with him and bore him 50 daughters. This, as the English classicist George Bean pointed out, 'might be thought enough to wake him'! The myth continued on into Christian times when Endymion was considered to be a local mystic saint, and Christian anchorites, discovering an ancient tomb on the site, pronounced it to be Endymion's and made it into a sanctuary.

This **sanctuary** can still be seen and lies at the beginning of the site just right of the road as you approach. It is an unusual and attractive construction with rock outcrops forming its back wall. If you are of romantic disposition, you can sit here remembering fragments of Shakespeare's *The Merchant of Venice*, Act V,

> Peace, ho! the moon sleeps with Endymion,
> And would not be awaked!

or Keats' *Endymion*,

> What is there in thee, Moon! that thou shouldst move
> My heart so potently?

117

Do not linger here too long, lest you should fall into a magic sleep yourself, but walk on beyond the shrine onto the headland where the ruins of a fortified **Byzantine monastery** stand. Here you can look down to the sea where rocks with oblong **pit tombs** cut into them are lying half-submerged in the waters of the lake.

Returning to the road and continuing towards the mountain, the most prominent building of ancient Heracleia can be seen. This is the **Temple of Athena** perched up on a promontory, a simple construction, but with beautifully crafted masonry walls. Inland from this lies the **agora**, where the school of the nearby village of Kapíkírí now stands. On the southern side of the agora is a well-preserved **market building** divided into shops. Just further inland is the charming **buleuterion** or council chamber, poorly preserved, but in a beautiful setting among the trees on the edge of the village. The **theatre**, about 300 metres away to the right up the mountain, is in poor preservation, as are the unidentified temples just above it.

Lake island churches

Christianity, although it arrived late on the scene — around the 4th C — spread rapidly into this region with many anchorites and hermits coming here to take refuge. In Byzantine times various religious communities came here, as is evidenced by the large number of **convents and churches** built on the many islets of the lake. These fell into ruin after the Turkish conquest and now add to the charm and mystery of the lake's atmosphere. It is possible to swim to the islet just by the restaurant at the foot of the site, though the abundance of reeds may cause a few uncomfortable moments.

Euromos

Elegant temple

About 20 km beyond Lake Bafa, just after the town of Selimiye, your eye will be caught by the elegant columns of a temple standing to the left of the road in the lee of three wooded slopes. This **Temple of Zeus**, in the Corinthian order and dating from the 2nd C AD, is one of the best preserved temples in Asia Minor today, and still stands with many of its columns complete with their architraves. One can only presume that its state of preservation is due to its sheltered position between the three slopes. The few unfluted columns were clearly never finished. On the south side is a piece of the cornice with a lion's head open-mouthed to serve as a water spout.

Excavations begun in 1969 revealed the foundations of an altar in front of the temple on the east, dating from the 2nd C BC, confirming that the present temple stands on the site of an earlier Hellenistic one.

The temple is in fact outside the **city walls of Euromos**, which was in early times the most important city in the region after Mylasa (Milas). It was minting its own coins from the

The Temple of Zeus at Euromos

2nd C BC to the 2nd C AD. The city itself lies to the north, where a fine *round tower* stands on a slope in the trees, about 100 metres north of the temple. This tower is part of the sturdy walls, which are nearly 3 metres thick, dating to at least 300 BC. In the plain over the hill, you can see the **agora** with some of the columns of its stoa or portico standing. There are also the remains of a poorly preserved **theatre** set into the hillside.

The walk to these additional ruins is not really warranted, and by and large it is enough to confine yourself to admiring the temple itself, and perhaps glancing at the underground **tomb chambers**, well-built and roofed in the Carian style with huge slabs, that line the track leading to the temple from the main road. The shapeless building near the road is of a later date and is probably a baths.

Headland City

South of Euromos at about 5 km a yellow sign points off 20 km towards the coast, along an untarmaced but driveable road to the ruined Carian city of **Iasos**. The site can also be reached by hiring a boat from Güllük (see below). An Italian team has been excavating here on and off since 1960, and their excavations have produced quantities of Minoan pottery pointing to an early Cretan connection, as well as some later Mycenean pottery and foundations.

The ruined city enjoys a striking setting on top of a headland described in the accounts of ancient historians as an
island, but now linked to the mainland by a narrow isthmus.
As you approach the village of Kuren which partly occupies
the site, you notice an aqueduct and a wide variety of **tombs**.
Some of the built Roman tombs have been converted by the
villagers into modern houses. The finest one, however, a
Roman mausoleum in the Corinthian order, has been
converted to house the pieces of sculpture and pottery found
on the site.

Strabo relates a tale to illustrate the extent to which the
ancient community here was geared to its fishing trade. A
professional musician visited Iasos and gave a performance in
the theatre. Half way through a bell rang to announce the fish
market was open. The audience immediately got up and
departed, leaving just one old man who stayed seated with his
hand cupped to his ear. The musician approached to thank
him for his devotion to art in not rushing off when the bell
rang. 'What? the bell rang did you say?' 'Why ... yes.'
Whereupon the deaf man excused himself and hurried off
too.

Along the coast of the mainland run tall powerful **defence
walls** probably built by Mausolus in the 4th C BC, nearly 2
metres thick, stretching for over 2 km and punctuated with
round towers and gates. On the **headland** itself the excavators
have cleared a theatre, a gymnasium, an agora with stoas, a
Byzantine castle, a buleuterion, a basilica and a Roman villa
with black and white mosaic floors and wall paintings. Till
the late 19th C the headland too was surrounded by a fine
defence wall, but nearly all of it was removed at that time to
build quays and other buildings in İstanbul.

Regional Crossroads

From Euromos, a pretty drive of a further 15 km brings you
on to the busy town of **Milas**. Set in a fertile plain surrounded
by wooded mountains at a natural crossroads, it is unusual in
that it has been a thriving centre since antiquity. The site of
ancient **Mylasa**, on which the modern town now stands, was
the capital of the independent kingdom of Caria around
350 BC when the Persian satrap Mausolus founded his
virtually independent principality here, away from the
domination of the Persian capital, before moving to the more
defensible site of Halicarnassus, the Bodrum of today.

The most visible remains of ancient Mylasa are the impressive **Roman gateway**, locally called Baltalí Kapí (the gate of
the Axe), and the handsome **Roman tomb** on the western
edge of the town called Gümüşkesen (Silver Purse). Built in
the 1st C AD, it was designed as a miniature replica of the
Mausoleum in Halicarnassus, with a pyramid roof supported
by pillars and columns with Corinthian capitals; today it

serves the local inhabitants as a cowshed.

More interesting, however, are the monuments which remain from the period of rule under the Menteşe Turks in the 14th C. They ruled southwestern Anatolia before the rise of the Ottomans, and were one of the many nomadic clans from parts of central Asia formerly under the Byzantine Empire. Their mighty stronghold here was **Peçin Kale**, situated on the dramatic flat-topped rock mountain just south of Milas, visible from far around, and reached by forking off right to Ören 500 metres after taking the Muğla fork. The governor of Milas was living here until the 17th C. The Menteşe fortress was built in the 14th C, and is entered by a gate under a tower decorated with sculptured lions. To the right inside on a flat area are the ruins of the residences of the Turkish governors of Milas. There is also the fine little madrasa (Koranic school) built in 1375, containing the tomb of Ahmet Ghazi, the last Menteşe governor of the citadel, who held out against a seige of a whole year by the Ottoman Beyazit I and his troops, before giving way in 1391 to Ottoman rule.

Pink mosque   There are three mosques of the 14th C left in Milas itself: the first two, **Orhan Bey Camii** (1330) and the **Ulu Cami** (1378) are both of the Menteşe period, simply built and difficult to find, but the most interesting is the larger fine **Firuz Bey Camii** built in 1394 just after the Ottoman conquest, with the elaborate pinkish marble of its facade borrowed from the ancient Greek temples. It stands by itself in an overgrown courtyard in the western part of the town. The river banks of the town are lined by exquisite but decaying 18th C **Ottoman mansions**.

Overnight accommodation in Milas is not great, and the traveller may prefer to drive on to Güllük (see below), a pretty seaside village with a good beach and hotel.

Just south of Milas is a major T-junction. Right leads down the peninsula to Bodrum, left leads on to Muğla and Marmaris. The visitor to Bodrum must retrace his steps to this junction before continuing along the coast, which will add about 65 km in each direction to his journey.

The Sacred Way from Mylasa

From Milas, a short excursion can be made to the atmospheric ruins of **Labraynda**, in a grove of sacred plane trees. Set high in the hills above Milas, this, the site of a sanctuary to Zeus, belonged in ancient times to Mylasa, the nearest city and Mausolus' capital, and was originally joined to it by a paved sacred way over 12 km long. At festival times processions from Mylasa would make their way up along this, but today it is reached by a driveable track. Apart from the sanctuary and temple festivals, athletics contests were held here, and a stadium has recently been recognised on a slope above the temple.

The suggestive setting is on a hillside, on steep that artificial terraces had to be built by Queen Ada in the 4th C BC. The other natural attribute of the site is its abundant water supply, and it supplies Milas with water even today.

Bejewelled fish

The sacred way arrives at the site with two magnificent **gateways** in Ionic style. The southern gateway was reserved for pedestrians, while chariots entered by the eastern gate. In between these two gates are the ruins of a 1st C AD **baths**, and a later **Byzantine church**. About 20 metres to the right of the apse a **mysterious marble building** has been excavated dating to the 4th C BC. The Swedish excavators who have been working here since 1969 dubbed it the Ablution Hall, but a French scholar recently offered a more interesting explanation, namely that the building housed the sacred pool where tame fish adorned with necklaces and gold earrings swam. The existence of such a pool at Labraynda is described in more than one ancient account, and it is thought to be connected with the delivery of oracles, where, according to ancient sources, fish were used as a primitive and rather limited type of oracle capable of yes/no answers: the response was favourable or not depending on whether the fish accepted the morsels proffered to them.

From the southern gateway a magnificent wide *stairway* of 23 steps leads up to the next terrace where the *fountain house* with its four columns stands. Further stairways lead up to the temple terrace and a large courtyard where the foundations of the great Carian **Temple of Zeus** stand. Zeus was regarded in Caria as a warlike military god, and is shown in early Mylasan coins as a bearded Greek standing with a double axe (*labrys* in Greek, from which the sanctuary name comes, and hence also the Gate of the Axe in Milas) on his shoulder and a long spear in his hand. In later coins, however, Zeus is represented most curiously, still with his beard and weapons, but wearing a necklace and breasplate with numerous breast-like objects, swathed in bands like a mummy from the waist down, and wearing a cylindrical headdress. It would appear from these coins that Zeus was fused with the Ephesian Artemis or with the Egyptian Osiris.

Behind the temple stands the most conspicuous building on the site, an **andron**, literally the mens' room, not a euphemism for the latrines but a room used rather like a club, where banquets and social functions were held at festival times. It still stands high with a large lintelled door and numerous windows set into its thick walls. Before the Swedish excavators began work it was thought that this was the Temple of Zeus. Adjoining it are a group of rooms that were probably houses for the temple attendants, and on the terrace below are two further androns but in a much more ruined state.

Tombs are scattered all around the sanctuary, but by far

the finest lies shortly above the temple on the steep hillside. It is a **monumental built tomb** containing no less than five sarcophagi, so large that the tomb must have been built around them.

BODRUM: ANCIENT HALICARNASSUS

Following the right hand fork from Milas, the Bodrum road is a winding drive, leading up through hills covered in olive groves. Strange domed buildings can be seen scattered here and there near the road; they are rainwater cisterns for irrigating the land as there are no streams in this area.

After about 18 km a sign points off right to **Güllük**, a pretty fishing town where you can break your journey for a restful night if the twisting 50-km road to Bodrum is more than you can face at this stage. Boats can be hired from Güllük to explore the lovely coastline, or for keen archaeologists the ruined Carian cities of **Iasos** and **Bargylia** (Varvil), 45 minutes and 30 minutes by boat respectively.

The drive from Milas to Bodrum takes about an hour of quite strenuous driving and you need your eyes glued to the bends all the way: it is not recommended at night.

Arriving in **Bodrum**, you are rewarded for your pains by the magnificent sight of the bay with its fine Crusader castle dominating the town and harbour. Pine-forested hills form a natural theatre facing out to sea, and the Greek island of Kos lies across the horizon.

Lively Port

Trendy resort

The first thing that strikes you about Bodrum is the liveliness of the place: people laughing and crowding the streets, colourful restaurants, pensions and cafés galore. It is a pocket of bustling youthful activity, contrasting strongly with the atmosphere of most other resorts. Its feel has become European Mediterranean, not Turkish, and its role as Turkey's yachting centre for the Aegean has given it a certain trendiness and ritziness not found in the other resorts, even Marmaris, its yachting rival. That said, it can in fact be a welcome change if you have been touring and want to revert to a taste of Europe for a while. Certainly for entertainment and night life, it takes some beating.

A stay in Bodrum for any length of time is really for boat people. The harbour has a new marina, stuffed full of yachts, and lining the remainder of the harbour front are rows of elegant Turkish caiques in golden wood, all for charter or daily hire. There is no real beach till you get 5 km out of town. If you are not on a yachting holiday, a stay of about two nights is fine to sample the night life and the restaurants and to visit the castle.

Ancient Traces

You can first spend a couple of hours dispensing with Bodrum's greatest, though distant, indeed all but vanished

Yet another Wonder claim to fame: as ancient **Halicarnassus** (the birthplace, incidentally, of Herodotus in about 485 BC) it possessed the **Mausoleum**, one of the Seven Wonders of the Ancient World (the others were the Pyramids of Giza, the Pharos or great lighthouse of Alexandria, the Colossus of Rhodes, the statue of Zeus at Olympia, the Artemision at Ephesus and the Hanging Gardens of Babylon). As there is not much to see of this or of Halicarnassus generally, you need to tread carefully or you will miss it altogether. Start at the castle; it was just here where the present harbour curve joins the neck of land leading to the castle that the ancient harbour was, and across the mouth of the present harbour, on the opposite point of land, were the ancient shipyards. Walk along the harbour road to the mosque with the pewter-coloured dome and silvery-tipped minaret on the water's edge: here you turn right and uphill. At the T-junction turn left and the Mausoleum is on your left.

What you see is a hole in the ground. It is a wonder that anybody comes to look at it at all. Some marble column drums, some foundation blocks, these are all there is to see. The site was discovered in 1856 by Sir Charles Newton,

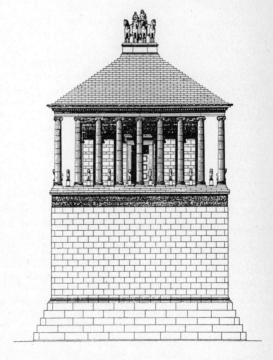

Reconstruction of the Mausoleum at Halicarnassus

whereupon he sent a number of its sculptures, including fine statues of Mausolus himself and of his wife Artemisia, back to the British Museum.

Mausolus was Persia's Carian satrap, but distant enough from his masters to assert his independence. He moved his capital from Mylasa (Milas) to Halicarnassus, regarding the site as well-suited to defence and commerce. When he died in 353 BC his wife (who was also his elder sister) Artemisia succeeded him. She is famous now for the building of the magnificent tomb called the Mausoleum (from which our modern word comes) in her husband's memory. It was originally about 40 metres high with beautiful friezes sculptured on all four sides: these are the fragments seen in the British Museum, and one block remains in Bodrum on display inside the castle. The Mausoleum stood for 1700 years, finally destroyed around the 14th C, presumably by an earthquake. The Knights of St John, arriving sometime after 1402, already found it in ruins and used it as a quarry to build their castle.

Rhodes deceived
But Artemisia was famous in her day not so much for the Mausoleum as for her prowess as a military leader. The Rhodians, hearing a woman was in charge of Caria, launched their ships to Halicarnassus, thinking Caria would be an easy capture now. Artemisia heard of their plan, and hid her own fleet in a secret harbour which Mausolus had had built under his palace, joined by a canal to the main harbour. The Rhodians sailed into Bodrum harbour and landed their men, and meanwhile Artemisia led her ships out to take over the unmanned Rhodian ships, taking them out to sea. The Rhodians were surrounded and defeated by another part of her army in the main market place. As stage two, the queen then manned the Rhodian ships and sailed to Rhodes where, believing it was their own men returning after an easy victory, the Rhodians allowed them to enter unchallenged. To commemorate this victory, Artemisia had a statue of herself erected branding the city of Rhodes. Ancient tradition in Rhodes stated that a monument once erected could not be taken down, so the Rhodians erected another building round it to hide the embodiment of their humiliation from the eyes of the world.

Above the Mausoleum you will see a mosque with a glinting metal-covered minaret cone: you walk up this street past the mosque and eventually over the main road that has come from Milas and continues to Gümbet to reach the **ancient theatre**. It is largely buried and overgrown, but you can nevertheless clamber up to its topmost row of seats for a fine view over the harbour. Halicarnassus had resisted Alexander the Great and much of the city was destroyed during the siege; the Mausoleum was spared, and there is this theatre and fragments of Mausolus' defence walls. Otherwise

Bodrum viewed from the ancient theatre

the rest is gone or lies beneath modern Bodrum, and part of the charm of the town today is stumbling across bits of ancient masonry set in walls, used as door-stops or lying about in gardens.

Crusader Toehold

So the main sight in Bodrum is the **Castle of St Peter**, built by the Hospitaller Knights of St John after they had lost their fortress in Smyrna (İzmir) in 1402 to Tamerlane. The Tower of France was the first to be built and the other towers and walls were added during the century. But when Süleyman the Magnificent conquered their base on Rhodes in 1522 the Knights were obliged, the following year, to fall back on Malta. What they left behind was one of the last and finest examples of Crusader architecture in the East. A tour of the castle takes two to three hours and it is best done in a leisurely way. It is open from 9am to 12 and 2 to 6pm daily.

The castle is set on a promontory on the site of an earlier Turkish fortress built by the Menteşe emirs. A series of fortress gates, seven in all and a moat as well, leads you into the castle proper and the citadel. Over the gates and in the walls, fragments of reliefs from the Mausoleum can be seen, mixed in with crests of the various Grand Masters of the Hospitallers.

The Knights Hospitaller

127

Entering the lower courtyard, on the right stands the elegant little **Chapel of the Knights**, converted into a mosque by the Ottomans. This lower courtyard was once separated from the upper courtyard by a wall and various buildings, in ruins today, inhabited by Janissaries after the surrender of Bodrum to the Ottomans in 1523. An **open-air museum** is here, with a portion of the frieze of the Mausoleum and some Mycanaean pottery. Tables have been set up among the trees and flowers of the courtyard and light refreshments are on offer.

At the entrance to the upper courtyard is the **main museum**, well laid-out in two sections, one showing collections of Greek statues, pottery and other finds from around Bodrum, and the other exhibiting the finds made underwater in the wreck of a ship, and illustrating the innovative techniques of the underwater archaeology used by the American team, with fascinating models. The ship sank 32 centuries ago and was resting on a reef 30 metres underwater. The cargo consisted mainly of 40 or so copper ingots, some of which had the Linear B writing of the Mycanaean or Minoan civilisations. This ship must have been trading between Syria or Cyprus and Greece towards the end of the 12th C BC.

Plantagenet arms

You now proceed to the upper courtyard and opposite is the two-storey **Serpents' Tower**. You then climb up onto the sentry walkway of the **escarpment walls**, with a lovely view down into the harbour and bay. In this inner part of the citadel the towers are named after the various countries of the Hospitallers. The tour of the walls brings you round first to the **English Tower** on the far corner of the citadel. The outer wall of this tower has a marble lion with the *arms of Edward Plantagenet* above, and a relief of St George and the Dragon; inside on the walls by the deep window seats, English Knights carved their names for posterity.

Steps lead on up to the **French Tower** and the **Italian Tower**. The views from the top are splendid. Returning down to the English Tower, you turn off left and continue on the sentry walk with a high bastion for defence from the land side, past the **German Tower**, via the Serpents' Tower to the lower courtyard and out again.

Around Town and along the Peninsula

The town itself, with its pretty whitewashed houses and abundant flowers, is always bustling with life, and it is pleas-

Warding off the evil eye

ant to stroll looking at the shops. The main bazaar area is around the foot of the castle: sponges and local blue lapis Lazuli beads to ward off the evil eye can be bought, as well as endless selections of rugs, carpets, embroidery and copper. Leisure clothes in soft cotton are also attractive. There is a bountiful selection of restaurants serving good sea-food, many having views towards the castle. At night, the Han restaurant in a beautifully converted 18th C caravanserai is a lively place to eat, with dancing in the central courtyard.

From the palm-tree lined crescent of the harbour, caiques can be hired to explore the local shoreline, which has a succession of sandy coves, many deserted and inaccessible by road. **Cnidos** can be visited in a long day trip.

Getting to the beaches

For beaches you must go out of the town. Many of the larger pensions and hotels are in fact out of town for this reason, mostly in **Gümbet Bay** 3 km distant. The nearest beyond Gümbet is at **Balíkcí Köyu**, 8 km away. Follow the Milas road for 3 km, then turn left for the remainder. It is a sheltered bay with a small deserted beach, and it is a pretty forest drive to get there. A further 9 km is the pebble beach of **Gigden** with some small restaurants, or you can go right to the tip of the peninsula, an additional half hour drive, to **Turgutreis** or **Karatoprak**.

At **Gümüslük** to the north, also on the tip of the peninsula, lies the ancient port of **Myndos**, on a headland with a well-sheltered harbour bay. Its remains amount to defence walls and a small Byzantine church.

Remote ruins reached only on foot

Scattered on the hilltops between Bodrum and the tip of the peninsula are the ruins of many ancient cities. All the sites are remote and can only be reached on foot. The most accessible is **Pedasa**, some 90 minutes' walk to the north of Bodrum, at the head of a pass overgrown with pine trees. Called **Gökçeler** today, the site is 2 km west of the village of Bitez and has a high citadel with an internal keep and some curious tumuli tombs.

TO MARMARIS AND AROUND

Returning from Bodrum up the peninsula to the T-junction just south of Milas and following the sign to Muğla, the road climbs up in sharp hair pin bends through pine forests. The scenery is lovely with spectacular views down into the valley below. Everywhere is a profusion of bee-hives; honey production here is taken very seriously. The land is lush and fertile as you pass the attractive Arslan picnic area with a restaurant set in the woods.

Diversions Along the Way

Worship of Serapis at Stratoniceia

On the plateau before the Yatağan turn-off, a yellow sign points off left to the site of ancient **Stratoniceia**, a Hellenistic city founded in c280 BC by Seleucus I of Syria. In Hellenistic and Roman times the city was rich and prosperous, but today very little remains standing. The modern village of **Eskihisar**, recently rebuilt after being destroyed by an earthquake, stands on the site. The **Temple of Serapis** is the most prominent monument in the centre of the modern village, and a little **museum** nearby houses the more important finds. Impressive quarry works lie just beyond the village, distorting the look of the hillside.

At **Yatağan** you meet the main Aydín-Muğla highway, and before continuing south towards Muğla those travellers fortunate enough to have the time at their disposal can make an interesting detour northwards to visit the evocative Carian ruins of Alabanda and Alinda, near the town of Çine, some 40 km to the north. The lack of formal excavations at these two towns, both capitals of Caria in their day, serves greatly to enhance the bucolic atmosphere of these sites, with sheep and goats grazing in their agoras and various fragments of centuries-old sculpture incorporated into the village houses. A visit to these sites would also be feasible as a long day trip from Kuşadasí or from Güllük.

The winged horse and scorpions of Alabanda

From Yatağan the excellent road leads through a beautiful river gorge before crossing a fertile highland plain to arrive at Çine. **Alabanda** lies 7 km west of Çine on a driveable dirt track. The name is said to mean horse (*ala*) victory (*banda*) in the ancient Carian language, and the city's early coins show the winged horse Pegasus. In historical accounts, apart from its equestrian associations, Alabanda was noted for a particular kind of red gem, like a garnet but darker and rougher, and for an abundance of scorpions. While no trace of the former has been found in modern times, the latter still rear their ugly tails from time to time.

The village of Araphisar lies on a corner of the site today, and the ancient city itself has suffered from plundering by the locals and flooding by the nearby stream. The **city walls** remain intact on the higher ground but have been largely washed away on the low ground. Alabanda's importance as a centre in antiquity is reflected in the size of its **theatre**, but the best preserved and most conspicuous building on the site is the council house or **buleuterion**, its walls still standing in part to 10 metres high. The site has not received the attentions of any excavators since 1905, and so the years of neglect and flooding have buried the buildings to some height. On an artificial terrace on the hillside stand the foundations of a **temple** in the Doric order thought, from a figurine of Artemis found here by the 1905 excavators, to be dedicated to that goddess.

Outside the city walls is a section of **aqueduct** and an extensive **necropolis** of sarcophagi, each citing the profession of its occupant — banker, architect, doctor, gardener, dealer in pheasants and even lamplighter.

An untouched Carian village

Returning to Çine, the adventurous traveller can hire a guide for the walk up to **Gerga**, a remarkable Carian village showing virtually no sign of Hellenisation and set in wild mountain country 6.5 km southeast of Eski Çine. Again, a whole day is required, but the ruins are so unusual that no one is likely to consider the time wasted. Among the most remarkable monuments, many of them unique, are the small but excellently preserved **temple**, quite plain but still complete with its roof, and fragments of vast statues.

Among the Finest Ruins in Caria

Continuing a few km north from Çine, a road then forks west for some 25 km to Alinda. Though historically less significant than Alabanda, the ruins at **Alinda** are far superior and George Bean even considers them 'among the finest in Caria'. The site, surprisingly, has never been excavated. Discovered by Chandler in 1765, his own account of the ruins was so dull that no one ever felt sufficiently inspired. Alinda makes her only appearance in historical records as the place to which Queen Ada, sister of Mausolus, was exiled, later to be released by Alexander the Great and made queen of the whole of Caria. Alexander himself lingered here while preparing for the siege of Halicarnassus (Bodrum), and he and the middle-aged Ada became close friends. He called her 'mama' and she offered to adopt him as her son.

Alexander lingers at Alinda with his 'mama'

The city is built on a double hilltop, steep on all sides and still heavily fortified by a wall surviving in many places, dating from Queen Ada's time in the 4th C BC. Climbing from the modern town of Karpuzlu, you arrive first at the **market building**, the finest of its type, better preserved than that at Assos near Troy or at Seleuceia near Side in the south. It still stands for its full length of 100 metres and to most of its original height of 15 metres. A three-storeyed building, its ground floor opens onto a narrow terrace cut partly out of the rocky hillside, and its top storey would have opened out on to the agora to the north. The bottom storey is divded into rooms which would originally have been shops, while the middle storey may have been used as storerooms for the shops below.

Climbing on up you next reach the well-preserved **theatre** with 35 rows of seats set into the steep hillside and now heavily but charmingly overgrown. The stage building, still deeply buried, looks to be in excellent preservation. Excavation would probably reveal it to be almost complete, but here, as so often in Turkey, you are torn between the merits of renovation and the attractions of the romantically overgrown aspect from which so much of the charm of the sites derives.

Just below the summit is a fine Hellenistic two-storeyed **tower**. Close by this is the entrance to a **tunnel** said to come out just above the theatre. No one has been through it, and its purpose remains a mystery.

Above the tower a saddle of hillside leads up to the second **acropolis** at Alinda, surrounded by well-preserved walls and entered by a fine gateway. Inside are extensive remains of private houses and a row of cisterns.

Beyond this second acropolis, a well-preserved **aqueduct** runs across the valley to the next hill, supplying the cisterns. The structure is still very strong and can easily be walked along.

All around the city are **tombs**, some of the Carian type cut into a boulder of rock with a separate lid, others of the built variety now converted to houses or storerooms by the local inhabitants.

Amyzon amid savage beauty

High in the hills above Alinda, and best reached from Koçarli via a road to the village of Gaffarlar, lies the ruined city of **Amyzon** in a mountainous setting of savage beauty. Inside the fine defence walls are the ruins of a temple on a terrace reached by a broad stairway, a theatre covered in vegetation, and a series of underground vaulted chambers for storage. The trip takes the best part of a day, but could be attempted from Kuşadasí.

Ottoman Interlude

Old Turkish houses

Set up on a plateau at 680 metres, the town of **Muğla**, capital of Muğla Province, was also the capital of the Menteşe emirs of the 14th C (see Milas). The town is large and sprawling with a clear divide between the old parts and the new wide boulevards with the Atatürk memorial. The **old quarter** lies to the left of the main road, and it makes a pleasant change from Graeco-Roman sites to wander in the picturesque bazaar and into the winding lanes where stand some of the most attractive houses of the Ottoman period in Turkey. The tourist office on the main square just left off the main boulevard will give you a map and directions. If the Ottoman period holds no attraction for you, however, the town can be by-passed as a new road now forks off right to Marmaris and Fethiye before you enter the town.

Arrival at Marmaris

After Muğla a long and spectacular descent to the sea begins. Arriving at sea level and just before the road turns right to cross the plain, you pass a group of **rock-cut tombs**, two of them with Ionic temple facades, all dating from the 4th C BC and belonging to the nearby Carian town of Idyma. From the plain the turn-off to Marmaris leads through a splendid avenue of eucalyptus trees, then on a further 30 km or so along a lush pine-forested peninsula. Once at Marmaris you must return by the same route along the eucalyptus avenue before continuing your journey southward.

Fjords and pine forests

Marmaris' situation, with pine forests reaching right down to the sea, has been described as fjord-like, for the huge bay in which it sits is almost landlocked. Nelson's entire fleet sheltered in this anchorage in 1798 prior to sailing for Egypt where it destroyed the French fleet in the Battle of the Nile. Like Bodrum, Marmaris is a main yachting centre and embarkation point for flotilla holidays, and despite the earthquake of 1958 it remains a pleasant town with a more Turkish feel than Bodrum. Both places have become particular favourites with the British. The harbour promenade is enjoyable for strolling and the older part of town has become a pedestrian precinct, lined with colourful restaurants and cafes. Parking along the main promenade has now been totally prohibited to avoid noise and congestion. This sometimes means that after checking into your seafront hotel, you find the car has to be parked 15 minutes' walk away, so it is worth asking first about the parking facilities.

Castle of Süleyman the Magnificent

In the old quarter on a hillock jutting out into the bay stand the remains of an **Ottoman castle** built in 1522 by Süleyman the Magnificent, with a cluster of crumbling houses roofed in red tiles huddled within its walls. The castle served as a staging post for the Turkish assault against Rhodes that year. Climbing up the steps to the battlements affords a good view of the town and bay. The market and shops nearby sell a good selection of Turkish crafts, including jewellery, leather and carpets, and the locally produced honey is delicious. Unlike Bodrum, Marmaris has beaches near the town or you can drive or take a dolmuş to one of the pretty bays nearby to find secluded swimming. Most of the larger hotels are situated in bays a few kilometres from the town.

As the site of ancient Physcus belonging to the Dorians of Rhodes, Marmaris was in antiquity a prosperous port on the commercial route between Anatolia, Rhodes and Egypt.

Rhodes lies directly opposite the Gulf of Marmaris and boats travel there daily, taking between two and three hours depending on the size of the boat.

The Rhodes connection

The link with Rhodes goes back a long way, and the forked Loryma peninsula west of Marmaris was the heartland of the area known as the Rhodian Peraea, as at various times this part of Anatolia, reaching north inland as far as Stratoniceia and Muğla, was under the control of Rhodes. From Marmaris, boats can be hired to explore the coast of the Loryma peninsula. Ruins of several ancient cities overlook the sea here and can be reached and explored far more easily by boat than from inland. Among these Rhodian ruins are **Amos**, heavily fortified with towers and gates, and having a theatre and a temple; **Gerbekse**, with several Byzantine churches; and the impressive Loryma castle in **Bozuk Bay**.

An Outing to Cnidos

Spectacular views

A pleasant day's outing from Marmaris is a trip to the site of Cnidos on the very tip of the peninsula. For the touring visitor who is on his way to the Lycian and southern shores, the detour does not really warrant the time it takes, as the ruins themselves are not that striking. But the drive down the peninsula is spectacular, climbing up through wooded hills, then descending to lush fertile meadows. During the mountainous sections there are some fine hairpin bends and perpendicular precipices; the road to this point is excellent. After about 1½ hours' drive, a road forks off right to Cnidos about 5 km before Datça. **Datça** is the site of old Cnidos, before it moved to its new site at the tip of the peninsula, but of this nothing more than rubble walls remain. The tarmac on the Cnidos fork soon peters out, and it is then a further hour's drive on dirt track to the site. The road is by no means totally straightforward, and there are some rough patches, but a private car (especially a hire car!) can manage well enough when driven carefully. The total drive from Marmaris to Cnidos is therefore about 2½ hours, and it is advisable to return before dark. At two points on the dirt track section there is no yellow sign — in both cases you take the left fork.

There are a handful of simple restaurants serving mainly fish along the harbour at **Cnidos** and there are usually a few yachts moored belonging to people who have sailed across from Bodrum (a 6-hour journey). About 2 km before reaching the site, the road takes you past an extensive **necropolis** scattered on the hillside. You then round the corner, gaining your first view of the twin harbour and lighthouse. About 600 metres before the restaurants a series of buildings will be seen on the right up the hillside. Clambering up the original steps of the street here brings you to the **Sanctuary of Demeter**. It was here that Sir Charles Newton, conducting excavations in 1857–59 discovered many sculptures, notably that of the seated goddess Demeter. This, along with several hundred other cases of sculptures and ancient stones, he duly sent back to the British Museum. From this point at the top of the sanctuary you can scramble up the hillside towards the cliff where you will find a very **ruined large theatre** set into the base of the cliff. But you can save yourself the effort: there is a lower and much **better preserved theatre** just 5 metres right of the road.

Without this diversion, it takes only about an hour to tour the ruins at Cnidos, which are not that extensive. The most interesting remains are the foundations of temples, particularly the circular marble base stones of the **Temple of Aphrodite**, reached by following the path from the restaurants up to the highest point of the excavations. The discovery of this temple was the highpoint of the American excavations carried out in 1969 by the aptly named Iris Love.

Irresistible statue of Aphrodite by Praxiteles

When Cnidos moved its site from Datça to here, new statues were needed for the temples at the new site. Aphrodite was the patron goddess of Cnidos, and so the city ordered a magnificent statue of a nude Aphrodite from the famous sculptor, Praxiteles. The statue was said to be so beautiful that travellers came from afar to Cnidos just to look at it, and Pliny declared it the finest statue in the world. There is a remarkable account in a work written by a man called Lucian in the 2nd C AD of a visit to see this Aphrodite. He and his friends were admiring the statue from all sides, when they noticed a dark patch like a stain on its inner thigh. They assumed it to be a flaw in the marble, but the old woman in charge of the key to the temple gave them a different explanation. A young man, she said, fell in love with the goddess and spent all day and every day in the temple hoping the goddess would love him. In desperation he one day hid himself inside when the temple was locked up for the night. In the morning the passion of his embraces had left this stain on the statue, where it had been ever since.

In 1970 a fragment of the statue itself was identified by the excavators nearby, a large very white marble block with an inscription with the beginnings of the names Prax (iteles) and Aph (rodite). Miss Love herself caused a furore by claiming that when poking around in the vaults of the British Museum among the sculptures sent back by Newton in 1859, she found the marble head of Praxiteles' Aphrodite, a claim which the Museum vigorously denies, pointing out that the head in question was found at the Sanctuary of Demeter, over 1 km away.

The other remains on the site are the small **odeon** near the submerged harbour walls on the mainland side, and the **Lion Tomb** on the lighthouse promontory, so called because it was surmounted by a recumbent lion, now in the British Museum.

The atmosphere of the site is pleasantly peaceful, with

animals grazing among the ruins. Swimming can best be done in the cove a 10-minute walk beyond the Temple of Aphrodite.

Originally founded by the Dorians from the Peloponnese a little later than Rhodes and Kos, Cnidos was an important member of the Dorian federation in the 7th C BC. Frightened by the impending approach of the Persians in the 6th C BC, the Cnidians planned to dig a defensive canal to cut off the headland on which the Lion Tomb and the lighthouse currently stand from the mainland. They consulted the oracle at Delphi about it, who advised them to give up this venture, and so they surrendered to the Persians without a struggle. Later Cnidos became a prosperous member of the Delian Confederacy under Athens. Conquered by Alexander in 334 BC, Cnidos later sided with the Romans against Antiochus III of Syria.

For a Taste of Lycia

Returning up the peninsula from Marmaris and joining the main Muğla-Fethiye road at the avenue of eucalyptus trees, follow the road towards Fethiye. It crosses a flat fertile plain, then begins to climb steeply.

Rock-cut temple tombs

After passing Lake Köyceğiz, there is a yellow sign off to the site of Caunus. A tarmac road leads 10 km to the fishing village of **Dalyan**, at the mouth of the river by the sea. The visit to Caunus can be a day's excursion from Marmaris (93 km each way), or a detour totalling about 3½ hours off the main route to Fethiye. It is to be recommended particularly for those visitors, perhaps based in Marmaris or Bodrum, who are not travelling on into Lycia, as it will give them, in the sight of its rock-cut temple tombs overlooking the water, their only chance of glimpsing the magic of the Lycian cliff tombs. But if you are proceeding on into Lycia it can be omitted if you are short of time as you will have ample opportunity to sample the delights of Lycia in such places as Fethiye and Myra. Many visitors to Caunus in fact make their approach from the sea, on caïque trips.

Arriving at the centre of the village, the tombs in the cliff can be seen on the other side of the river, and in the season numerous boatmen are waiting on the bank to ferry visitors across. Near the bank are restaurants serving excellent, if somewhat expensive, sea bass and mullet. These fish swim up from the sea to spawn in the lake, and in making their return to the sea some two months later are caught in large quantities here. There are a few simple pensions for basic accommodation.

A healthy enough place for the dead

Caunus has been surprisingly neglected until recently. This may have been due to the lingering reputation of the unhealthiness of the place in ancient times. Caunus is now some 3 km from the sea, but was in antiquity a Carian port.

However, the marshiness which has built up over the centuries with the silting of the river, already existed at that time and was a perfect breeding ground for mosquitoes. As a result, most of the population suffered from malaria, giving their complexions a death-like greenish tint. The link between mosquitoes and fever was not, of course, understood in ancient times, so to them it just seemed that the place itself was unhealthy. Stratonicus, famous for his sharp tongue, visited Caunus in the 4th C BC and observing the unhealthy colour of the inhabitants commented that he now understood what Homer meant when he said 'humans pass on like leaves'. When the Caunians protested at this rudeness, Stratonicus retorted 'What! How could I dare to call a city unhealthy where even dead men walk the streets?'

Strabo, surprisingly, states that Caunus was unhealthy in the autumn because of the abundance of fruit. Doctors at that time in fact regarded fruit as dangerous to the health, and Galen, greatest physician in antiquity after Hippocrates, believed that fruit caused fever and insisted that his own father, by abstaining from it, had lived to be 100. You may rest assured however, that Caunus is not malarial today, as in 1948 a serious campaign to eradicate malaria was begun in Turkey.

Murderous work force Lying on the borders of Caria and Lycia, the history of the town was very mixed. It was considered Carian in classical times, and its language was similar to Carian, yet its customs were said to be closer to those of Lycia (eg burials in temple-type rock tombs). It existed already at the time of the Persian invasion in the 6th C BC, belonged to the Delian Confederacy under the aegis of Athens in the 5th C, was fortified by Mausolus the Persian satrap in the 4th C, and was then under Syrian, Rhodian and Roman rule like the rest of Caria. The site has benefitted from excavation by Turkish archaeologists since 1967, using, according to a Turkish guide, convicted murderers as their labour force.

Approaching the site from the river meandering among the giant reeds, you have leisure to examine the **rock tombs** in the cliff. They are in two uneven rows, the upper row of Lycian style tombs with the facade of Ionic temples (as at Fethiye), and a lower row of simpler cut chambers with square doors. Some of the upper row are quite easily reached, but others are virtually inaccessible. The only decoration on the temples is on one of the pediments, a pair of lions face to face.

A climb of about 10 minutes from disembarking takes you up towards the theatre, passing the ruins of a **Byzantine basilica**, then a huge **Roman bath** which will be converted into a museum after restoration. The fortified **walls** of the city, built by Mausolus in the 4th C BC, are well-preserved in places. At the foot of the acropolis hill, crowned by the ruins of a **Carian fortress** of the 4th C BC, lies the **theatre** in the

Greek style, slightly more than a semi-circle. It is the best preserved of the buildings of Caunus, the southern half cut into the hillside with the two arched entrances therefore on the north side. From the seats of the theatre you can see the original port, in a cove now covered in reeds. Descending towards this you will see the high walls of a **nymphaeum** dedicated to Vespasian and a Hellenistic **gateway** pointing towards the pool known today as the Pool of Leeches. You can also look at the remains of statue bases, an interesting structure thought to be a shallow outdoor bathing pool with a marble semi-circular bench and the scattered column drums of various temples.

Swimming is not generally indulged in at the site, but those in boats can go on to swim in the fresh water of the lake, after first calling off to visit nearby hot sulphur baths.

PRACTICAL INFORMATION

GÜLLÜK
Pelit Pansiyon, 13 rooms, on beach beyond Milas.

BODRUM
At the end of a peninsula, Bodrum is 4 hours' drive from İzmir and 2 hours from Dalaman airport. It can be used as a base to visit Ephesus, Priene, Miletos and Didyma, but there is no escape from the long drive up the peninsula. There are no large or luxurious hotels, but a myriad of small pensions and hotels, usually family-run. The choice on arrival is bewildering, and it is as well to have decided in advance which one to aim for. All the ones listed here are 1-star. The tourist season runs from April until November.

TMT, bungalow-style, 15 minutes' walk from town. Best hotel in Bodrum, 2 pools, good grounds and water sports facilities. Open-air disco.

Manzara, chalet-style. Set up 10 minutes' walk from the centre with views of the castle. Tiny pool, pretty flowers, rooms have small kitchen area.

Merve, large rooms, roof terrace for breakfast.

Mylasa Pension, 12 rooms all with WC. English owners, 10 minutes from centre. Roof terrace for breakfast.

Artemis, 16 rooms, beach.

Halikarnas, open April–October, 20 rooms, beach.

Herodot, open March–November, 15 rooms, a few with shower. Good views of castle and bay from balconies.

Kaktus Motel, June–September, 16 rooms, 8 km from centre on the road to Karatoprak, on the beach at Ortakent.

Gala, 13 rooms with WC, opposite the marina, family run. Carpeted rooms and corridors, unusually.

Restaurants: many along the front and in the town at the foot of the castle. Han Restaurant, a converted caravanserai, is a pleasant environment for evening meals, with music and dancing.

There is no beach, but dolmuş taxis run to the nearest **beaches** frequently.

Boats go twice a week to Kos, Mondays and Fridays. In principle it is possible to do the return journey in a day, leaving a few hours for the visit.

Art and Culture Week, early September. Held in Bodrum castle, including classical Turkish and Western music concerts, exhibitions, fashion shows and examples of Turkish theatre. Many local artefacts of Bodrum craftsmen are on sale.

GUMBET
Small resort 5 km west of Bodrum, where larger hotels with beaches are situated.

Water sports are available and small boats can be hired to take you to Bodrum or one of the remoter bays. Dolmuş taxis link it with Bodrum.

Hotel Taraca, 2 minutes' walk from the beach, luxuriously fitted rooms with own fridge. Pool. Good views to Kos.

Hotel Sami, right on the beach, all rooms with shower, WC and balcony. Family-run. Good restaurant.

Pension Pay, 18 rooms, private facilities but very small rooms. Owner-run. Friendly.

Pension Levant, 17 rooms, private facilities, breakfast on roof terrace.

MARMARIS

Motel Marti (3-star), 9 km beyond Marmaris on Datça road. Open April–November, water sports, private beach.

Lydia (2-star), open April–November, 5 km beyond Marmaris on the Datça road. Private beach, gardens, 300 rooms.

Otel 47 (2-star), in Marmaris town on seafront. No beach, but very modern. Excellent value.

Yavuz Hotel (1-star). On the seafront. Roof terrace for breakfast with small pool. Family-run.

Atlantik (1-star), 40 rooms. In town centre.

Many **restaurants** lining the harbour front and in the older pedestrian area.

Beaches are outside the town, at least 5 km away.

Boats run to Rhodes in summer daily except Sundays, the journey taking 2–3 hours, depending on the size of the boat.

Music and Art Festival in June.

DATÇA

Small town with a few hotels and restaurants round a small harbour. Very quiet.

Dorya Motel (2-star), open mid-April to mid-October, 32 rooms, private beach, pool, gardens.

INLAND TO PAMUKKALE (ANCIENT CARIA: THE HINTERLAND)

ANCIENT CARIA: THE HINTERLAND

The hinterland of the region of Caria can best be explored either from the base of Kusadaşí or on the return leg of a circular tour of the southwestern Turkish coastline.

Following the Maeander

The main road leads inland shortly south of Selçuk following the Maeander river valley upstream. From antiquity this route was always one of the main channels from the Aegean coast inland to Anatolia and the Taurus mountains. The early Greeks settled along the valley, establishing cities, some of which, notably Aphrodisias, rivalled their sister cities on the Carian coast in importance.

Avenue of Greek settlement

The drive inland is not initially very exciting, the scenery being fairly flat with fig trees, olive groves and vineyards all along the valley. **Aydín**, by far the largest town today, can be bypassed as it holds no interest for the traveller. On a plateau just north of Aydín is ancient **Tralles**, famous for its pottery and its distinguished citizens, among whom was Anthemius of Tralles, one of the architects of Haghia Sophia in Constantinople. In the last century there was quite a lot to see at Tralles, but the site is currently occupied by the military (requiring a special permit from the local municipality to visit) and little now remains to be seen.

The road leads on to Sultanhisar, from where a yellow sign points off left 3 km to the site of Nyssa, set in the hills above the modern town.

Neglected Nyssa

The **Nyssa** site, excavated some years ago by local people on funds from the Turkish government, is now very overgrown again, but this in itself lends a lot of charm, especially to the **theatre**. It is here that the visitor arrives first, with numerous mature olive trees growing out between the rows of seats. The site is very peaceful and is usually deserted.

Trees in the theatre

Founded in the beginning of the 3rd C BC by a Syrian Seleucid king, it was a relatively insignificant place until Roman times when it prospered and from when most of its monuments date. It was probably abandoned at the time of Tamerlane's advance toward İzmir in 1402, when the inhabitants dispersed and moved down onto the plain.

Approaching the site, to the right of the road is the **gymnasium**, hardly visible now, just a flat area about 150 metres long. At one end is a better preserved building thought to have been a **baths** originally, then converted to a church at a later date.

Parking at the theatre, a stream can be seen running

141

through an **ancient tunnel** about 100 metres long just below. Then walking on up the track for about 200 metres, a small path leads off right to the **buleuterion** or council chamber, which is the most attractive building remaining on the site. It was completely excavated, although foliage is taking root again fast, and is in good condition with 12 rows of seats and five stairways. Behind the speaker's platform are three entrances, beyond which are the bases of a row of eight columns. Nearby is a marble bath with a plug hole. Of the **agora**, just beyond the buleuterion, there are just a few column stumps to be seen.

Buried library   The other building of interest, but difficult to find, is the **library**. Returning down past the theatre, it is about 100 metres, up the hill off the track to the right. It dates from about AD 200 and originally had two or three storeys. The top storey is almost totally destroyed, and most of the ground floor is still buried. The niches in the walls for the books are still visible. Hopefully this building will one day be excavated, as the buried ground floor has probably been well preserved; the building would then be second only to the Library of Celsus at Ephesus.

APHRODISIAS: AN ARCHAEOLOGIST'S LABOUR OF LOVE

About 30 km beyond Sultanhisar you reach the turn-off right to the ancient city of Aphrodisias, clearly signposted. It is a total of two hours' drive or so from Kusadasí along the main route inland to this point. The detour from here off the main road to the site is considerable, 38 km each way, but the route is attractive and with the extensive and continuing excavations the city has increased in importance to the extent that it has now become a compulsory stop for coach tours between İzmir and Pamukkale.

The road winds along the course of the Maeander valley for most of the way. Just 2 or 3 km before the site near the village of Dandalaz are several prettily situated restaurants at the side of the river offering fresh trout, so fresh that they may even be fished out of a pool and cooked specially for you.

Echoes of columns The ruined city lies on flat fertile ground in the lower Maeander valley ringed by distant mountains. The setting is not spectacular but there is in the atmosphere bucolic charm. The green and peaceful surroundings are admirably suited to the city of Aphrodite, originally an indigenous fertility goddess, later the Olympian goddess of love and beauty. Two aspects of the site are peculiarly Aphrodisian: the beautiful marble, often blue in colour, quarried from the local hills; and the tall poplar trees echoing the slender columns of the temple and the porticoes. This effect is especially lovely at sunset and by moonlight.

Victim of a violent earthquake in the 7th C AD, the city went into a gradual decline and was finally abandoned completely after the Mongol incursion of 1402. The earliest excavations on the site were carried out somewhat randomly in 1904–5 by a French enthusiast who removed a number of fine sculptures. Though this was without the permission of the Turkish authorities it was not at that time downright illegal, as the first restrictive law on the removal of antiquities was not until 1906. In 1937 a brief burst of Italian excavations took place, but it was left to Professor Kenan Erim, a Turkish national attached to New York University, to conduct serious excavations and to disentangle the aftermath of earthquakes and amateurish excavators.

The struggle to continue excavating A generation ago, Aphrodisias was regarded as an attractive but unexciting site, of interest primarily to archaeologists. The labours of Kenan Bey, as he is affectionately called, began in 1961. He returns each summer in the university vacation. The National Geographic Society helped until recently with the funding, and the Turkish authorities built the site museum, but the future of the excavations depends largely on Professor Erim's labour of love, with funding being pursued from a variety of sources. He is trying to persuade the authorities to preserve the site as an Archaeological Park, with any development of restaurants and hotels kept a healthy distance from the site itself. He bemoans the current trend in Turkey of using the ancient monuments as the venue for modern festivals.

Transformed now by the extensive excavations, which have revealed many exceptionally well-preserved monuments, it is easy to relive the grandeur and wealth of the city. The site was inhabited from the beginning of the Bronze Age in 3000 BC, as the excavations in the hill at the back of the theatre have shown. The city with its famous temple was dedicated to the cult of Aphrodite in the 6th C BC. Because of its faithfulness to Rome, Caesar and Augustus protected it and conferred on its Temple of Aphrodite a right of asylum equal to that of Artemis at Ephesus. It was declared a free city and enjoyed a number of privileges such as freedom from taxation, making it very prosperous.

With the arrival of Christianity its name was changed to Stavropolis, City of the Cross, and the pagan Temple of Aphrodite was converted to a church. At the end of the 5th C the Byzantine Emperor Leo I made it the capital of Caria and it became the seat of a bishop. The town was already in decline when it was taken by the Seljuks, then ravaged by the Mongol Tamerlane in 1402, after which it remained a field of ruins.

Touring the Aphrodisias Site

At the site is a hut selling refreshments, and tickets are bought at the **museum** which opened in 1979. Here are housed the many fine sculptures and statues (many of Aphrodite herself) found on the site. Two hours should be allowed as a minimum for an enjoyable tour of the site, which is open daily from 8.30am to 5.30pm.

The blue marble of Aphrodisias

The path from the museum leads first across what used to be Geyre's village square. The village had to be removed 2 km away to allow excavations to continue. Geyre is a Turkish corruption of Caria, Aphrodisias' name during Byzantine times when it was capital of Caria. Here in the former square is the **theatre**; the carved seats for prominent people in the bottom row have survived well. In the far chambers through the stage building arches are an abundance of carved blocks with bulls' heads on them. The area in front of the theatre has only recently been excavated: it is a **second agora** (for the main agora, see below) with a *colonnade of blue marble columns* and a large theatre baths beyond. The blue marble looks particularly fine when wetted. Photography of these areas is forbidden because of the continuing excavations. The excavators had been puzzled by the existence of this second agory, but they now think it likely that the main agora was flooded after an earthquake in the 4th C AD. In the **theatre baths** is a large basilical hall with fine scrolled pillars covered in elaborate reliefs, and these have been re-erected.

After the theatre the path leads off over the hill with a lovely view right down onto the columns of the **main agora** standing picturesquely among poplar trees. In the back of the hill behind the theatre are **Bronze Age excavations**. The path then leads down past the **Portico of Tiberius** which once housed a series of shops and latrines (photography forbidden). The portico was originally 250 metres long and an elaborate garlanded frieze ran the length of it. Many sections of this frieze are in the old Basmahane museum in İzmir where air pollution has damaged the surfaces over the years. Professor Erim has re-erected many columns of the portico and has asked for the İzmir frieze to be returned. Excavations have also begun on the northern portico in the poplar trees, on the eastern side of which a large **gateway** with two towers on two storeys, later converted to a nymphaeum, was found. This had originally been thought to be the agora gate, but though the excavators still call it that, *faute de mieux*, it has now become clear from the direction it faces that the gate was not the entry to the agora, but rather to another building whose identity is as yet unknown.

Labour of love: sticking the bits back together at Aphrodisias

Beyond this are the **Baths of Hadrian**. It was in this area
that the French archaeologist in 1904 carried out his brief
flurry, and the sculptures and reliefs he did not take himself
are now in the İstanbul Archaeological Museum. One item
taken by the Frenchman, part of a life-size sculpture of a
man's head, was in turn abducted by Professor Erim from
Paris, and as if in vindication, he recently excavated the other
half: the two joined pieces make up a remarkably skilfully
carved Roman head of a bearded man with a squint in his left
eye (dated to the 5th C AD). The baths are very extensive with
a series of a chambers; the three chambers in the far southwest
corner are thought to be the *women's baths*, which were often
separate from the men's. To the side of the baths the path
passes what looks as if it would have been the *plunge pool*, a
shallow square pool with four columns, one in each corner,
all in marble, to the left of which is a large handsome
palaestra or open courtyard for exercise paved with black and
white squares.

Walking on, the path leads through a two-column door
into an open field with poplar trees and undergrowth which
was the main agora. Forking right off the main path beyond
this, leads to the charming little **odeon** built in the 2nd C AD,
one of the most perfect structures of its type in Asia Minor.
The orchestre had a mosaic pavement, but now has water and
lilies in the bottom with the odd frog. The seats are still very
well preserved in lovely marble, especially those on the top
row with lions' feet. The stage backdrop was adorned with
statues and reliefs, now on display in the museum. Adjoining
the western outer wall of the odeon is a curious **heroon** or
tomb of a distinguished citizen. It is circular with three steps
leading up to a platform with a decorated altar. North of the
odeon, between it and the Temple of Aphrodite, large numbers of unfinished statues and marble carvings discovered by
the excavators pointed to this being the famous **sculptors'
workshop** of Aphrodisias.

Next door to the odeon on the west you will find a track
leading to the **Bishop's Palace**, an interesting structure with a
courtyard of extraordinary blue marble columns. It was
dubbed this by the excavators when the found a seal in it
referring to the seat of the bishopric of Caria, and because of
its closeness to the temple (then the church), it seemed likely it
was the residence of the Bishop of Stavropolis.

The main path continues on to the huge **Temple of
Aphrodite** itself, thought to date from about 100 BC, with
many well-preserved columns and friezes in the Ionic order
still standing. In the late 5th C AD the temple was destroyed to
make way for a Christian basilica, the apse of which is still
standing on the far side of the temple. At that time the tall
Ionic columns were moved to form a nave and two aisles. The
structure was heavily damaged by the earthquake in the 7th C

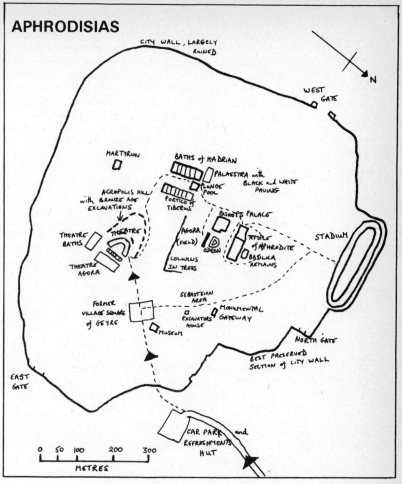

APHRODISIAS

CITY WALL, LARGELY RUINED

N

WEST GATE

MARTYRION

BATHS of HADRIAN

PALAESTRA with BLACK and WHITE PAVING

PLUNGE POOL

ACROPOLIS HILL with BRONZE AGE EXCAVATIONS

PORTICO of TIBERIUS

BISHOPS PALACE

THEATRE BATHS

THEATRE

AGORA (FIELD)

ODEON

TEMPLE of APHRODITE

STADIUM

THEATRE AGORA

COLUMNS IN TREES

BASILICA REMAINS

SEBASTEION AREA

FORMER VILLAGE SQUARE of GEYRE

EXCAVATORS HOUSE

MONUMENTAL GATEWAY

NORTH GATE

MUSEUM

BEST PRESERVED SECTION of CITY WALL

EAST GATE

0 50 100   200   300

METRES

CAR PARK and REFRESHMENTS HUT

and extensively re-worked again in the 11thC, leading to considerable confusion in the architectural plan. During recent excavations in the northern aisle of the church, marble slabs like paving stones were found which, on being turned over, were found to be elaborate Byzantine sarcophagus panels carved with figures and the garlanded friezes so common in Aphrodisias.

The main path then leads on to the final, furthest monument, the **stadium**, before looping back towards the museum. The stadium is magnificent, one of the best preserved in the Graeco-Roman world, with 25 rows of seats still standing and the curved ends almost perfectly intact. Its seating capacity was 30,000. In the middle of the far side is the *Royal Box*.

Eros exhausted   Returning in the direction of the museum, the path leads past the **tetrapylon** a monumental gateway of four sets of four columns standing at the entrance to the city (until recently the entrance to the village of Geyre as well). This structure with its lovely spiral fluted columns was dismantled in the summer of 1985 and extensive work has been carried out to stabilise the foundations around it which were heavily waterlogged. About 90 percent of the elements of the architectural design have been found, and the intention is to reconstruct the gateway starting in summer 1986 on the new firm foundations. Among the *reliefs* found here were a charming series of capitals showing Eros engaged in combat with various animals including a snake, a bear, a lion, and a mythical chimaera. The final capital in the series shows him, suitably exhausted from his labours, lying on his back, fast asleep with mouth open and eyes tightly closed.

Also in this vicinity recent discoveries have been made of a large and elaborate **Byzantine house**, its inside walls decorated with frescoes. One of the rooms has a courtyard with the characteristic blue marble columns. Also in this vicinity two statuettes of Egyptian gods were found, the first Egyptian finds to be made at Aphrodisias.

Returning beyond the tetrapylon through the trees to the excavators' house you come to another major area of excavation, though little is visible to the layman at the moment. First discovered in 1979, the **Sebasteion** consists of two porticoes enclosing a processional way, the whole about 100 metres long and 80 metres wide. The construction, dating to the 1st C AD, was grandiose, with porticoes in three storeys, the lowest one Doric, the second and third Ionic, and with elaborate scenes in relief between the second and third storeys. Numerous fragments of statues, heads, statue bases, and various limbs of statues — have been found here. The whole area was heavily waterlogged, and excavations were below the water table.

The path now returns past the museum and back out into the parking area.

Poplars and columns: the unexcavated agora at Aphrodisias

AROUND PAMUKKALE

After returning to the main İzmir-Dinar road you continue east to Denizli, a modern town appearing to consist of an endless string of car repair workshops. Just after Denizli at the same point as the turn-off to Pamukkale is a second turn-off to Laodiceia, indicated with a yellow sign. The site is about 4 km up a track.

The City of Compromise

Limited excavation was done at Laodiceia by Laval University of Québec from 1961 to 1963, but there is not a great deal to see, especially in comparison with the ruins at Hierapolis. Most people make the detour not for the ruins themselves, but because at Laodiceia was one of the Seven Churches of the Apocalypse.

'I will spew you out of my mouth'

Founded in the 3rd C BC by Antiochus II of Syria, Laodiceia had a large Jewish population and converted early to Christianity. But it seems that the citizens were slackers, compromising their faith in Christ by participating in the imperial cults. St John got very cross with them, and seizing on the nearby tepid waters of Hierapolis (modern Pamukkale) for his metaphor, he sent this stinger to the church at Laodiceia: 'I know your works; you are neither cold nor hot. Would that you were cold or hot! So, because you are lukewarm, and neither cold or hot, I will spew you out of my mouth'.

The city was visited by a number of earthquakes, and the Seljuks took it in 1094 only to be ousted by the Byzantines, but repeated sackings of the city and massacres of the Christian population at the hands of the Turks led to its depopulation. In the 14th C the Arab traveller Ibn Batuta recorded that the Moslems, in control of the city already for a century, 'buy beautiful Greek slave girls and put them out to prostitution, and each girl has to pay a regular due to her master. The girls go into the bath houses along with the men'. A century later it was no more than a village. The main **monuments** remaining are a *stadium*, in a fair state of preservation, a large *gymnasium* dedicated to Hadrian, an *odeon*, a *nymphaeum* (the only building excavated) and two *theatres*, both poorly preserved.

Arriving at Pamukkale

The white mass visible on the hillside does not look like much from a distance. But travellers should make the effort to visit the fantastical rock formations and hot springs at **Pamukkale**, 'The Cotton Castle'. From the İzmir-Dinar highway, at the same point where you can turn off for

The calcified 'waterfalls' at Pamukkale

Laodiceia, there is a turning left just after Denizli leading after 14 km to Pamukkale. The total distance from Kuşadasí is 217 km and takes about three hours by car.

It is when you are close to, walking among the rock pools and standing in the hot running streams, that the wonder of Pamukkale hits you. The limestone deposits in the water are continuously building on to the structure, changing it slightly year by year. The formations have been 14,000 years in the making, if a constant rate of deposit is assumed.

Wallowing in the waters

Even though the spot is now highly commercialised, with stalls selling rubbishy souvenirs and big hotels having enclosed the best rock pools within their grounds, it still retains a special festive, holiday atmosphere. Turks themselves, always keen on natural wonders, are particularly fond of it, and it is a popular place for day outings from far around. If you are camping or not intending to spend the night, there is a public bathing area that is just like a normal swimming pool, and is therefore not very exciting. It is the Tusan Model which has the best pool, and is to be recommended for that reason only; it consists of a couple of deep joined pools, constantly overflowing and running off down the hill, situated right on the edge of the chalky rock formations. From this pool you can indulge in hanging your arms over the raised limestone wall edge staring at the other visitors passing by in their explorations of the rock pools, looking back

151

enviously at you in yours. You will be overcome by a strange sensation of not knowing who is in the zoo and who is the spectator. The water is bath temperature, and has a heavy quality about it which induces the desire to wallow about like a hippo. Swimming in it seems inappropriate and altogether too much effort. The properties of the water as recorded throughout history seem to be limited to making the colours fast when dying sheep's wool. Nowadays it is claimed that the waters are suitable for bathing as well as drinking, benefitting heart and circulatory complaints in particular, as well as digestive, rheumatic and kidney diseases. Their main property is to induce extreme sloth and lethargy, as lingering in the soporific waters has the effect of rendering you devoid of all will to do anything else.

Holy City

The ruins of **Hierapolis**, also situated on the plateau, take second place to the natural phenomemon of Pamukkale. It is pleasant, however, particularly at dusk, to stroll off to look at the ruins and the small **museum**, housed in part of the original Roman baths. Distances are big though, and a complete tour of the site would total around 5 km, so unless you have a lot of time and lots of energy, it may be advisable to have transport.

Mystical springs The hot springs were credited from the beginning with religious and mystical qualities, and so it is not surprising that the city which grew up on the site centred around the baths. Hierapolis means Holy City. Nothing remains of the original Hellenistic city founded by Eumenes II, King of Pergamum c180 BC, and the ruins we see today all date from the Roman period. There were major earthquakes in 17 AD and 60 AD and so most of the buildings we can see would have been rebuilt after then. The population was mainly made up of Graeco-Romans with a sizeable community of Jews, which helps to explain the early spread of Christianity here. The Apostle Philip lived here and was martyred in AD 80. Hierapolis remained a sacred city up to the time of the Crusades and the Seljuk invasions, and was finally abandoned in 1334 AD after another violent earthquake.

The ruins of the city lie either side of the original long main street running in a straight line for over 2 km. It is this street that you stroll along today. Near the beginning, the most prominent building, not surprisingly, is the **baths** on the right side of the parking area. The two large vaulted rooms now housing the **museum** were in Roman times reserved for the emperor or for special ceremonies. At the back part of the baths is an adjoining **palaestra** or open area for exercise and gymnastics. Behind the palaestra are the remains of a vast **basilica** with three naves, which is thought likely to have been the cathedral erected in the 6th C when Hierapolis became the seat of a bishop.

Beyond the Turizm Hotel and its sacred pool with its columns and pillars in the shallow water, you will see the ruins of a **nymphaeum** or monumental fountain, recently restored. Here also is the **Temple of Apollo**, the most famous shrine of Hierapolis, excavated by Italians, and recognisable by its wide flight of steps. Below the temple on the right you will see a small vaulted door which leads to a chamber under the temple. This is the infamous **Plutonium grotto**, much described in accounts of ancient historians such as Strabo, which exuded noxious fumes said to be deadly.

Eunuchs with bated breath

The discovery of this was the most exciting result of the Italian excavations, undertaken from 1957 onwards. The Temple of Apollo was almost completely buried, and when in clearing its south side the Plutonium was unearthed the Italians found it corresponded very closely with the ancient accounts. The excavations were in fact made very difficult and unpleasant by the foul fumes issuing from the grotto. The Greek historian Dio Cassius visited the temple in the 2nd C AD and reported that the fumes killed all living creatures who entered the Plutonium grotto except eunuchs (who were particularly good at holding their breath, says Strabo).

Backing into the hill to the right is the Roman **theatre**, its large well-preserved cavea of seats dominating the site. The stage building is partially standing, but the decorated stage wall had collapsed into the orchestra, and the Italians, in digging it out, discovered splendid reliefs dating from the time of the Romans Emperor Septimius Severus (c200 AD) illustrating the myths of Dionysus, Apollo and Artemis. The magnificent facade of the hyposcaenium (lowest relief on the stage wall) was found practically intact. The sculptures of the podium are mouldings and the originals are in the museum in the baths.

Beyond the theatre, a road leads out of the walls up to a vast building, also discovered by the Italians, built around the beginning of the 5th C, which houses the **tomb of the martyred Apostle Philip**. The plan of the building is complex, with an octagonal central chamber.

Retracing your setps to the baths at the entrance of the site, you can now walk right up the main street of Hierapolis, finally reaching, after about 2 km, the well-preserved northern **monumental gateway** with a triple arch and two round towers. (You can drive to this point if you prefer). Just inside the gate is a small **Byzantine chapel**, and between the gate and the city wall the street is lined with **private houses**, some of which have recently been excavated. Near the monumental gateway the excavators have unearthed a handsome tomb belonging to the merchant Flavius Zenxis, the inscription claiming that he made 72 voyages round Cape Malea to Italy. Beyond the gateway is an imposing brick building, a former bathing establishment, which was converted into a **church** at the beginning of the Byzantine period.

Curses from the tomb Beyond this again is the most striking feature of the site, the vast necropolis, one of the most extensive and best preserved in Asia Minor. Over 1200 tombs, many of them Hellenistic, have been counted lining the beginning of the ancient route to Ephesus. Strolling along this street littered with its jumble of tombs on a moonlit evening is an experience. Many of the epitaphs, ironically, invoke curses on all and sundry if their tombs are not looked after or if they are overshadowed or the approach to them is not kept clear. One is particularly all-embracing: 'may he who commits transgression, and he who incites thereto, have no joy of life or children, may he find no land to tread nor sea to sail, but childless and destitute, crippled by every form of affliction let him perish, and after death may he meet the wrath and vengeance of the gods below. And the same curses on those who fail to prosecute him'.

The Seljuks, as Moslems objecting to the representation of the human form, defaced most of the bas reliefs originally decorating the tombs when they overran the city in the 11thC.

Ak Han

Caravan routes east Just 1 km after the turn-off to Pamukkale as you continue eastwards towards Dinar, an impressive Seljuk caravanserai faced in pinkish marble stands just on the left of the road, called **Ak Han**. It was built in the 13thC on the route from Denizli to Konya, the Seljuk capital. It has an interior square courtyard and one can still walk up onto the roof. An inscription carved on the handsome door attributes the completion of the building to Karasungar in the reign of Sultan Keykavus on 19 July 1254. There are at least 50 of these handsome Seljuk caravanserais on the main trade routes of central Anatolia, all built in the 13thC when the Seljuk Turks were the dominant power in Anatolia.

PRACTICAL INFORMATION

PAMUKKALE

Many **hotels** with pools, some like rock pools, others more like normal swimming pools. There are also some **campsites** lower down on the plateau, but they have no pools. There is one public pool, like a swimming pool in feel, or else the open water cascades which are for wallowing or paddling rather than swimming.

Many of the hotels make half board compulsory, which is a shame as service then tends to be poor.

Tusan Motel (2-star), 47 rooms, best of the rock pools and with a good situation on the edge of the plateau. Half board compulsory, service atrocious. The pool compensates.

Belteş Hotel (2-star), also on the edge of the

plateau with the pool divided into individual sections for each room. Good views. Half board not compulsory.

Turizm Moteli (1-star), 16 rooms with simpler accommodation between the museum baths and the public pool. Its charm lies in its courtyard pool, once the Sacred Pool of the baths, full of fluted Roman columns and capitals.

Restaurants: most in Pamukkale are linked to hotels. There is a handful of excellent restaurants for fresh trout on the side of the Maeander river enroute to Aphrodisias near Dandalaz.

Denizli Pamukkale Festival early June.

FETHIYE TO ANTALYA (ANCIENT LYCIA)

ANCIENT LYCIA

Wild Lycia

Crossing from Caria to Lycia you are immediately aware of a change in atmosphere for there is in Lycia a sense of the wild and the primitive. Ancient Lycia, the bulge in Turkey's southern coastline that lies between Fethiye and Antalya, has throughout its history held itself aloof from its neighbours. An isolated and mountainous region, always sparsely populated, its inhabitants were fiercely independent to the extent that the men of Xanthos, Lycia's principal city, fought to the death on two occasions rather than submit to the yoke of foreign rule. They were not in fact warlike or violent by nature, but simply determined to defend their freedom.

A Remote Province

Until 1981, the tarmac road stopped at Fethiye and recommenced at Antalya, leaving Lycia impassable for all but Land Rovers. Even in this century only the hardiest of travellers have ventured here: Freya Stark travelled by boat, Land Rover and horses, and George Bean, redoubtable man that he was, did most of his travelling on foot. Long neglected by travel guides, Lycia has now, with the completion of the new road, emerged from is isolation and today's visitor is fortunate to be able to experience the magnificence of Lycia and its ancient cities without the hardships previously entailed.

Lycian Magic

Lycian landscapes, the savage beauty of their mountains, the haunting tombs of their remote cities contrasting with the peaceful loveliness of the Xanthos river valley, hold a magic unequalled elsewhere in Turkey. The bewitching quality of these landscapes is timeless, and travellers from Fellows in 1838 to George Bean in 1946 and Freya Stark in 1952 all confessed to having fallen under its spell.

The modern visitor need not be anxious about difficulties in finding accommodation in the area. There are as yet no luxury or star-rated hotels, and the official list of hotels supplied by the Turkish Tourist Office does not even admit to anything between Fethiye and Kemer/Antalya, but there are many small hotels and pensions, notably in Fethiye, Kalkan and Kaş, whose modest facilities are amply compensated for by their cheapness and their excellent and attentive service.

The ruins of some 40 ancient Lycian cities have now been identified. Many of these are extremely remote, perched up on rocky outcrops, invariably requiring difficult and arduous walks to reach them from the nearest road or village. The following accounts confine themselves to those sites that are worth visiting and accessible by private car. Sometimes a short walk is necessary, but never more than half an hour, and on these occasions the effort will always be amply rewarded, both by the satisfaction of personal achievement and by the spectacular setting of the ruins.

Earliest times

The origins of the Lycians are somewhat mysterious, with theories that they are the Lukka referred to in Hittite records or the Lukki mentioned in Egyptian documents as one of the 'Sea Peoples' who were so troublesome to the pharaohs of the 19th and 20th dynasties. We know that the Hittites made an incursion southwestwards from their capital at Hattusa (east of Ankara) into the hinterland of Antalya and Fethiye around 1370 BC, though no trace of Hittite civilisation has yet been found in Lycia. It is generally agreed, however, that the Lycians were not an indigenous people but came, as Herodotus said, from Minoan Crete in c1400 BC under the leadership of Sarpedon who was thrown out of Crete by his brother King Minos after losing a power struggle.

Who were the Lycians?

Cultural distinctness

The Lycian people were always distinct from the other races of Anatolia, very different to their neighbours the Carians or the Pamphylians, and they were always prepared to fight to retain this separateness. Lycia was the last region in Asia Minor to be incorporated into the Roman Empire. It had its own language, even now not totally understood, with an alphabet of 29 characters, 19 of them Greek, the remaining 10 unique to it. The Lycians presumably invented these characters to represent sounds used in Lycian but not in Greek. Some have seen in it a resemblance to the Hittite language.

Another peculiarity of Lycia in its early history, according to Herodotus, was its matrilineal society. Lineage was reckoned on the mother's side, not the father's, and a Lycian when asked who he was named his mother and his mother's mothers. The offspring of any female, citizen or slave, were legitimate, whereas those of a male citizen by a foreigner or concubine were illegitimate.

Part of the Greek World

The first mention of the Lycians in Greek literature is in Homer's *Iliad* where they fought as allies of the Trojans in the Trojan war. In the 6th C BC the whole of western Asia Minor was under Lydian rule with exception of Lycia and Cilicia. When the last Lydian king, Croesus, fell to the Persians in 546 BC, the Persians were not content to leave Lycia free. Such was the Lycians' determination not to be conquered that the men of Xanthos, the principal Lycian city, on realising they could not win, burnt their city with their women and children inside and then marched out to fight to the last man.

Mass suicide No. 1

Persian allies

Persian rule was in fact not arduous: the country merely had to pay a tax and was left to govern itself. In 480 BC when

Xerxes was collecting his huge fleet in preparation for the conquest of Greece the Lycians contributed 50 ships. After the Persian defeats at Salamis and Plataea the Athenians founded their maritime league, the Delian Confederacy, requiring tribute from each city. Tribute from Lycia seems to have been erratic and only Phaselis, not a proper Lycian city at the time, paid regularly.

When Sparta defeated Athens in the Peloponnesian War in 404 BC the Delian Confederacy was dissolved and Lycia came again loosely under Persian rule but was in practice virtually independent and continued issuing its own coinage. The Persian satrap Mausolus, taking advantage of the laxness and distance of Persian rule, established himself in Caria as an independent ruler, and tried to extend his rule to Lycia as well. The Lycians under their local dynast Pericles resisted Mausolus, and only Phaselis, still not a true Lycian city, concluded a treaty with him.

Alexander   The arrival of Alexander the Great on the scene in 333 BC wiped out the independent province of Mausolus' successors and after destroying Halicarnassus (Bodrum) he continued to Lycia. He made a treaty with Telmessus (Fethiye), then received the surrender of Xanthos, Pinara and 30 minor cities. Phaselis was characteristically grovelling, offering Alexander a golden crown.

Part of the Roman World

After the death of Alexander Lycia came under his general Ptolemy, who had established himself as king in Egypt. During the following century of Ptolemaic control the Lycian language died out and was replaced by Greek. In 197 BC Antiochus III of Syria took the country but was shortly afterwards defeated by the Romans at the battle of Magnesia (Manisa, north of İzmir). In recognition of the support Rhodes had given against the Syrians, Rome gave the whole of Caria and Lycia (with the exception of Telmessus) to Rhodes in 189 BC. In the years that followed there was fierce fighting in resistance to Rhodian rule and in 167 BC the Roman Senate decided to withdraw Rhodian rule and return Caria and Lycia to freedom.

Lycian millionaires   It was in the long period of freedom after 167 BC that the Lycian League flourished. The Lycians had always had an instinct for unity, a strange phenomenon for those times when most cities were separate city states constantly fighting one another. To defend their region the ancient Lycians formed themselves into a League of 23 cities. They had a system of proportional representation so that at their meetings, held in a different city each time, the major cities had three votes (Xanthos, Patara, Pinara, Tlos, Myra and Olympos), the middling ones two votes and the minor cities one vote. The taxes they levied from the League members were also calculated in these proportions, each city according to its importance. The country was prosperous and huge fortunes could be amassed by private individuals, usually merchants, some of whom like Jason of Cyaneae and Opromoas of Rhodiapolis were millionaires, making lavish gifts of money to their own cities, but also to other cities in Lycia. The population of the whole of Lycia was at this time estimated to be no more than 200,000, which gives an average of only 5000 inhabitants per city.

Mass Suicide No. 2

During the Roman civil wars in the 1st C BC the men of Xanthos, in resisting Brutus who had murdered Caesar in 44 BC, committed their second dramatic mass suicide. Brutus was raising money and forces for his impending confrontation with Mark Antony and Octavian, and when Lycia resisted him Brutus laid seige to Xanthos. After a lengthy and complex battle Brutus gained the upper hand and the Xanthians, rather than give in, slaughtered their women and children and burnt themselves alive. Brutus was said to have wept at the spectacle.

When Brutus was defeated by Antony and Octavian, Antony was given the East as his share of the Roman world and he allowed Lycia its freedom. But in AD 43 the Emperor Claudius joined Lycia with Pamphylia as a Roman Province, an unlikely union, as the character and people of the two regions were totally different. Lycian freedom was for a short time given back under the Emperor Nero (AD 54–68) until Vespasian (AD 69–79) reinstated the joint province of Lycia and Pamphylia. Then in the early 4th C the province was divided by Diocletian and a slow decline set in.

Greek ghost towns

The Arabs hastened the decline by their invasions in the 7th C. With the subsequent drop in population and cultivation following the break-up of the Byzantine Empire malaria spread through the valleys. Catastrophe was completed by the upheavals of the exchange of Greek and Turkish populations in 1923 which was Atatürk's drastic solution to the bitter struggle between the new Turkish republic and the Greeks who had lived for millenia in western Anatolia. The Lycians were essentially Greeks so they went to Greece, leaving a small population of Turkish farmers to move in behind them. The Greek ghost town of Kaya in the hills behind Fethiye is the most dramatic reminder of this exodus, but derelict Greek houses can also be seen at Kalkan, Kaş and Demre.

A Legacy of Tombs

Enduring monuments

The chief legacy of ancient Lycia is its tombs. Here as elsewhere the original buildings have been overlaid by Hellenistic and Roman ones but the Lycian tombs, often still in excellent condition, date in many cases to before Alexander. They have survived the ravages of battles, earthquakes and pillaging, and are remarkable today for their profusion, their size and their often dramatic settings cut into cliff faces, littered over hillsides or even submerged in the sea.

Types of tombs There are four types of tomb: pillar tombs, temple tombs, house tombs and sarcophagi. The pillar tombs are the oldest and rarest and are peculiar to Lycia. Used largely for important dynasts, they consist of a tall stone pillar set on a rock base, with the grave chamber on the top, its sides often decorated with reliefs. The most notable examples are at Xanthos. The temple tombs are large and cut into a vertical rock face with the facade of a temple, usually in the Ionic order, and the grave chamber inside. These are not specifically Lycian, but are also found in Caunus and in other parts of Anatolia. Fethiye has the best examples of these. The house tombs are smaller, also cut into rock faces with the grave chamber inside, and are very numerous especially in Myra. They were in imitation of the wooden houses of the ancient Lycians and much care has been taken to imitate in the rock carving the exact form of the houses with the beam ends projecting and the smooth layers representing the wattle and mud put in between the wooden struts. Freya Stark, travelling in the 1950s, said that some of these types of traditional houses could still be seen in the remoter mountain valleys of Lycia, but they have now unfortunately all but disappeared. House tombs are often decorated with reliefs on the walls, on the pediments, or on the adjoining walls, as at Myra.

The sarcophagi are the most prolific of the tombs, scattered everywhere in the most unlikely places. Sarchophagi are common all over the world of course, but the early Lycian type is distinctive. It is in three parts, a base, a grave chamber and a curved, crested 'Gothic' lid, and is remarkable for its enormous size. The lids and sides were often decorated with reliefs, while the base was often used as a secondary grave chamber for the main occupant's dependants or slaves. In the Roman period the sarcophagi became much smaller and simpler with a rounded lid.

Veneration of the dead and the importance of the funerary monument is something which was universal in the ancient world, from the Pyramids onwards. Much care was taken in the preservation of the tomb, and in an invariably unsuccessful attempt to protect it from damage and misuse the epitaphs threatened fines and curses for anyone violating them.

The Lycian Pantheon
As far as the religious beliefs of the Lycians are concerned, we know of their 12 gods, based on Greek gods, among whom
Artemis and Apollo the main figure was an Artemis equivalent. She is represented as a huntress accompanied by dogs. The Lycian national

shrine was the Letoon, near Xanthos, where Leto was said to have given birth to Artemis and Apollo, and annual festivals were held here every autumn. The cult of Apollo seems to have been minor by comparison with that of his sister, as indeed was the case in much of Asia Minor where goddess cults were dominant. The role of oracle, however, seems to be reserved for Apollo, notably at Patara.

Over 20 examples of the 12 Lycian gods have been found in various parts of Lycia, especially in the north. They are all carved on stone slabs less than a meter long, and usually show 14 figures, the 12 gods on the top row in two groups of six with a single figure in the middle, and in the bottom row a smaller figure between two groups of dog-like creatures. The smaller figure is thought to be the citizen making the dedication, but the central figure above is unknown when male. When female, the dedication tells us it is Artemis. From the abundance of dogs must all be hunting deities.

Haunting eyes Examples of these 12 gods are on display in the Antalya museum, and are in fact one of the most noticably different displays in their style. Contrasting strongly with the elaborately carved sarcophagi from Perge, they are primitive and formalised with no individual features for each god. All have staring vacant eyes and the effect is quite haunting. They are very much smaller than any Hittite carvings, but otherwise their powerful but primitive simplicity is strongly reminiscent of Hittite art, with their square shields and spears.

Lycia Today

In the Middle Ages Lycia was a region of exceptionally large concentrations of nomads whose settlement in this area was **Nomads and resettlement** greatly encouraged by the Seljuk sultans. Throughout the Ottoman period this country of Uch (the frontier) was a centre for the migration of the nomads and semi-nomads who moved for the winter from their summer *yaylas* (pastures) in the mountains down onto the coastal plains. Initially mosquitoes and malaria were still a problem, but obviously not in the winter. Later, however, malaria died out, and especially since 1948 when the Turkish authorities conducted a campaign to eradicate it people have gradually been returning to the coastal cities. In many cases the nomads' winter settlements became permanent villages, and thus the resettlement of the Lycian lowlands whose ancient towns like Xanthos had disappeared without leaving any direct successors has begun again. Nomads' black tents and many camels can still be seen here today, even in the Xanthos valley.

Bean Bey George Bean, the English classicist and archaeologist, in his visits to the region in the 1950s and 1960s was one of very few foreigners to know Lycia well. He would sit in the villages talking in perfect classical Turkish and go through the formalities of enquiring about the crops, the quality of the

Kas: the Lion Sarcophagus in the town

water, and the village school, while the villagers for their part enquired in the charmingly direct way that is quite normal in the East but so rare in the West his age, his salary and his marital status. Only after half an hour's talking would Bean get to the point of his visit and ask for details of the local ruins. On one occasion he remembers building up the courage to ask the question 'What do you do in winter?', to which he received the unashamed and disarmingly open reply 'We sit'.

The new generation

This is unlikely to be the answer today, and Professor Cook, co-author of various publications with Bean, laments the change, recalling the advent of 'the new generation of archaeologists who drive round the countryside in jeeps, pausing in the villages only for long enough to enquire whether there were any ancient remains'.

The growth in population and prosperity, with the export of timber, tomatoes and citrus fruits, has been marked in Lycia in the last 20 years, but the region nevertheless retains its distinctive character and charm.

FETHIYE (TELMESSUS), KAYA AND ÖLÜ DENIZ

From Caunus and Lake Köyceğiz eastwards the road involves another steep and spectacular climb passing numerous roadside springs enroute before an equally steep and winding descent to the plain of Fethiye. Set in a large sheltered bay backed with mountains, **Fethiye** was always the principal port of Lyica. The town grew considerably at the end of the 19th C, and until the exchange of Graeco-Turkish populations in 1923 it had a large Greek population. Its name at that time was Makri in modern Greek. The port has since the Middle Ages been concerned with the timber trade, the principal clients being Egypt and Syria, whose small boats can often be seen loading their cargoes.

Fethiye built upon its ancient site
Nothing is known of the origin of **Telmessus**, the ancient city on the site. Five inscriptions in the Lycian language have been found here, yet in the first historical references it was clearly not considered a Lycian city, always being mentioned separately. It possessed a sanctuary to Kakasbus, a Lycian horseman deity identified with Hercules. Alexander came here in 333 BC and made a peace treaty with the Telmessians before proceeding on to Xanthos. Only later under the

Rock-cut tombs in the cliff above Fethiye

Roman Empire did Fethiye become a normal member of the Lycian League. No excavations have been carried out, and the new town has now grown over the ancient settlement.

Looking Around Fethiye

Earthquake legacy

A lot of the hotels in Fethiye are not in the town itself but line the bay in the approach to the town. A road forks off to the right from the main road about 3 km before Fethiye and takes you along the seashore from where you can inspect the many hotels and pensions. The whole stretch of the bay is sandy with good swimming. The Fethiye seafront, from where caiques can be hired for the day to visit the excellent beaches nearby, is pretty enough with a stretch of municipal gardens: behind that however it becomes a bit of a dusty sprawl.

A fine sarcophagus

Yellow signs lead off to the various tombs, notably the **sarcophagus** in the middle of the road in front of the town hall left there since the severe earthquakes of 1956 and 1957. This sarcophagus is one of the finest in Lycia. One hundred years ago it was standing in the sea so the water level after rising since antiquity has evidently fallen again more recently. It is huge, mounted on a stone pediment, and represents a two-storeyed Lycian house with square imitation wooden beams and a curved 'Gothic' arch-shaped lid, perhaps to represent a tent with a pitched roof or a development of the temporary houses of sailors made from a boat turned upside down set on legs. Both sides of the lid and of the surmounting crest have reliefs of rows of warriors. The destruction these earthquakes wrought explains the newness of the town, only the buildings set up in the rocky slopes being spared. If you stroll among the houses on these rocky slopes you will come across various tombs, mainly sarcophagi, perched in unlikely places among cowsheds and chicken runs.

Temple tombs at sunset

The most spectacular sight in Fethiye is however without doubt the group of splendid **rock-cut temple tombs** in the cliff face above the town; they are all that now remains of the ancient city of Telmessus. A visit to these involves climbing lots of steps, but it is well worth the effort. As the first glimpse of what is to come in Lycia they make a particular impression, especially when seen at sunset when the cliff glows red. The steps and path take you straight to the **tomb of Amyntas**, the most magnificent of the group, and the best example of a Lycian temple tomb. Its Ionic portico, funerary chamber and monumental gate with bronze leaves reproduced in the rock down to the last detail give an impression of great size. Half way up the left pillar the name of Amyntas (an unknown citizen) is inscribed in letters of the 4th C BC. The door to the main grave chamber has four panels with imitation iron studs; the bottom right panel has been broken open by robbers. Inside the chamber are three benches where corpses would have been laid out.

The peaceful lagoon of Ölü Deniz

In the cliff face to the left are two further temple tombs, similar to that of Amyntas, which are fun to clamber up to if you fancy yourself as a mountain goat. Beyond and below these, cut into the cliff are numerous simpler pit graves, difficult to reach and unrewarding of the effort, for there is nothing to see inside.

A ruined **mediaeval castle** attributed to the Knights of St John stands just above the older houses on the rocky slopes, on the original acropolis hill of Telmessus. In the east face of the hill is a pair of rock tombs similar in type to that of Amyntas, but smaller and simpler. The town's theatre stood near the shore on the west of the town, just inland from the stone jetty of today, and Fellows in 1838 described it as 'in tolerable preservation'. As no trace of it now remains it has presumably been an earthquake casualty.

Once out of the sprawl of Fethiye you enter Lycia proper and the countryside changes. Coach tours do not yet penetrate here and the traffic is generally very light. The road climbs gradually through very lovely woods with a fast river rushing beside the road, and verdant grassy banks with pink Oleander bushes flowering most of the summer.

An Excursion from Fethiye
An interesting excursion from Fethiye is a trip via the Greek ghost town of Kaya to the lagoon of Ölü Deniz. Leaving

Fethiye on the main road to Kemer and Antalya (the only road out in fact apart from the one you came in on), before the sprawl of the town has finished there are two roads leading off right to Ölü Deniz, the first about one kilometre before the second. Although signposted they are easy to miss as they just look like dusty tracks leading to suburbs of the town. After a pothole-ridden 2 km the two tracks meet and become a good tarmac road leading all the way down to Ölü Deniz. The total drive from Fethiye is only about 20 minutes.

Modern Greek ruin   About 3 km from the start of the tarmac road a signposted forest track leads off to Kaya. The track is fine for a private car and runs through the woods to a cleft between two hills. **Kaya** (The Rock) is a modern ruin, a thriving Greek community until 1923 when the exchange of Greek and Turkish populations took place on Atatürk's instructions and all the 3500 Greeks abandoned the town. The empty town covers three hillsides and there are now just a handful of inhabited Turkish houses right at the bottom. The subsequent earthquakes have added to the air of destruction and decay. It is eerie to walk round this derelict place, the only signs of life the animals penned in the occasional disused courtyard. Crops are grown now in the fertile gardens of the larger Greek houses. There are two main **Greek basilicas** in Kaya, most of their murals defaced, though in the lower and more recent of the two (dated 1888 above the entrance), the faces of Christ and the Apostles on the altar piece are still intact.

Calm lagoon   Returning on the forest road to the fork and continuing another 3 km brings you to **Ölü Deniz** (the Dead Sea, so called because it is a lagoon with only the narrowest of inlets from the sea.) This is a particularly peaceful spot and good for few days' rest and relaxation if you have the time. A favourite haunt of yachters, the number of motels, pensions and restaurants in the bay is increasing but it is still very tranquil. The swimming here in the calm and salty water of the lagoon encircled with pine-forested mountains is one of the finest of the many fine swimming spots along the Turkish coast. Beyond the lagoon (reached by turning right on reaching the sea) 2 km of sandy beach called the Bay of Belceğiz stretches off towards a cliff along which a track leads to yet more beaches. Even in the height of the season these remote beaches offer privacy to the few who venture that far. The nearby island of **Gemili** has *ruins of Byzantine churches* which can be explored by boat.

ON THE WAY TO XANTHOS

A visit to the ruined Lycian city of **Tlos** can be made by the traveller touring between Fethiye and Xanthos, or in a five-hour return trip from Fethiye. One of the oldest and most powerful cities in Lycia, it is referred to in Hittite records of the 14th C BC as Dalawa or Tlawa, and possessed the maximum of three votes reserved for the six most prominent cities in the Lycian League. The charm of the city today lies in its particularly splendid setting high on a rocky promontory. Taking the fork left off to Kemer about half an hour's drive out of Fethiye, a yellow sign points off right 15 km to Tlos immediately after crossing the bridge in Kemer itself. After about 11 km of narrow but mainly tarmac road an unmarked gravel track turns off left at a right angle up towards the hills for a further 4 km. The fortress summit is visible from afar on the top of the rocky outcrop, with Lycian tombs cut in the rock face below, so you are reassured that you are on the right road. The track is rough and bumpy in parts but a private car driving slowly will have no real problems.

There is a tiny hamlet at the base of the city and the local children, who are particularly charming, will take you all around the ruins, pointing out Lycian inscriptions and carvings you would never have spotted yourself on a first visit.

First Essentials for the Visitor at Tlos

The first must is a climb up the acropolis and the rock cut steps to the summit of the Turkish **fortress**, site of the original Lycian fortress, from where the view is breathtaking; westwards down into the Xanthos valley or eastwards towards the mountains where the theatre can be seen covered in undergrowth about 500 metres away. It was in this castle in 1842 that Lieutenant Spratt, sent from Britain to collect the carvings from Xanthos that Charles Fellows had reported two years earlier, was entertained by the pirate Kanli Ali Ağa, the Ağa's brother, who dominated the region during the 19th C, using the castle as his winter palace. Tlos was one of the few Lycian cities to remain inhabited right through till the 19th C. The site was discovered by Fellows in 1838, and Spratt, his envoy, wrote of the setting that 'a grander site for a great city could scarcely have been selected in all Lycia', praise indeed in a region like Lycia with an abundance of magnificent settings. On the path to the summit traces of the **city wall** can be seen, along with picturesquely scattered Lycian **sarcophagi**.

Splendid setting

Tomb scrambling

The next compulsory item on the agenda is a scramble down a goat track to the cluster of rock-cut tombs in the cliff face which you saw on the approach to the site. Of these it is the **tomb of Bellerophon** which is the noteworthy one, with carvings and reliefs. If you find the path tricky the children will always offer a hand even though most appear to be less than five years old.

The tomb is of the temple type with three *doors* on the front wall. The two side doors stand on raised blocks, each of which has a relief of a horse on it. Above the left door is a leopard- or lion-like animal facing left and on the top part of the left wall of the porch is *Bellerophon, mounted on the winged horse Pegasus* with his right arm raised as if attacking the animal. This recalls the legend of Bellerophon slaying the mythical beast, the Chimaera (see Olympos).

Myth of Bellerophon and the Chimaera

According to ancient mythology, Bellerophon, son of King Glaucus of Corinth, was accused of murder and forced to flee to the court of Proetus, King of Argos. The king's wife fell in love with him but when he rejected her she accused him to her husband of rape. Proetus, unwilling to mete out too harsh a punishment, sent Bellerophon away to his father-in-law Iobates, King of Lycia. With him he sent a sealed letter which begged Iobates to kill Bellerophon for the attempted rape of his wife. Iobates, however, reluctant to kill the youth outright, instead set him the seemingly impossible task of killing the Chimaera, a monster that lived in the mountains of Lycia. With the aid of Pegasus, his winged horse, Bellerophon miraculously succeeded in slaying the monster whereupon Iobates set him a second seemingly impossible task of battling with the Solymi (the people of Termessus) and the Amazons, races infamous for their warlike character. Belatedly realising Bellerophon's innocence, Iobates relented and gave his daughter in marriage to Bellerophon, who then ruled on over Lycia. There is further evidence of the Bellerophon myth in Tlos, and the first rulers of Tlos claimed descent from Bellerophon.

Inside the tomb itself are four *benches* carved in the stone for the corpses. The one on the right has a pillow in stone for the dead man's head and a niche for offerings, clearly where the most important member of the family was laid, with his dependants around him.

Elsewhere Around Tlos

The flat open area, now cultivated, which lies between the road and the acropolis hill, was thought by George Bean, the classicist and archaeologist who visited in the 1960s, to have been the ancient agora. On the acropolis side of it a few rows of seats are visible in the hillside, the remnants of a **stadium**. Opposite, on the road side of this flat area, is a long building, heavily overgrown, which Bean presumes to be a market complex next to the agora. In fact, as he himself comments, it is very unusual indeed, not to say unheard of, to have the stadium next to the agora, and it is far more likely that the space was not the agora and that the long, overgrown building was a gymnasium leading into a palaestra, leading in turn into a baths complex, three buildings which were usually grouped together in ancient cities. No excavations have been carried out on the site, but they will certainly clarify the position when they are undertaken one day.

Millionaire's gifts

A short walk on up the road brings you to the large, handsome Roman **theatre**, charmingly overgrown, with many carved blocks of actors' masks among the collapsed stage building. The other building well worth looking at, on the return from the theatre, is the **baths**, which have a lovely setting with seven windows looking out over the Xanthos valley. Both the theatre and these baths were built from the money of a generous gift from the millionaire Opramoas of Rhodiapolis in AD 150. He was a wealthy Lycian merchant who made numerous lavish gifts for the construction of public buildings throughout Lycia.

At the end of your escorted tour, having forgotton to come armed with bags of sweeties, you might try to make amends by buying all the children a fizzy drink at the local coffee house cum post office. There is no restaurant in the village, so a picnic lunch is advisable if travelling over midday. The return trip could be done in a long afternoon from Fethiye if leaving straight after lunch around 2pm.

The Climb to Pinara

Jeeps only

Returning to the Kemer/Antalya junction, follow the Antalya sign: the road now follows the course of the Xanthos valley. This stretch is particularly beautiful with lovely forests and grassy meadows in between the trees. Camels are often seen with nomads tents nearby.

The first yellow sign you come to indicates Pinara off to the right. Do not be deceived by the easy looking flat track. It soon begins to climb up rocky hillsides and is not suitable for a private car. For those with jeeps the excursion is worthwhile but strenuous as the ruins cover a large area and a visit to the site involves a detour of at least 3½ hours off the main road.

The track brings you to the village of Minare, from where a climb of half an hour on foot takes you on to the ruins. As you climb you will see above you the great round outcrop of rock which has given the city its name, **Pinara**, meaning 'round' in Lycian. At the foot of this outcrop, which rises up about 600 metres, lies the ancient city, one of the largest in Lycia, spreading over long, overgrown terraces. The cliffs of the outcrop are perpendicular and the summit is only accessible by a difficult path on the south side. It was on the broad flat summit of this rocky crag that the earliest city of Pinara was founded. The ancient Lycians, like the modern Turks, made light of a climb of a 600 metres or so at the end of a day's work in the fields below. Only slight traces of this original city remain now, mainly cisterns and flat rock foundations for houses that would originally have been made of wood and mud brick.

It is the extraordinary east rock face of this crag, however, which is the most bizarre feature of this hill, honeycombed with hundreds of rectangular **pigeon-hole tombs**, completely inaccessible without mountaineering equipment. These tombs evidently date from the city's earliest days and must have been cut by hanging on rope ladders, an extraordinary feat.

Village guides

The extensive ruins of the classical city are situated around the lower acropolis hill at the foot of the rocky crag. The remains are scattered among rocks and vegetation and a thorough exploration requires considerable time and effort. The villagers from Minare, who will invariably insist on accompanying you up to the ruins, will always guide you to the major remains.

Among the ruins, the most impressive are the various groups of rock-cut tombs, three in all, largely of the house type. Many of them have curious reliefs of a type not found elsewhere in Lycia. The **southern necropolis** is particularly noteworthy. The **theatre** too, purely Greek in form, is well-preserved with parts of the stage building still standing.

In ancient Lycian times Pinara was an important city, possessing three votes in the Lycian League. A series of newly discovered pillar tombs points to the fact that the settlement existed as early as the 5th C BC. According to the 4th C BC Xanthian historian Menecrates, Pinara was founded as an extension of Xanthos which had become overpopulated. In 334 BC the city was, along with Xanthos and Patara, among Alexander's most important conquests in Lycia.

Sidyma: for the Enthusiast

Returning to the main road, the next yellow sign is off 12 km to the right to Sidyma. Representing a considerable detour of at least 5 hours from the main road, this is a trip only for the devoted Lycian enthusiast with plenty of time. The ruins are not that spectacular, and if short of time, it is better to leave Sidyma in favour of more accessible and more rewarding sites.

Long detour

Steep climb

The road is tolerable for the first 6 km, then the final 6 km is suitable only for a jeep. This is followed by a fairly steep 300 m climb of about an hour by a good stony path. The village of Dodurga is now in the middle of the ruins, and this has caused damage to the city centre. A public convenience has been set against the wall of the stoa, and a mosque has been constructed largely out the stones of ancient Sidyma.

All the ruins date from the Roman period. Near the top of the climb, a large number of open pigeon tombs cut in the cliff are to be seen, reminiscent of those at Pinara, though much less numerous and less impressive. Their age is uncertain. On reaching the top, the ruins of Sidyma are at once in view, consisting largely of groups of varying types of tombs, some sarcophagi, some large Roman tombs, and a remarkable temple tomb. One is a small pillar tomb, the only material evidence of Sidyma's existence in the Helenistic period. The Roman theatre is badly overgrown and poorly preserved.

Enchantment at the Letoon

Continuing on the main road, another sign forks off right 4 km to the Letoon, the national sanctuary of ancient Lycia. In order to see this site at dusk when it is at its most lovely **of** travellers may prefer to continue 2 km on to see Xanthos first, then make the short journey back. The approach road is tarmac all the way and the detour is a must for the site of the **Letoon** is one of the most delightful in all Lycia.

At the sanctuary to Leto and her two children, Artemis and Apollo, the main remains are their three temples and the nymphaeum: the existence of the theatre, the only other major building, reflects the Letoon's dual role of sanctuary and central meeting place fo the Lycian League. Leto, Artemis and Apollo were the national deities of Lycia; national festivals were held here, the ceremonies conducted by the chief priests of the League.

The greater part of the site is underwater which lends a particular charm especially at sunset when the frogs abounding in the pools croak for all they are worth. Other wildlife living in the sacred pools are miniature tortoises and crabs which are enormous fun to tease with nearby pieces of bullrush. It is an enchanting place just to sit and watch the sunset. The guardian, Osman, is charming and justly proud of his ruin, and will gladly show you the unusual Lycian mosaic in the centre of the Temple of Apollo of a lyre, the sun and a bow and arrow. This is the only Lycian mosaic still to be seen, as most date from the later Byzantine period. The visitor will notice that the blocks of stone and columns lying about the site are all numbered: this represents the labours of the French excavators who began work on the site in 1962. Before then only the theatre and a jumble of blocks marking the site of a temple were visible. Osman assures you that they will return to complete their work and erect the columns in a few years' time. Some very fragmented statues have already been painstakingly reconstructed and are on display in the Antalya museum.

The site is small and a tour of the ruins is not at all arduous — a rarity in Lycia where visits to most sites entail varying degrees of hardship. To appreciate and enjoy the atmosphere, however, at least an hour should be allowed, even by the cursory ruin-visitor.

Sanctuary Leto

Underwater wildlife

Touring the Letoon Site

The car can be parked immediately on the edge of the site; and the natural course is then to walk straight over on a track between the submerged ruins either side to the bases of the **three temples** lying side by side in a row, the furthest (easternmost) one nearly set in the foot of the rocky hill. The *closest (westernmost) temple* is in the Ionic order, surrounded by a single colonnade. During the excavations a small round sacrificial stone of marble was found with a dedication to Leto. The discovery of a large number of Lycian coins in the foundations enable the building to be dated to the middle of the 2nd C BC.

Shepherds into frogs

The cult of Leto was widespread on this part of Turkey's southern shore. According to legend she was loved by Zeus by whom she had her children Artemis and Apollo. She was therefore jealously persecuted by Hera, wife of Zeus, and forced to flee while still in her pregnancy. Many cities refused her entry, fearing the gods' wrath, and she finally arrived in Lycia, where she gave birth to her twins (the more famous variant of this story is that she gave birth to the twins on Delos). While washing them in a spring near the Letoon she was driven away by local shepherds whom she subsequently turned into frogs in punishment and whose descendants we hear today. Wolves then guided her to the river Xanthos where she bathed her children and drank. In gratitude she dedicated the river to Apollo and called the land (previously known as Termilis) Lycia for the wolves, *lykos* being the Greek for wolf.

Lycian mosaic

The *temple nearest the rocky face* on the east is in the Doric order and is nearly the same size. This is the temple with the *mosaic*, with the bow and arrow representing Artemis, and the lyre and sun for Apollo. The mosaic and temple date from the 1st and 2nd C BC.

The *smallest and oldest temple* lies in the middle and is unusual in that a large rock has been incorporated into its foundations. It has been identified by a Lycian dedication to Artemis (Ertemit) and dated to the 5th or 4th C BC.

Immediately south of the three temples are the low ruins of a **Byzantine church and cloister**; both were destroyed towards the middle of the 7th C in the Arab raids.

Underwater excavations

Just west of the church, romantically submerged in water and covered in bulrushes is the monumental **nymphaeum**. This is the area alive with frogs or metamorphosed shepherds. The original structure consisted of two buildings separated by a pool of water: the eastern part is Hellenistic while the western section is thought to be Roman since a dedication for a statue to Hadrian was discovered in a central niche. The excavations of this area were very tricky, being conducted largely underwater, and the whole area is now permanently flooded.

On the other side of the track the second submerged area is the **northern stoa** or portico for public promenade and the exedra (semi-circular recess or alcove with a bench). The scale of this structure is at first surprising, though it is in keeping with the role of the Letoon as the sanctuary and meeting place of Lycia.

Beyond the flooded areas of the site, 50 metres to the north, is the **theatre**, not really visible from the site as it is tucked round the side and partly built into the hillside. In Hellenistic style, the cavea of seats is remarkably well-preserved but the stage building has gone. A vaulted passage leads into the cavea from either side and the frieze above the far tunnel has a row of 16 face masks representing, among others, Dionysus, a satyr, a girl and an old woman. Just beyond the tunnel, slightly up the hillside beside the theatre, is a large **tomb**, sunk to mid-height in the ground.

Garden gnome

The Letoon is also notable for the discovery by the French excavators near the rocky ledge by the three temples of a remarkable inscription in Lycian, Greek and Aramaic (a language probably spoken by Christ). This trilingual inscription was of great importance in deciphering the Lycian language. George Bean also mentions a curious stone figure he found here in 1946 lying on top of a thorn hedge. It seemed to be an unfinished statue about one metre tall and was taken away and set up in a local garden in Fethiye, like a gnome, but since the earthquake of 1957 no trace of it has been found.

XANTHOS

Continuing scarcely 2 km on the main road from the Letoon turn-off, a bridge leads across the Xanthos river (today's Eşen Çay or Koca Çay) to the unsavoury-looking town of Kíník from the middle of which a yellow sign points up left to Xanthos. The dirt track leads about one kilometre up the hill and there is a cleared parking area on the right past the theatre. On hot days the guardian is to be found here under a tree, but he will only hail you in an attempt to sell you dubious booklets on Lycia. Cool drinks may also be on offer out of a cold box but there is no restaurant.

Magnificent site

Xanthos is a magnificent site as is fitting for what was always the greatest city of Lycia. It is, however, very extensive and a thorough visit takes a good three hours and requires a fair bit of walking and scrambling, but those who make the effort will not be disappointed.

Excavations and History

The site was made familiar to the western world by Sir Charles Fellows, who was greatly impressed by his first visit in 1838 and who visited it again two years later. The subsequent publication of his journals aroused so much interest that in 1842, Lieutenant Spratt was sent off in HMS Beacon to bring back to the British Museum the Lycian sculptures and carvings described. The operation continued for two months on site, with sailors stripping and carrying off the monuments. Spratt built a camp beneath the ruins and Freya Stark speculated that here, perhaps, cricket was played for the first time in Lycia. When eventually the 70-odd huge cases of sculptures and inscriptions arrived in England, they caused almost as much of a stir as the Elgin Marbles had done 40 years before. A visit to the Xanthian room at the British Museum is recommended whether before or after a visit to the site; it certainly helps the visitor to appreciate the magnificence of the Lycian carvings.

Xanthos has always been the greatest city of Lycia; Herodotus writes almost as if Lycian and Xanthian were the same thing. Certainly the inhabitants of Xanthos personify the qualities of Lycia with their fierce love of freedom which they were prepared to defend at all costs. The splendid setting of the city overlooking the Xanthos valley bears testimony to its elevated status with three votes in the Lycian league.

Apart from the digging of Spratt's sailors, no serious excavations were carried out here till 1950 when the French began a thorough campaign. As a result of these excavations the ruins of Xanthos, in spite of their despoilation for the benefit of the British Museum, are still the most impressive in Lycia.

The pillar tombs at the Xanthos theatre

Xanthos' first mention in history is in connection with the Trojan War (thought to have occurred c1200 BC) when the Lycians fought on the side of the Trojans. Their leaders were Sarpedon and Glaucus, grandson of Bellerophon; Homer's *Iliad* describes them as coming from the distant swirling waters of the Xanthos.

Hopeless valour Archaeological finds on the acropolis hill date back to the 8th C BC but the first real mention is when the Persian general Harpagus arrived in Lycia after his conquest of Asia Minor. Xanthos, always fiercely independent, resisted him even though the Persian armies were far superior and so Harpagus laid siege to the city. Realising they could not win, yet determined not to surrender, the Xanthians collected their wives, children, slaves and property on the acropolis and set fire to it all, then marched out and fought to the death.

Following this defeat, Xanthos, like the other Lycian cities, was incorporated into the first Persian satrapy, but the Persians left no garrison behind so what remained of the city's population was able gradually to recover and govern itself again. As all the main buildings had been destroyed in the fire much re-building was done. It is to this time that the first pillar tombs of Xanthos date. Their shape, considered barbaric by the Greeks, possibly has Persian influence.

After Alexander the Great's conquest of Lycia in 333 BC

Xanthos shared the succession of rulers from Syria, Egypt and Rhodes with the rest of the region but was able to expand and erect many new buildings.

Brutus weeps Tragedy once again befell the city however when in 42 BC during the Roman civil wars, Brutus lay siege to Xanthos to force it to pay his extortionate taxes which he was raising to buy soldiers and weapons for his showdown with Mark Antony and Octavian. The Xanthians, again realising they could not win, set fire to everything, threw their women and children on to the fire, and killed one another. Hearing their lamentations, Brutus was suddenly overcome with pity — some accounts say he wept — and offered his soldiers a reward for each Xanthian who was found alive: because of this 150 Xanthians survived.

Under Hadrian Xanthos regained its position as the first city in Lycia and entered another period of prosperity. The buildings of this period are the arch of Vespasian, the new theatre and new agora. In Byzantine times the city walls were renovated and a monastery was built on the top of the hill. The city had its own bishop but he ranked low under the Metropolitan of Myra.

Reading the historical accounts of the changing population in Lycia, it strikes you forcibly how recently these lowland areas have been resettled. In Fellow's description of his arrival at Xanthos he found that one hut and two barns constituted the city. Freya Stark writing in 1956 said there were just a few small cottages. Since that time the towns of the lowland like Kínik and Kaş have mushroomed, with nomadic settlers increasingly staying in the lowlands rather than returning to the highlands for the summer, mainly because of the wiping out of malaria since the government campaign of 1948.

Searching Among the Ruins of Xanthos

For a tour of the site the obvious and best place to start is the theatre, made distinctive by the extraordinary pair of Lycian **pillar tombs** rising 8 metres at its side. Much has been written about these tombs, particularly the one which has come to be called the *Harpies Tomb*, with its elaborate reliefs on all four sides of the grave chamber at the top. The originals were taken off to the British Museum, with the result that the pillars looked severely mutilated till the Turkish authorities installed the plaster casts we see *in situ* today. On each side is a seated figure receiving a gift, variously seen as a bird, a cock, an egg, a pomegranate or a helmet. The creatures who have given the tomb its name are on the north and south sides on either side of the seated figure. They are half bird, half woman, with wings and tails, yet with female heads. In their arms they are carrying children. Views about what these reliefs represent differ widely: Fellows saw in them the

Harpies Tomb

Harpies of Greek mythology, carrying off the orphaned daughters of Pandareos as described by Homer. Hera, Athena, Artemis and Aphrodite assumed care of the children, but when they were left unguarded for a time the evil Harpies, winged monsters with the face of a woman and the body of a vulture, snatched the children off and gave them as servants to the Furies. Pandareos, a Lycian hero, in fact had only two daughters, whereas four are shown in the reliefs which is why later scholars have said these winged figures have nothing to do with the harpy myth but are the Sirens, the other bird-women of mythology, carrying off the souls of the dead to the Isles of the Blessed. The seated figures could be gods of the dead or members of the dead person's family receiving funeral gifts. The tomb has been dated to 470 BC.

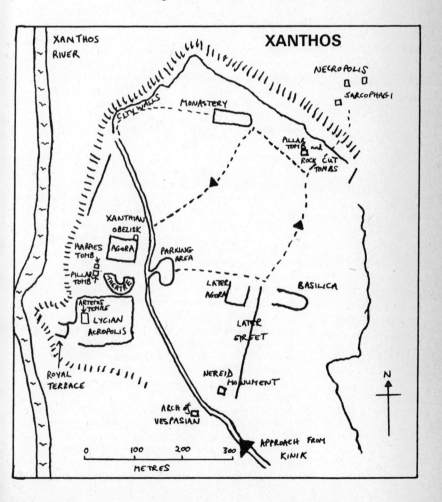

The *second pillar tomb* is a sarcophagus standing on a pillar, inside which was a second grave chamber. The pillar section is a similar age to the Harpies tomb, while the sarchophagus is of later date (3rd or 4thC BC). This curious arrangement is unique in Lycia.

The **theatre**, immediately adjacent, is Roman, standing on the site of an earlier Hellenistic one. It dates from the 2nd C AD and an inscription records that it was again Opromoas of Rhodiapolis, the Lycian millionaire, who donated the money for its construction. Although well-preserved, many of the upper seats were removed in Byzantine times and incorporated into the city wall. The orchestra is full of blocks from the once two-storey high stage building.

Lycian acropolis

Climbing up behind the theatre through a breach in the back wall you reach the original Lycian acropolis. This was the original city centre, twice burned to the ground in Xanthos' chequered history. In the far southeastern corner (the furthest corner away from the river valley), are the remains of a square building with several rooms, thought to have been the **palace** of the early Xanthian kings. Further west (towards the river), on the highest point beyond a large cistern hollowed out of the rock, are the scanty remains of the **temple** to the Lycian equivalent of Artemis, its foundations cut into the rock.

Royal terrace

Heading off towards the river valley beyond the temple, you reach a concrete platform on the edge of the acropolis, overlooking the valley. The view over the wide Xanthos river is superb and this spot gives the best impression of the magnificent setting of the city. It is said by the locals to be the site of the royal terrace, from where the Xanthian kings strolled in the evenings looking down onto the plain below.

Returning to the foot of the theatre you notice in a cleared area which is the Roman **agora** a large *obelisk-like pillar* covered in inscriptions. This monument, in fact another type of pillar tomb with a grave chamber inside, and with over 250 lines of writing, has the longest Lycian inscription known. The text seems to relate the heroic deeds of the dead person.

Crossing the road and walking on past the parking area, a path leads off to the residential sections of the Hellenistic and Roman city. The main excavated area shows a large **Byzantine basilica** with extensive abstract *mosaics*. Its foundations show many blocks reused from the original Lycian city.

A rest among tombs

Another path, not easy to find, leads up the hill for several hundred metres, passing some free-standing **sarcophagus tombs** in the woods on the way, arriving then at an extraordinary cluster of rock-cut **house tombs** dominated by one tall **pillar tomb**. This spot is very attractive and quite shady, making a good place for a welcome rest. The path leads on past these tombs and beyond the city wall to the **necropolis** where a dense scattering of sarcophagus tombs are to be found on the hillside, some with attractive decorated reliefs. The scene of two lions killing a bull is particularly noteworthy. The path takes you past all the most interesting tombs.

For the traveller who is still not worn out, a climb can now be made up on to the hilltop to see the ruins of a **Byzantine monastery** built among the remnants of a large **Roman temple**. You can then make the descent over on the river valley side of the hill following the line of the city wall: this route is spectacular but something of a scramble and only suitable for those with sound ankles and scratch-proof legs. Alternatively you can make a gentler and more direct descent to the parking area.

Maybe you should be in London   At the lower end of the city, as the road descends towards the village, you pass the site of the famous **Nereid Monument** on the right. Originally the most beautiful tomb in Xanthos, with exquisite marble carvings, all its original parts are now in the British Museum, leaving only the foundations *in situ*. Like the Harpies Tomb it dated to the 5th C BC.

Driving back down the dirt track to Kínik you also pass the remains of the **south gate** of the Hellenistic city, behind which the Roman **triumphal arch**, still standing, is dedicated to the Emperor Vespasian.

ALONG THE COAST TO KAŞ

The sign 6 km off to **Patara** is reached after only a 10-minute drive from Xanthos, and is the last and southernmost of the sites in the Xanthos valley. Originally situated in a natural harbour, now sanded up, it was the port for Xanthos. The sign points off the main road to the right just before a small bridge over a stream, a tributary of the Xanthos but once a much larger river which flowed into the sea at Patara: it is this stream which the road follows initially. Though dirt track, the road is all right for a car.

Sandy beach   A visit to Patara is best done as a relaxing day's outing from Kalkan, only half an hour's drive further on, rather than as the finale to a day spent visiting the other sites in the Xanthos valley. Lunch can then be taken at the simple but pretty restaurant set back from the sea at Patara. The beach, not visible from much of the site, nor for that matter from the restaurant, is a long and broad expanse of sand, and swimmers must expect a few minutes' walk across the sand to reach the sea.

History of Patara

In Roman times Patara was the principal port for the whole of Lycia and most of the monuments surviving today date

Birthplace of Santa Claus   from that period. Patara was the birthplace of St. Nicholas Bishop of Myra (whose legend evolved into that of the modern Santa Claus), and among the famous people who stopped here in Patara's days as a great port were Hannibal, St Paul and the Emperor Hadrian who built the colossal granary which is still one of Patara's most impressive monuments.

Oracle to rival Delphi   Patara also owes its fame to the temple and oracle of Apollo here, which was compared to that at Delphi for riches and reliability. It was this oracle which told Telephus, a hero of the Trojan War wounded by Achilles, that his wound would only be healed by its inflictor. He was later indeed healed by the rust from Achilles' sword. According to Herodotus the oracle was active only when Apollo resided in his temple during the six winter months as he spent the summer months at Delos. There seems to have been a gap in the oracle's performance, as we have in an inscription the statement that Opromoas, the Lycian millionaire, gave 200,000 denarii to the people of Patara 'for Apollo, the god of their ancestors, whose oracle, after a long silence, has once more begun its prohesy'. The only find relating to the god in the ruins so far has been a large head of Apollo, but there is no trace unfortunately of the temple or oracle in the ruins extant today. The site has never benefited from excavations and so the temple may at some future point be discovered.

Founded in the 5th or 6th C BC, Patara was one of the oldest and most important cities in Lycia. It was saved from destruction by surrendering to Alexander, but after his death the city entered a period of confusion, falling later into the hands of the Egyptian Ptolemy II. For a time it bore the name Arsinoë after Ptolemy's sister-wife, but this name did not survive beyond Patara's capture by Antiochus III of Syria in

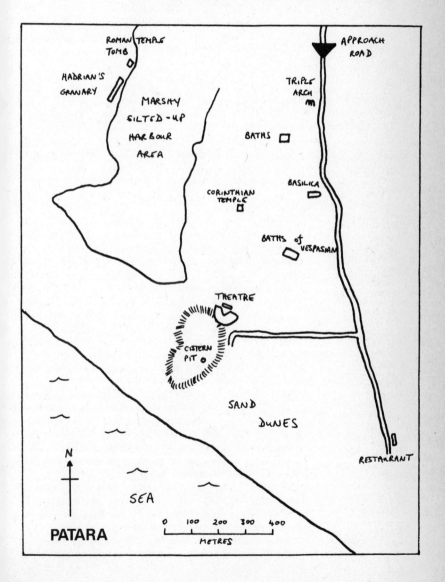

196 BC. In the Lycian League it had along with Xanthos, Pinara, Tlos, Myra and Olympos the maximum three votes. The League often held its meetings at Patara, presumably because it was the most centrally placed of the six major cities.

Under Roman rule Patara became the seat of the governor of the Roman province of the area, and the port from which the Roman fleet maintained its contact with the eastern provinces. In the 4th and 5th C AD Patara became an important Christian city. St Paul set out for Rome by ship from Patara. The decline of the city took place around the 14th and 15th C, when the harbour began to silt up.

A Tour of Patara

The charm of Patara today lies in the fact that most of the site is sanded up. The original city and harbour were at the head of a river, the successor of which is the stream the track follows from the main road. The river has gradually silted up over the centuries, blocking the harbour entrance and forming the vast sandy beach you see today. The theatre, now half-filled with sand, is strangely attractive. The distances involved in seeing the ruins are, however, considerable and are made trickier by having to walk through sand with occasional marshy areas.

Engulfed by sand

The approach to the site takes you past the triple-arched **triumphal gate** built in AD 100 by the Roman governor of the province of Lycia and Pamphylia as the entrance to the Roman city. Nearby are several tombs of Roman and Lycian sarcophagus type, as this is the edge of the necropolis, situated as always just outside the city walls.

Continuing on towards the sea, the track goes straight on to the restaurant and beach, or turns off right towards the theatre, passing the ruins of a baths complex and a basilica to the right. It is best to leave the car at the end of the track to the theatre, and to climb to the top of the **theatre** first, from where you can survey the extent of the ruins and assess the effort required to reach each part. From here it is worthwhile to climb on up the hill at the back of the theatre to see the amazing **pit** in the hilltop with a square pillar in the middle and steep stairs cut in the rock leading down to the bottom. This has been variously called the oracle of Apollo, a cistern, a lighthouse, or a sacrificial pit by confused writers in the past. From its location, a cistern seems the most credible as the water could then be distributed by aqueduct to the city below. There are also good views from this hilltop of the old harbour, and one can visualise the layout of the original port well. There are views also towards the sea over the extensive stretch of beach, several kilometres long.

Corinthian temple

From the theatre you can walk inland through the sand towards a temple building in the Corinthian order about 500 metres away in the undergrowth. Paths are difficult to find and it is often a case of making a direct scramble through the undergrowth towards the buildings you want to reach and then finding, once there, that there is a path leading back out which you could have followed in much greater comfort in the first place had you been able to find it. The **temple**, though small, is remarkably well-preserved with the front door lintel beautifully decorated. It dates from the 2nd C AD. The undergrowth is taking its toll however and cracks are starting to appear which suggest the lintel may fall before long. As the only temple on the site found to date, the local people are keen to call it the Temple of Apollo, though it is in fact far too small for a building of such importance.

Following the path back out, it passes the **Baths of Vespasian** which are quite well-preserved with five chambers joined by doors.

Colossal Roman grain store

For the really indefatiguable, undeterred by walks through sand and marshes, a trek can be made right across the silted harbour to the **Granary of Hadrian**, a colossal building, still intact apart from its roof, now covered in vegetation and undergrowth. It can be reached with somewhat less effort by taking the fork left as you leave the site, about 700 metres after the monumental triple arch. This track leads to the far bank of the original river, passing numerous *tombs*, one of which, just north of the granary, is built in temple form approached by steps from the harbour side, and must originally have been rather splendid.

The granary is spectacular for its sheer size, over 65 metres long and 25 metres wide, like the other Roman granary on the river bank at Andriake, the port for Myra. This latter is easier to visit, so travellers may prefer to pass over the granary at Patara in favour of that at Andriake.

Pausing at Kalkan

The only place offering accommodation between Fethiye and Kaş, **Kalkan** is a very welcome port of call, especially after the scramble of Xanthos. It is a fishing village with a growing number of small family-run pensions and is also a frequent stop for flotillas and yachts which can sometimes stretch the resources of the local restaurants to capacity in the evenings. Though the village is expanding fast to cope with the increasing number of visitors, it is still a pretty spot and many of the pensions have idyllic roof terraces where generous quantities of breakfast are served.

Pretty fishing village

The steep slopes on which the village is built run down to the rocky harbour; the only beach is that which the owner of Pasha's Inn built himself, which he takes guests to and then charges them for the privilege. On the harbour front are a few very fine but crumbling Greek houses, deserted since the Greeks were forced to abandon their ancient ties here with the transfer of popultions in 1923.

Development project Kalkan, mainly because of its lack of beaches, is a stopping place rather than a destination in its own right, and so most visitors will only stay one or two nights before moving on to Kaş. The drive from Kalkan to Kaş is an easy half hour. The road clings to the coast all the way and the route is therefore level but very winding. Just before Kaş a curious chateau-style building can be seen, the only building on the snake-like peninsula. It was built by the group of journalists organising the tourism development project for the Kaş headland, and this house and the road round the headland were the first things to be built. The development project includes plans for ten nightclubs, but fortunately progress is slow and the plans date from some years back. Fodor's guidebook, evidently carried away by the ambitious plans, has invented a fictitious Club Mediterranée village here.

Arrival at Kaş

The town of Kaş is the main resort of Lycia with many small hotels and restaurants. It is easily the most sophisticated place
Chic resort on the coast between Fethiye and Antalya, its harbour-front lined with cafés and restaurants which feel distinctly chic after the homeliness of Kalkan. The bay in which it is situated is lovely and enclosed with high mountains behind; immediately opposite is Kastellorizo (Megiste), the most easterly of the Greek islands, a 40-minute boat trip away. Once the finest harbour between Piraens and Beirut, Kastellorizo is all but abandoned now. The islanders had land around Kaş but they were forced out in 1923. Their large church has now been converted to a mosque with a minaret and whitewashed walls.

The harbour at Kaş is bustling and is the frequent destination of Club Mediterranée private charters, yachts and flotillas from Bodrum or Marmaris. There is a good daily boat trip to the sites of Aperlae, Simena and Kekova (see below). Tickets can be bought at a very reasonable price on the harbour front. If preferred, a private boat can be hired with its skipper at much higher cost, though unless your Turkish is good you will see no more than aboard the public boat.

The main bay does not have a swimming beach, but there are small rocky swimming areas to both sides of the bay where the town has now spread, and many of the hotels or camping areas have their own private bathing areas.
Ancient port The modern town of Kaş, called Andifli till the last century, stands on the site of **Antiphellus**, an ancient Lycian city of the 4th C BC. It was the port for the city of Phellus whose location is still not known for certain. It grew in importance in Hellenistic times and under the Roman Empire was one of the major cities of the region. It would have traded largely in

timber from the Lycian forests, and Pliny particularly cites Antiphellus for the soft quality of its sponges.

The extant ruins today are limited to the small but extremely well-preserved theatre, and some notable Lycian rock tombs and sarcophagi. On entering the town, a fork leads off right past the converted Greek church to the **theatre**, just right of the road. Although small, with only 26 rows of seats, it has a lovely setting looking out to sea at the island of Kastellorizo. Local inhabitants have used it as a venue for wrestling matches, a common sport in southern Turkey. Walking over the hill above the theatre for a few minutes takes you to an extraordinary rock tomb on the hillside, unique in style, and known as the **Doric tomb**. Cut from a huge rock, it stands about 5 metres high and has a passage all around and a single chamber inside. On the bench inside, a *frieze* of about 20 small dancing figures is carved. The tomb is thought to date from the 4th C BC.

Lion sarcophagus

Returning to the town, the scant foundations of a **temple** can be seen not far from the harbour but it is not known to whom it was dedicated. There are several Lycian **sarcophagi** in the town, notably the one on the harbour front and the one near the town centre which is remarkable for its size and its excellent state of preservation. It is raised up on a high base and the sarcophagus on top has the 'Gothic-style' curved lid with the stone carved to resemble the beams of old-style Lycian houses. On each side of the lid are two lion's heads jutting out, resting on their paws. The inscription on the base is in a peculiar poetical form of Lycian and has not yet been deciphered.

In 1842 Spratt counted over a 100 sarcophagi at Antiphellus but most of these have been destroyed over the years by the local inhabitants as the flat sides make useful building stones. The curved lids however are less easily incorporated into buildings and can often be seen lying alone as a result.

In the rocky cliff wall northwest of the town centre are a number of Lycian **rock tombs**, simple in style and not very spectacular in comparison with those at Fethiye, Tlos or Pinara.

Boat Trip to Kekova (Aperlae, Simena and Teimiussa)

Although with a jeep it is possible to reach these sites by land, the journey is uncomfortable and not in itself interesting, so a boat excursion from the harbour at Kaş is a far more enjoyable and relaxing way to see them. The boat leaves at 9am and generally returns around 6pm. The trip is touted as a chance to see the underwater ruins of Lycian cities and tombs, submerged as a result of earthquakes. In fact the submarine sites are not very spectacular and the traveller should not expect to see any Atlantis-like city: just enjoy the trip as a day out on a boat.

Leaving the harbour and passing Kastellorizo, you first reach the ruins of **Aperlae**, a Lycian town dating from the 5th and 4th C BC. It lies on the coast at the head of a long thin bay after about 1½ hours sailing. A member of the Lycian League, Aperlae headed the group of small cities that included Simena, Apollonia and Isinda, and together they had one vote. Now the spot is uninhabited apart from one house on the shore, and the nearest village is an hour's walk inland.

The **walls** are the best preserved of the remains of Aperlae, and the *main gate to the most ancient town* with a 3-metre block lintel is visible about 75 metres above the shoreline. The newer town is below this, closer to the shore, and the *new city gate* is now nearly in the water. A whole section of the town is submerged under the water and was discovered by the American Robert Carter and his wife on his private yacht in the 1960s. It can be clearly seen when pointed out from the boat and whole **streets** and the outline of **buildings** can be made out in the turquoise shallower parts of the water. An indented **quayside** can be seen right on the edge of the submerged town. Mooring close by is difficult for larger boats, and the coast is rather too rocky and tarry to make swimming attractive. The daily boat trip does not in fact even stop here to let you disembark, which is not really a loss as the area of ruins enclosed by the walls is very rocky and overgrown and is difficult to explore. Outside the walls, especially by the east side, are scattered numerous **sarcophagi**. From the absence of a theatre or a temple on the site, it is clear that Aperlae was never a particularly important place.

A further 3/4 hours on the boat brings you to a beautiful cove on **Kekova island** itself, with a Byzantine apse standing just on the shore. This is the site of the ruined village of **Tersane**, and is an excellent spot for swimming. A handful of yachts is usually moored here. To one side of the cove **submerged ruined houses** are visible, but swimming among them requires caution as they have their fair share of sea urchins. Swimming carefully over them, you can then stand in the water to waist height on a flat paved floor of a house. After the swim, the boat skirts the coast of Kekova island where half-submerged ruins are visible for a few hundred metres along the edge, part on land, part underwater, evidence of the upheaval wrought by earthquakes centuries ago. Foundations of houses, rock-cut staircases and the occasional lintelled doorway can be seen. A notice forbids skindiving.

The boat crosses the strait back to the mainland opposite, where the site of Simena stands above the current village of **Kale** (castle), named for the Byzantine fortress on the summit

A cove on Kekova island

of the hill. Lunch can be taken here at one of the simple restaurants in the small harbour, and there is now even a small pension offering basic accommodation.

The site of **Simena** has in the past often been mistaken for that of Aperlae: while not particularly surprising in the case of Fodor's and Nagel's guidebooks, as their authors have clearly never visited the region, it is more surprising in the case of the travel writers Freya Stark and John Freely who have.

Snorkelling for ruins

What appears to be a rocky island just off the harbour is what the locals claim are the remains of baths, with visible steps cut into the rock. Other Turkish sources however say these islets were used as stone quarries for local sarcophagi, hence their flat surfaces. Snorkelling with masks and flippers is recommended in this harbour; a good look can be taken at the **foundations of buildings** and at the occasional Lycian **sarcophagus** lying on the harbour bottom. Watch out for the urchins though.

After lunch a climb up through the mediaeval village of Kale to the top of the **Byzantine fortress** is worthwhile for the views and to see the charming tiny Lycian rock-cut **theatre** near the top. Its size, with seven rows of seats and a capacity of 300, is testimony to Simena's small population. Looking over to the west of the summit, many Lycian **sarcophagi** can be seen scattered around the hillside, some with carving. There are also two **tombs** of the house type.

The boat returns taking a brief look from the sea at the site of **Teimiussa**, immediately next to the small village of Üçağíz, just a few minutes east of Kale. Many scattered sarcophagi can be seen on the shore, while the oldest funerary monument is a **house-type tomb** with a relief of a nude boy.

The return boat journey to Kaş takes about 2½ hours, arriving around 6pm.

BETWEEN KAŞ AND FINIKE

Rough road

The drive from Kaş eastwards to Demre takes about an hour and involves a steep climb up a winding road recently widened and improved. At the top of the climb yellow signs point off right to Kekova and Teimiussa (Üçağíz) (19 km) and Apollonia (17 km). This road is long and uncomfortable, and is suitable only for a jeep. Kekova is recommended rather by boat from Kaş, as described earlier. **Apollonia**, lying 300 metres inland from Üçağíz and a 20-minute walk above the village of Siçak (Kinlínçlí), has a poorly preserved theatre, a large vaulted reservoir and many cisterns. Sarcophagi are abundant as usual, but there are also six Lycian pillar tombs, a Lycian rock tomb and a handsome Roman tomb.

Cyaneae

The main road climbs up to the pretty plateau of Yavu at the top of the pass. For the energetic, a 2-km climb can be made up to the site of **Cyaneae**, signposted up left from the main road through Yavu village.

Steep climb

Leaving the car in the village at the foot of the hill, the climb up to the site takes about 45 minutes. The effort is worthwhile because of the tombs and their setting, but be prepared for the total excursion to take at least three hours. The present path up follows in part the ancient route to the city; at the top the city is surrounded by a **wall** on three sides with the prescipitous cliff face as sufficient defence on the fourth (south) side. The site is heavily overgrown and rocky, making it difficult to explore, but hidden in the undergrowth within the walls are a **library**, a **baths** and a **reservoir**, all dating from the Roman period. An avenue leads from here to the **theatre**, quite well-preserved.

Abundant tombs

The most impressive remains at Cyaneae however are the **tombs**. A temple tomb cut in the precipitous cliff face is conspicuous during the climb up but difficult to reach. Lining the climb up from Yavu and at the summit on the approach to the theatre are numerous sarcophagi, perhaps more numerous than at any other Lycian city. Many have reliefs and date largely from the Roman period, one of which, depicting soldiers with spears, is now on display in the Antalya museum. The city's name is Greek, meaning dark blue, the colour of lapis lazuli.

Trysa and Other Remote Sites

Six kilometres northeast of Cyaneae, remote and not easily accessible, lies the site of **Trysa**. The discovery here of an extraordinarily beautiful tomb, called the **Heroon** and dating from the 4th C BC, was one of the most exciting events in Lycian archaeology. The elaborate friezes on the internal walls of the sarcophagus depicted scenes from the *Iliad* and the *Odyssey*, the exploits of Theseus, and the battles of the Greeks and the Amazons. These reliefs were removed in the last century and are now on display in Vienna, with only the walls of the Heroon surviving *in situ*.

Rarely visited sites Throughout this region there are many remote sites of small Lycian cities, very rarely visited except by enthusiasts like George Bean. Most require a jeep and then a long steep climb. They are often interesting however, and show the pattern of occupation in this wild central region of Lycia, where living conditions have not changed materially from what they were 2000 years ago.

The Plain of Demre

From the Yavu plateau the road then winds on to a descent into the flat alluvial plain of Demre. The plain is not a pretty sight, particularly in May and June when the plastic roofs of tomato sheds disfigure the landscape. From a height these roofs look like mud flats. Tomato growing is a recent phenomenon in this region, within the last 25 years, and has meant that the town of **Demre** itself has grown fast and untidily, a dusty sprawling mass surrounded by tomato sheds everywhere. In the early 1950s Freya Stark said the population was a mere 200.

It is worth rising above your first impressions of the town, for the visit to the site of **Myra** with its Roman theatre and Lycian necropolis is truly spectacular and is not to be missed. If you take the turn left at the bottom of the descent just before the well-preserved 15-metre high Roman temple tomb at the side of the road, you will in fact avoid the worst of the town. Following the first gravel road which branches left off this past more tomato sheds will bring you after about one kilometre straight to the site of Myra, nestling at the foot of the cliff behind the town. There is a place for refreshments at the entrance, but no restaurant, and for lunch it is best to drive out to the small harbour near Andriake, the port of Myra, described a little later.

Myrrh-breathing city The origin of the name Myra has always been associated with myrrh, and one Roman emperor described it as 'the thrice blessed, myrrh-breathing city of the Lycians, where the mighty Nicholas, servant of God, spouts forth myrrh in accordance with the city's name'. Myra was indeed unusual among Lycian cities, as it retained its fame and prosperity into Christian times because of St Nicholas, Bishop of Myra in the 4th C. The Apostle Paul met here earlier in AD 60 with his followers on his way to Rome. In Byzantine times Myra became the Lycian centre of religious and administrative affairs. But by the 7th C Arab raids began to take their toll on the city, and with the silting up of the plain and the ever present danger of earthquakes Myra was eventually abandoned.

Myra's beginnings date back to the 5th C BC; in the Lycian Leage it was one of the six major cities with three votes. It enjoyed its golden age during the Roman imperium; in the 2nd C AD the theatre was rebuilt on donations from the lavish benefactor and millionaire Opromoas of Rhodiapolis after the city had been badly damaged by an earthquake in AD 141.

Exploring Myra

It is to the **theatre** that the path leads first, at the foot of the cliff, on the summit of which remains of Byzantine fortifications against the Arab raids are visible. It is large and remarkably well-preserved. The particularly impressive thing is being able to walk up inside the huge *vaulted paradoi* with little rooms off where vendors would have been selling the Roman equivalent of popcorn and ices before the show. With a total of 14 stairways, it has a very broad diazoma (horizontal walkway around the cavea) with a 2-metre wall backing it on which are painted names, apparently reserving seats. In the centre of the wall is a small *statue of Tyche*, protectress of the city. The stage building has been partially cleared and is still in quite good order: the facade facing the audience was highly decorated. There is something slightly barbaric about the atmosphere that makes it easy to recall that the audience were enjoying, not plays or music, but gladiatorial spectacles with beasts.

From the theatre, paths lead up to the cluster of **rock-cut tombs** set in the cliff face above. The paths lead to the most noteworthy tombs with reliefs and carving, but the way across the rock-face is fairly precipitous and not suited to those with a fear of heights. The guardian, with his typically lugubrious Lycian face, will always offer a helping hand if required.

The tombs vary in size and form but most are of the house type with roofs carved out of the rock to resemble the ends of logs. Later versions of this became dentil friezes. Most of the inscriptions visible are in Lycian, not in Greek. One of the house tombs is especially remarkable because of its beautiful reliefs: the rock above the roof shows, on the far left, a soldier in full armour, left hand raised resting on his lance, receiving a helmet offered by a small boy. The main central relief shows the scene of a funeral banquet. The figure reclining on the couch is probably the deceased, while those around him are his family. The relief is dated to the middle of the 4th C BC. Another house tomb, not in the cliff face but right at the foot of the cliff partially under ground level is decorated in an unusual way: the borders of the relief give it the appearance of a window; two warriors are shown in

Popcorn stalls

Western necropolis

Funeral banquet

heated combat, with the victor on the right grasping the shield of his fleeing opponent with his right hand while holding his own shield tightly with his left. This is a motif often found in Lycian art, where unlike Greek art it is not the moment of triumph after the battle that is shown but rather the dramatic climax.

The interiors of the tombs also vary greatly, and some of the benches are carved to imitate bedsteads. One tomb has a grafitti saying 'Moschus loves Philiste, daughter of Demetrius'.

Eastern necropolis

There are two main groups of tombs at Myra; this above the theatre which is the *western group*, and the eastern group which is not visible from the main site but is 2 km further round the cliff. Allow at least 1½ hours for the western group of tombs and the theatre, and about one hour for the eastern group. Do not be misled by the small middle cluster of tombs, which look quite tempting but are difficult to reach and do not repay the effort. The way to them involves walking along the top of the wall at the back of the theatre and then following a very vague path through rocks and brambles, and you are likely to rewarded only by a close encounter with a snake or a hornet. To reach the *eastern group*, follow the gravel dirt track east past the main site to a T-junction and then branch left through fields and yet more tomato sheds. Keeping your eyes on the cliff face to the left of the gravel track, stop when you are directly opposite the cluster of tombs in the cliff. From the road a path leads in a straight line across the field to the bottom of the tombs.

The so-called **Painted Tomb**, one of the most remarkable tombs in all Lycia, is at the top of a staircase cut into the rock which you will notice on closer scrutiny running from bottom left to top right of the cliff. Scrambling up this is not totally straightforward, being mildly precipitous, but presents no real problem unless you suffer from vertigo. The scenes of carved reliefs on the rock face in front of the tomb are striking, though the only colour which now remains is the blue and red background of the reclining man on the left side, raising a wine cup in his right hand. Fellows in the last century saw red, blue, yellow and purple in the scene, giving an idea how brightly painted it must have been. The figures in the porch of the tomb seem to represent the indoor life of the deceased and his family, while the ones outside on the rock face shows them dressed for outdoors. Among the grouping of figures on the far right-hand rock face, the young man leaning on a staff, feet crossed, catches the eye with his unusually casual pose.

The other tomb in this cluster which used to be worth clambering to, the **Lion Tomb**, is now disappointing, because the relief of two lions killing a bull in the pediment above the lintel has recently fallen away.

Myra: the eastern necropolis

From Artemis to Santa Claus

Missing temple
Artemis, Apollo and their mother Leto were worshipped above all others in Lycia. In Myra the main cult was dedicated to Artemis Eleuthera, a distinctive form of Cybele, the ancient mother goddess of Anatolia, as was Artemis of Ephesus. On the Myran coins her effigy was represented as that of Artemis Ephesia, many-breasted as a sign of her fertility and giving of life. We know there was a magnificent temple of Artemis Eleuthera, famous as the largest and most beautiful building in Myra, but no trace of it has yet been found. An inscription on the tomb of Opromoas, the wealthy Lycian benefactor, tells us he donated the money for the temple to be rebuilt after it was heavily damaged by the earthquake of AD 141, or, as legend would have it, Nicholas, Bishop of Myra, had the temple destroyed after a divine inspiration.

The **church of St Nicholas** can be visited today after a visit to Myra. Signposts point to it from the centre of Demre where it stands up a side street in the town. Despite its sanctity and historical interest the church is not a remarkable building. It stands slightly away from the street sunk down in a hollow; in the last century it was often submerged in up to a metre of water. A church of some kind has probably existed here since the 3rd C AD when St Nicholas died but has been heavily and frequently restored, so that the church as it stands today dates from a variety of periods. St Nicholas was buried in the crypt, but in 1087 his body was stolen by sailors from Bari in southern Italy where it now lies.

Patron of children

Nicholas, born in Patara around AD 300, achieved fame by resurrecting three children whom a butcher had cut up and put in brine. His association with children was matched by that for gift-giving: hearing of a man, once wealthy but now fallen on hard times, who was unable to find dowries for his three daughters, Nicholas entered his house secretly by night and left three purses of gold. Hence the three daughters were able to contract suitable marriages and avoid a more public fate. Many stories are also told of Nicholas' miraculous powers in rescuing prisoners, shipwrecked sailors, lost travellers, recovering lost property, and generally answering the prayers of those in distress. Now, 1700 years later, his cult has reached alarming proportions among children, who await his benificience each Christmas morning.

Andriake: the Port of Myra

The town of Demre offers no recommendable accommodation. It is possible to stay in a room in a local house but it is preferable to camp on the beach away from the town by the small harbour of Andriake, port to Myra. This spot is worth visiting anyway for lunch at the pleasant restaurant on the beach at the river mouth.

The harbour is reached by returning to the large Roman temple tomb on the main road and turning left. This road skirts the town for about 2 km and then, where the main road bends sharply left, a straight, dead flat tarmac road leads off towards the sea. It follows the course of a river estuary and along its left side the ruins of Andriake can be seen across the water, overgrown, with foliage. These ruins are mostly minor, with the noteable exception of **Hadrian's Granary** (see also Patara).

Another granary of Hadrian

To reach the granary involves a 10-minute walk. A path leads across from a wooded area at the left of the road, across the sand. You continue through the sand till you reach the very edge of the estuary and then fork left to walk through the ruins, passing through an arch among crumbled buildings which appear to be mainly Byzantine. As you approach the granary from the side you can see the huge blocks of stone, and then as you round its corner you see that the eight storage chambers stretch on and on sideways, facing the river. Above the central doorway are reliefs with busts of Hadrian and the Empress Faustina, where the Latin dedication also survives.

It is refreshing to bathe in the icy fresh water at the river mouth, and a welcome rest to sit in the restaurant reached by a footbridge over the river. The owner of the restaurant also hires out boats for trips to Kekova island, but it is cheaper and generally preferable to do this trip from Kaş. Free camping is offered on the beach, with simple open-air showers and a WC. There are also a few caravan-huts which seem to be used by Turks on holiday. The site attracts mosquitoes, so you are wise to go armed with repellent.

AROUND FINIKE

Eastward from Demre the road continues through a flat coastal stretch and skirts an inland sea-lake. It then winds round bays and headlands for about a 30-minutes drive to reach Finike.

Working harbour

The town of **Finike** is now one of the largest on this stretch of Lycian coast till Antalya. Fellows described it in the last century as consisting of three houses, and Freya Stark in the 1950s said it was a main street with a few lanes off it, but noticed the nomads from the highlands gradually beginning to settle here. In the last 25 years however it has developed as an agricultural town with an active harbour shipping out cargoes of locally grown tomatoes and oranges. Tourism has yet to make its mark here. There are no yachts or private cruising boats in the harbour, and there are just a handful of basic small hotels and pensions. The extreme flatness of Finike's setting, contrasting sharply with the mainly mountainous Lycian coast, also helps to make the town seem unexciting.

Inland to Limyra

Inland however the scenery soon becomes very attractive with lush orange groves in the valley and steep hills rising either side. The Lycian city of **Limyra**, lying a few kilometres back from Finike, is right on the edge of the coastal plain with its necropolis rising up the mountains behind. Limyra is something of a mystery as the Turks do not seem to want to admit to it. It has one of the most extensive necropolises in Lycia and yet it is never signposted, nor is it even mentioned in official tourist publications while other far lesser sites are given coverage. The most likely explanation for this is that the site used to be on the old road along the coast to Kumluca, but since the new tarmac road was built it requires a special detour.

Drive-in theatre

For the traveller who does want to visit Limyna, it is reached by forking inland left from the centre of Finike and continuing for about 6 km up the Elmalí road. At the village of Turunçova an unsignposted road turns off right over a small bridge which takes you through the small village. After about 4 km along mainly untarmaced road (forking right whenever there is a choice) you will reach Limyra with the **theatre** so close to the road that you can even park inside the vaulted parados for shade. This theatre, small but with an unsually large orchestra, is all that remains of the ancient city besides the tombs, and was built by that now familiar benefactor of the arts Opromoas, who gave 20,000 denarii to Limyra in AD 141 for the reconstruction of the theatre after its destruction by an earthquake.

As there is no sign announcing Limyra, so it is not surprising that there is no guardian and no refreshments. On the
opposite side of the road is a pleasant stream with the
picturesque ruins of a **Byzantine nunnery** and several other
large but unidentified Byzantine buildings. Of the extensive
necropolis, the main feature of Limyra, however, it is very
difficult to get a feel from below. The occasional sarcophagus
tomb can be seen on the hillside near the road, notably that
raised up on the hillside slightly behind the theatre. This is the
tomb of Catabura it was thought to have been a brother of
Pericles, ruler of Limyra. Built in the 4th C BC, the sarcophagus is mounted on a huge ornamented base with reliefs of
the traditional funeral banquet, and an unusual scene of the
judgement of the dead. The deceased person is shown in the
nude with his clothes draped over his arm, appearing before
the court in the world of the dead.

A few rock-cut house tombs are also visible from the road,
walking on beyond the theatre, but the majority of the tombs
lie out of sight above the ridges and involve climbing across a
series of endless and uncomfortable rocky ridges with no
path. As Bean says, it would take a stay of three days to do an
extensive tour of the site. You may well feel by now, as even
the indefatiguable Freya Stark did, when travelling the region
with her companion David Barrow: 'The day came when D B
and I looked at each other and said: Must we go up and look
at that tomb?'

The town of Limyra dates back to the 5th C BC and was a
prosperous trade settlement, exporting agricultural produce
from its port as Finike does today. During the 5th and 4th C
most of Anatolia was under the administration of local
governors or satraps linked to the Persian Empire. It was at
this time that the dynast Pericles made the city of Limyra his
capital from where he resisted the Persian satrap of Caria,
Mausolus, hence forming the Lycian League. Any Persian
pretensions to rule of Lycia ended in 333 BC with the advent of
Alexander the Great. The interesting heroon recently
discovered high up in the necropolis at Limyra is almost
certainly the **tomb of Pericles**. The ascent directly across from
the theatre is not recommended as it is tougher than it looks.
Instead retrace your steps back towards the Elmalí road; at
the first little village there is a path leading up to the heroon,
built into the natural rock on a platform at about 250 metres
above sea level and looking over the plain of Limyra. Only the
large rocky base about 20 metres square with the lower stones
of the construction remain on site, as the relief and caryatids
which decorated it are now either locked in the depot nearby
or are in the Antalya museum. The war-like scenes on the
reliefs show both Greek and Persian influence, as one might
expect given its date of construction in c370 BC when Lycia
stood between East and West with the Persians attempting to

dominate the native Greek population. The Nereid Monument at Xanthos dates from the same period.

Returning to the main Elmalí road and continuing up the valley, after about 2 km high up on the cliff face to the right of the road a remarkable cluster of about eight rock-cut **house and temple tombs** will be seen. The setting is extraordinarily precipitous and the tombs look totally inaccessible. It is possible that they are the topmost grouping of the extensive necropolis of Limyra.

Further to Arycanda

A more worthwhile detour and infinitely less strenuous is to be had by continuing further up towards Elmalí for about half an hour's drive (35 km from Finike) to the splendid site of Arycanda, the most reminiscent of Delphi of all the Lycian sites. The drive from Finike climbs up through a pretty valley with gorges and a fast-flowing river, the ancient Arycandus. Allow $3\frac{1}{2}$ hours for the excursion from Finike and back.

Turkish Delphi

The road is excellent and a clear yellow sign points up right, 1 km, to Arycanda just before a cascading waterfall at the side of the road. There is no place for refreshments here but you can eat passably at a basic café about 2 km before Arycanda where many truck drivers stop. Alternatively Arycanda is an excellent site for a picnic. To reach the site leave your car parked on the main road and walk the easy 15 minutes up the signposted forest track.

Arycanda has benefited from recent excavations beginning in 1978 by teams from İstanbul University which have brought many more buildings to light than there were in George Bean's day. The setting of the site is magnificent, backing into the lee of a high cliff face overlooking a beautiful green valley with pine forests to one side. Fellows said of the setting: 'All is grand yet lovely'.

Pleasure lovers

The ancient city dates from the 5th C BC and was for a time under Persian rule, later to be part of Alexander's empire. The Arycandans were a pleasure-loving people. Their prodigality, profligacy, sloth and love of pleasure led them into debts which they could not repay. When, therefore, the Seleucid Antiochus III was engaged in taking Lycia from the Ptolemies in 197 BC, the Arycandans supported him in the hope of being rewarded by the remission of their debts. In the 2nd C BC Arycanda became a member of the Lycian League and minted its own coins, remaining in the League till it was dissolved by the Roman Emperor Claudius in AD 43 whereupon it came like the rest of Lycia under Roman rule. Christianity appeared here by the end of the 3rd C AD and the city existed throughout Byzantine times and right up to the 19th C. The site is now totally deserted, and the village below is not visible once you start to climb.

The first building you come to, just to the right of the path, is on the newly excavated **acropolis**, a small hillock. The five steps leading up through the gateway are impressive and the high stone walls are surprisingly white in colour. Inside are the remains of several rooms with the remnants of the underfloor heating still visible. Continuing up the path passing the main site buildings on the hillside to the left, you come among pine trees to the scattered remains of **Roman temple tombs**, some with carvings, which used to line a street approaching from that side.

Below the tombs the colossal **baths** with their two rows of huge windows overlooking the valley dominate this whole area of the site and are, as so many baths, remarkably well-preserved, still standing to a height of over 10 metres. Next to them stands a **gymnasium** with an open area in front like a palaestra.

One of the finest settings in southern Turkey

Crossing the stream bed, dry in summer, and following the vague path further up towards the cliff face, you soon arrive at a large open area to the left of the path with buildings off it on the cliff side. Bean in the 1960s speculated that this was a gymnasium, but with the benefit of further excavations it now

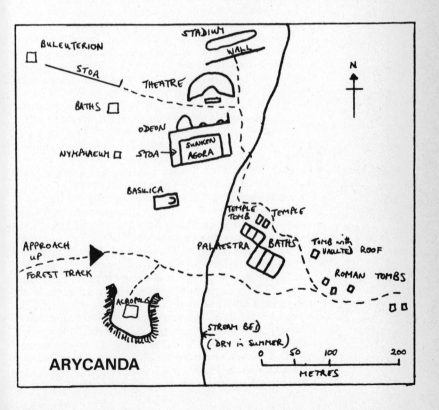

ARYCANDA

seems more likely to have been a large sunken oblong **agora** with a raised walkway or stoa on three sides. On its cliff side is a high wall with five arches set into it, the furthest three leading into a small **odeon**. Immediately above this is the **theatre**, in the Greek style slightly more than a semi-circle and in an excellent state of preservation, again the subject of recent excavations. There is no diazoma and there are several sets of paths leading up through the seats. The stage building has survived quite well. The setting of this theatre is, after Termessos, the most magnificent in all of southern Turkey, with the cliff face as its natural backdrop, facing out into the valley and the snow-covered mountains opposite.

Climbing out above the theatre, a crumbling stairway with shored-up walls leads on up to the **stadium**, the highest of all the buildings in Arycanda. It is not particularly well-preserved, but the setting is magnificent and very peaceful with the wind rushing in the pine trees. A few rows of seats on the cliff face side are all that is visible, but further excavation could well reveal more. Heading off west at about the same height as the theatre terrace, a long **stoa** leads up to what was presumably the **buleuferion** (council chamber) with its seats carved from the rock. Between this and the agora is a ruined **baths**, and lower down, the remnants of a **nymphaeum**.

Returning down the hillside, below the sunken agora area are the foundations of a large Byzantine **basilica** still with remains of its *mosaic flooring* in abstract patterns of blue and red. Up on the hillside on the right as you return to the main path, the impressive built-up blocks of the stoa's retaining wall can be seen, almost resembling fortifications from below.

Waterfalls Once down on the tarmac road it is worth walking on some 50 metres to the waterfalls at the side of the road for a refreshing splash. Here too, above the road, can be seen the only evidence that Arycanda was a Lycian city, in a few rock-cut tombs of Lycian style carved from the cliff face.

A Strenuous Expedition

High in the hills above Arycanda at a height of about 1000 metres lies the site of **Idebessus**, a good example of the extraordinary remoteness of some of the Lycian cities. George Bean, climbing there from Arycanda in 1953, recalls the journey as the most exhausting day's walk throughout his time in Turkey, which is certainly enough to make the average mortal think twice about a visit. Barely 18 km as the crow flies, it took all day on a track that was virtually non-existent in places, with an old man acting as guide who had followed the track 20 years earlier and thought he might still remember it. Freya Stark did the journey by mule in the reverse direction, and even downhill found it hard going. The rare visitor is rewarded by ruins of a theatre, a baths, and many fine sarcophagi with reliefs of cupids and animals.

The spectacularly sited theatre at Arycanda

BETWEEN FINIKE AND ANTALYA

Returning to Finike, the road (dual carriage-way even) continues eastwards along the exceptionally long, flat and fetureless bay of Finike. Set back from the road is the occasional very large expensive-looking house in extensive grounds, presumably the dwellings of newly rich tomato magnates.

Dismembered cities

Right at the end of the bay, the road passes through the agricultural town of Kumluca, an unpleasant dusty place, and shortly afterwards forks left to Antalya. Once east of Limyra, the peculiarly Lycian character of the ancient sites is less noticeable. Their foundation legends are Greek or Rhodian: **Rhodiapolis**, the city of the millionaire Opromoas means Rhodian city. It lies high in the hills above Kumluca, at least an hour's walk with a guide. Its claim to fame is the Opromoas funeral monument, the walls of which were covered in inscriptions narrating the honours poured on him; the whole amounts to the longest single inscription in Lycia, perhaps even in the whole of Asia Minor. The tomb is now in total ruin, its carved blocks scattered about the area. In the remoter sites it is fairly common for this kind of damage to be done, and often the stones of the ancient cities are carried away in truck loads to serve the needs of the local inhabitants. Kumluca and its neighbouring villages are full of the dismembered parts of various Lycian cities, and many carry inscriptions, like the one set in a new house in Kumluca, which carries a bilingual Lycian and Greek text.

Mountain Crossing

After Kumluca, the newly constructed road on to Antalya follows a very steep climb, one of the steepest in Lycia, up into the mountains. The scenery throughout this mountain cross-

Spectacular climb

ing is very beautiful, with a good view back down over the Finike and Kumiuca bay. The mountainous stretch between here and Phaselis is particularly prone to storms, and the whole area is almost entirely uninhabited. There are no signs off until, shortly after the summit of the pass at the beginning of the descent, a sign points off right, 9 km, to the site of Olympos and the Olympos National Park. The detour from the main road for the visit involves about three hours.

Pink oleander valley

The visit to **Olympos** is an enjoyable one as the site benefits like many others in Lycia from a lovely setting, overgrown in summer with pink oleander bushes where the river estuary meets the sea. The traveller should however be warned that there is a dearth of places to stay and he should be prepared to camp. The road leading off from the main road starts off as tarmac but soon degenerates into gravel track which is fine as far as the village of Çavus; the final 3 km along the river valley to the sea are a bit uncomfortable in parts, but a car can do it if driven carefully. If your nerve fails you, or if you are in your own rather than a hired car, you can always leave the car and walk. In some ways, walking through the lush oleander valley with high forested mountains on either side gives you a better appreciation of the magnificent landscape of these parts.

Thrashing about Olympos

Ruins overgrown or submerged

You come to Olympos more for its setting and for its good beach than to see the ruins themselves. These are mainly covered in dense undergrowth, partly underwater, and very difficult to explore. It is questionable whether exploration repays the effort involved. It is a very peaceful spot and, mainly because the locals themselves come here, there are a couple of shack-like restaurants on the shingle beach where the willing owners will serve you a simple lunch.

No excavations have ever been undertaken at Olympos, but persistent enthusiasts have found in the undergrowth the collapsed ruins of a theatre, a baths and a basilica. The most notable and striking monument is the **temple** whose 6-metre high doorway complete with decorated lintel can be seen rising above the vegetation. An inscription on the base of a plinth nearby tells that it was built during the reign of the Emperor Marcus Aurelius AD 172. The **necropolis** is on the slopes of the hill on the south side of the river. There are many scattered tombs, some of the sarcophagus type, others of a type not characteristically Lycian at all: they are in the shape of a vaulted chamber with a small square doorway.

History: from Unknown Origins to Extinction

The name of the city comes from the nearby mountain of the same name (today's Tahtalí Dağ, 2400 metres) one of more than 20 mountains of the same name throughout Greece and Asia Minor which were known in antiquity as the homes of the gods. Nothing of the origins of Olympos is known, and the first evidence of its existence are the silver coins struck in the 2nd C BC. These show that Olympos was a member of the Lycian League, and by 100 BC it was one of the six major cities of Lycia, possessing the maximum of three votes. Of these six cities, four (Xanthos, Tlos, Pinara and Patara) were in the Xanthos valley, the heartland of Lycia; one (Myra) represented the centre; and Olympos represented eastern Lycia. The choice of Olympos seems strange, given that Phaselis, a much greater and more important city, lies just to the north, until it is remembered that Phaselis was not at that time a member of the Lycian League but had its own constitution.

Pirate stronghold

Around 85 BC Olympos (and Phaselis) was captured by Cilician pirates and their leader Zeniketes made the city his stronghold. Olympos remained in the grip of the pirates till the Roman Proconsul of Cilicia, Servilus Vatia, conquered and plundered the city. Realising his defeat, Zeniketes set fire to his stronghold, burning himself and his family alive. After this the area was classed as Roman property and sold off or leased to private citizens. During this period Olympos lost her position in the League and only recovered it again under the Roman Empire in the 2nd C AD. Olympos then prospered on trade and in AD 129 Hadrian visited the city during a tour of the empire, in honour of which Olympos took the name Hadrianopolis for a while. The wealthy Lycian citizen Opromoas is known to have donated money for the construction of many fine buildings during this time.

Its golden age came to an abrupt end when in the 3rd C AD it was again sacked by pirates from Cilicia after which the city declined and became a modest settlement. It had a brief revival under Venice, Genoa and Rhodes but during the period of Ottoman domination over the eastern Mediterranean in the 15th C Olympos was completely abandoned.

The Chimaera

The principal deity worshipped in Olympos was Hephaistos, the Roman Vulcan, god of fire and forging. He was the unloved son of Zeus and married Aphrodite. Hephaistos was not one of the major Greek gods and his worship here was due to a natural phenomenon, the Chimaera, in the hills above Olympos. This is described from the 4th C BC onwards as a mountain on which burns an eternal flame. Homer in the *Iliad* calls the Chimaera the fire-breathing monster of the underworld, which the youth Bellerophon was sent to slay by the King of Lycia (see Tlos): 'Chimaera the unconquerable ... of divine birth was she and not of men, in front a lion and behind a serpent, and in the midst a goat, and she breathed dread fierceness of blazing fire'.

The origins of the Chimaera give rise to speculation on the origins of the Lycians and their possible link with the Etruscans of ancient Italy. The Etruscans are a little known people of uncertain beginnings, yet the most civilised people in western Europe at their time (around the 6th C BC). Among extant Etruscan art, most of which has come from their underground burial chambers, is a beautifully crafted Chimaera monster in bronze, conforming in every detail to Homer's description.

The site of the Chimaera, the **Sanctuary of Hephaistos**, can be reached by a 1¼ hours' walk up the mountain to a point about 250 metres above sea level. The perpetual flame, called *yanar* in Turkish, still burns today in a cave barely a metre in diameter, and certainly seems to have dwindled considerably from the reports of earlier travellers. The ancients claimed that the flame could not be put out, whereas now a small quantity of earth or water will extinguish it — though it flares

Bad breath

Etruscan-Lycian link

The 6th C Etruscan bronze Chimaera

up again after about 10 or 15 seconds. It looks its most impressive at night from out at sea when it can be seen glowing in the hills. In recent years commercial interest has been aroused by the Chimaera as it was thought there might be oil or gases in the surrounding earth. In 1967 a group of Turkish scientists was sent to carry out tests but nothing seems to have come of them so far.

Zoroastrian link   Another curious cult at Olympos is related by Plutarch: 'The pirates conducted strange sacrifices in Olympos and celebrated certain secret rites, among which one in particular, to Mithras, was first introduced by them; it has remained popular to the present'. Mithras was the Persian Zoroastrian god of fidelity and the pure spirit of light. The concepts of the immortality of the soul, the resurrection and the last judgement were prevalent in the cult of Zoroaster. The cult of Mithras was more widespread than Christianity in the 2nd C AD throughout the Roman Empire. Mithraism was introduced from the East by the returning Roman legions, but it is curious to find Cilician pirates helping to spread the cult westwards.

Back to the Madding Crowd
From the Olympos turn-off the drive on to Phaselis is only about 30 minutes. Just a couple of kilometres beyond Phaselis on the coast is the village of **Tekirova** with the first

decent accommodation along this stretch of coast since Kaş, in the form of a cluster of motels and a private holiday village mainly for Germans. A further 7 km on is **Kemer**, a holiday resort for Antalya, with a range of hotels and restaurants, something of a shock to the system after the emptiness and virtual absense of people and hotels experienced in Lycia.

A shock

The site of **Phaselis** also seems a far cry from the sites of the rest of Lycia. Because it is in easy reach of Antalya, only 30 km away on a good road, it is a popular place for school outings and picnics (despite the large signs forbidding camping and picnicking). It has been extensively excavated and a new complex of buildings has been built at the entrance, complete with souvenir shop, tea house and large administrative office: the real shock is that you will need to buy an entry ticket, the first site asking for this since the Priene-Didyma-Miletos cluster. Having said this, the site is nevertheless extremely beautiful, on the sea and just 2 km off the main road, and you can drive on a track right through to a Roman aqueduct among the trees. The site has three natural harbours; the small central one is a lovely spot for a swim. Most yachts, boats and picnickers seem to favour the furthest harbour and it is certainly true that the view from there inland to the mountains with the pine forests coming right down to the shoreline is particularly fine. Two hours is ample for the site — longer if swimming and sunbathing.

The Character of the Phaselians

The history of Phaselis bears witness to the ingratiating nature of its citizens. Demosthenes said of their devotion to commerce: 'They are very clever at borrowing money in the market, then as soon as they have it they forget that it was a loan, and when called on for repayment think up all sorts of excuses and pretexts, and if they do repay it they feel that they have been done out of their own property; and in general they are the most scoundrelly and unscrupulous of men'.

Scoundrels...

Founded from Rhodes in the 7th C BC (Phaselis means chick-pea in Greek), the city enjoyed excellent harbours, a heavily wooded hinterland and the flowers and plants that allowed it to produce rose oil and scented ointments, so that it flourished as a commercial trading centre and was the most important port on Lycia's eastern coast. The Phaselians happily accepted Persian rule, then bent to Athenian hegemony after Salamis and Plataea, sided with Mausolus against their fellow Lycians and grovelled before Alexander. Ultimately Phaselis became part of the Roman Empire, and only then did it become properly Lycian — inscriptions show a change in personal names from Greek to Lycian as though there had been a resettlement. But otherwise there is little of the Lycian in their history or character; everything was up for sale, including citizenship which was offered to all comers at

100 drachmae.

Arab raids around AD 650 brought destruction, but in the 7th and 8th C Phaselis revived and was a major port of the Byzantine Empire. With the Seljuk conquest during the 12th C the city declined finally, its trade lost to the favoured ports of Antalya and Alanya.

...and freaks A hairstyle, the 'sisoe', associated with Phaselis, found its way into the Bible: in Leviticus (19:27) is the prohibition: 'Ye shall not make a sisoe of the hair of your heads'. A modern English version translates this as: 'Ye shall not round the corners of your heads'. Nobody knows what the sisoe style was like exactly, and the 'round corners' does not help; an excavated statue is needed to reveal all.

Looking Around Phaselis

In the first harbour where you arrive at the site Roman **sarcophagus tombs** are lying in the shallow water, and some on the shore. One lid on the shore under a pine tree is particularly fine, cracked now but with a good carving of a headless woman. Past the aqueduct and towards the sea you come to the small central harbour, from the far side of which the main **paved street** of ancient Phaselis leads across the headland to the far harbour and the large **gateway** set up in honour of a visit from Hadrian. This street is the most fascinating feature of the ruined city, and strolling along it, lined with shops, gives a vivid feel for the life that once was in the old city. In the past some early travellers imagined the street to be a stadium, even though it is far too long and narrow. The **theatre**, reached by a stairway off the main street, is still pleasantly overgrown and shady, making a cool haven from the sun in summer. On the opposite side of the street are extensive **bath complexes** with their central heating systems plainly visible.

PRACTICAL INFORMATION

FETHIYE
30 minutes' drive from Dalaman **airport**.

Many **hotels** lining the bay on the approach to the town, among the best of which is the Letoon Motel (1-star), pretty chalets back from the sea with abundant flowers. The public sandy **beach** opposite is good for swimming.

In the town itself the Likya Hotel (1-star) is the best, on the harbour front with a small private beach for swimming and a quay where a caique is moored for the use of guests. 22 rooms with private facilities.

The Likya has the best setting for an **evening meal**, on its terrace at the water's edge.

ÖLÜ DENIZ
Dolmuş **taxis** run to Fethiye regularly, but **buses** are very infrequent. Kaya is walkable, but **car hire** is necessary to visit Xanthos or anywhere further afield.

Peaceful lagoon, excellent swimming, wooded shoreline. Very popular with yachts.

Motel Meri (1-star), 75 bungalows all with

WC, prettily built into the hillside. Simple but adequate. Pretty gardens and trees. Some water sports available.
Camping Deniz, best of the few campsites.

KALKAN
Handful of small **pensions** in the village. Pasha's Inn used to be recommended but has now become overpriced and ritzy. The best are Balíkçí Han and King Pension, where facilities are basic but with lovely roof terraces for breakfast. All have a view over the harbour but there is no **beach**.

KAŞ
Again there is no **beach** in town, though the **camping sites** beyond the theatre have access to rocky beach. All accommodation is very simple, though usually clean. The group of **pensions** over the hill beyond the town centre are quiet, some with balconies over the sea. Most are family-run. You can try the Andifli Hotel, 6 rooms, Akdeniz Pension, Nur Pansiyon, Lale Pension, Hotel Likya and Antiphellos Pension.

DEMRE
Festival 6–8 December in honour of St Nicholas.

FINIKE
Hotel Sedir, 13 rooms on main street. Basic, but offering the only reasonable accommodation between Kaş and Kemer.
Self-sufficient **camping** possible at Olympos, and on the beach at Demre/Andriake.
Restaurants: at Patara, near the beach. At Demre near Andriake on the beach.

TEKIROVA
Near Phaselis, a few kilometres before Kemer, Motel Akman (1-star), very quiet, quite lush gardens. All rooms with private facilities and balconies.
Restaurant on edge of beach.
Good **swimming**.

KEMER
Extensive resort, many large **hotels** and a private holiday village linked with the Club Mediterranée, which has to be booked in advance.
Motel Beytur, (1-star), on the beach.

Antalya to Alanya (Ancient Pamphylia)

ANCIENT PAMPHYLIA

Turquoise Coast

The route from Phaselis on to Antalya clings to the coast all the way with the mountains rising up so close to the shoreline that the road has to pass through several tunnels. Once you leave the mountains behind you are entering what is known as the Turquoise Coast or the Turkish Riviera, stretching for 500 km from Antalya right through to Iskenderun near the Syrian border. Although the coastline changes dramatically, the whole stretch shares the benefit of an excellent climate with 300 days of sunshine per year and a clear turquoise sea.

Mixed Multitude

Turkey's southern shore falls into several distinct regions, so different that as you pass from one to another it is like entering a different country. So it is as you leave the wild mountains of Lycia for the flat, well-watered coastal plain of Pamphylia. This plain extends for about 80 km from Antalya to Side, and in classical times supported five great cities: Attaleia (Antalya), Perge, Aspendos, Sillyon and Side.

The Greek origins of all these cities date back to the time of the Trojan War in the 13th C BC. When Troy fell, a 'mixed multitude' of Greeks migrated across Asia Minor and settled on the coast, mainly on the Pamphylian plain, some moving further eastward to Cilicia. The Greek name Pamphylia means 'land of the tribes', which confirms the mixed groupings of the origins of the settlers. The three main leaders of this migration were Mopsus, Calchas and Amphilochus. To judge from the close resemblance which the Pamphylian dialect of Greek as found on coins and inscriptions bears to the dialect spoken in southern Greece before the Dorians invaded, driving out many of the native inhabitants, many of this 'mixed multitude' came from southern Greece. Following Alexander's conquest of the region, standard Greek gradually spread over Asia Minor and the local dialects died out.

A Small Role in History

Cut off from the main east-west trade routes by mountains to each side and behind, Pamphylia played a small role in history, and records of the cities are not as complete as those of the Aegean coast like Ephesus and Miletos. Our first knowledge of the region's history dates from the 6th C BC, when the last king of Lydia (at Sardis), Croesus, extended his empire to cover Pamphylia. This domination was short-lived though, and in 546 BC Croesus was utterly defeated by the Persians. Under the period of Persian domination and the Persian wars against the Greeks, the Pamphylians, like the Lycians and Carians, fought against the Greeks, contributing 30 ships to the Persian fleet.

Alexander achieved his aim of driving out the Persian
power from Asia Minor remarkably quickly. He advanced
through Lydia and Ionia unopposed by any large army, and
only Miletos and Halicarnassus (Bodrum) offered him any
resistance in Caria. He then passed on through Lycia,
arriving in Pamphylia less than a year after he had crossed the
Hellespont. Attaleia did not yet exist, so his first stop was at
Perge where he was received warmly, and he also took
Aspendos and Side with no opposition. At Sillyon however,
naturally strongly defended upon its acropolis in the plain, he
met resistance and his first attack failed. Since however, his
purpose in capturing this part of Turkey was to prevent the
Persians from using it as a naval base, he decided Sillyon, not
being a port or even on a river, was not worthy of a siege.
Needing to go north to meet up with the other part of his
army, Alexander returned to Perge and past the mountain
fastness of Termessos, the Eagle's Nest. Here too, he thought
better of a lengthy siege and moved on northwards.

Alexander went on to conquer the Persian empire, but his
premature death at Babylon in 323 BC left his new empire
without a ruler, and his generals spent the next 40 years
squabbling among themselves for control of it. By the end of
that period, three main kingdoms had been established:
Greece and Macedonia, Egypt under the Ptolemies and Syria
under the Seleucids. After 280 BC a fourth kingdom emerged
at Pergamum, ruled by the Attalids. Pamphylia was claimed
by both the Seleucids and the Ptolemies, though in practice
any control was nominal and it remained largely independent.

Around 158 BC Attalus II, King of Pergamum, sought to
extend his empire and capture a port on the south coast of
Pamphylia. The Pamphylian cities had, however, been
allowed their freedom by the Roman Empire by this time,
and so Attalus, not wanting to offend Rome, founded a new
port named after himself, Attaleia, the Antalya of today.

In 133 BC Attalus III, the last king of Pergamum, died,
leaving his empire to Rome. The Romans were not keen on
saddling themselves with a troublesome eastern empire, and
they retained only the core of Ionia and Caria, but gave away
Lycia, Pamphylia and Cilicia. They were never particularly
interested in the south coast, and it was only the activities of
the pirates here which eventually roused them to send
Pompey in 67 BC to eradicate the pirates from the whole of the
south coast for once and for all.

The three centuries of Roman rule were in general peaceful
and prosperous, and many of the most splendid monuments,
such as the theatre at Aspendos, date from this period.
Christianity did not take hold in the region till the end of the
3rd C when a considerable Christian community built up.
Side and Antalya had also Jewish communities.

ANTALYA AND THE INLAND RETURN TO İZMIR

The initial approach to Antalya from Lycia is not very salubrious as the road takes you past the industrial port area. In the peak holiday period the long beach which runs up from the port to the city is packed to bursting with thousands of holiday-makers' tents. A few US Navy ships usually stand in the bay, and in the seafront restaurants American naval personnel are often to be heard talking ship.

A place to avoid   **Antalya** is a generally unpleasant place. It is more expensive than comparable towns, fraught with hassle and unfriendly lethargic inhabitants — a rude shock after emerging from the charm and hospitality of Lycia. The traveller would do best staying outside it somewhere along the Lara beach road near the **Duden Falls**. These waterfalls are a spectacular sight with the Duden river cascading over the vertical cliff edge down into the sea. About one kilometre west of the falls are the scant remains of ancient **Magydus**, a port pre-dating Antalya, now partly occupied by a small Nato establishment.

At **Lara** there is a good choice of hotels and pensions, some set in small coves with private beaches. The road to Lara branches off from the main road to Antalya at a major junction with traffic lights just east of the clock tower. This road does not unfortunately rejoin the main coast road further on, so the traveller must return to this junction before continuing on to Perge.

Antalya's Seljuk and Ottoman Heritage

Founded by Attalus II of Pergamum in the 2nd C BC (later than the other cities of the Pamphylian plain), Antalya has been the main port on the south coast of Turkey for the last 2000 years, taking over from Side. During the Crusades, Antalya was the point of embarkation for the Christian armies who sailed from here to the Holy Land to avoid the long and difficult journey across Anatolia. However, as so often when a city is inhabited continuously, the original buildings have disappeared and only a few Roman monuments remain from antiquity. The chief interest of the town today lies in its later Seljuk and Ottoman monuments. Antalya was first captured by the Seljuk Turks in 1207, who lost it about 100 years later to the Hamitoğlu emirs of Eğridir. Then in 1391 it was taken by the Ottomans under Murat I and remained under Ottoman rule till the end of the empire in 1922.

The two centuries of Seljuk rule in Anatolia produced some of the loveliest architecture to be seen in Turkey today. The style is always highly distinctive, with its red brickwork

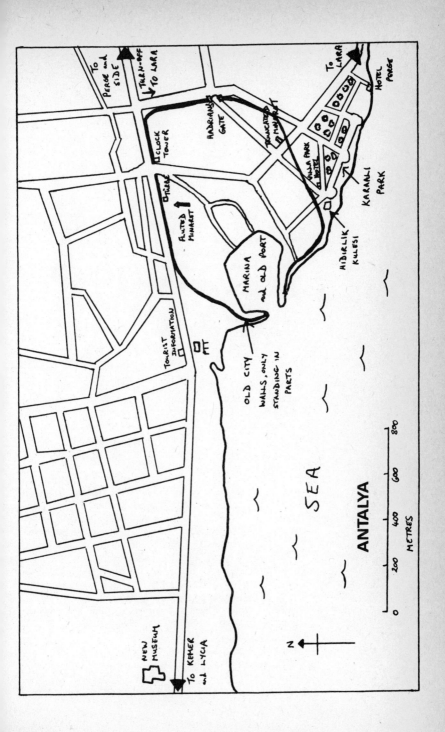

and often elaborate carving in wood or stone on the interiors and entrances. With the notable exception of the famous fortifications of Alanya, most of their architecture is found in the form of public buildings, particularly mosques, hans (caravanserais) and madrasas (Koranic schools). A tour of the monuments of Antalya can be done in a half day, and it is pleasant to spend a morning walking around the old part of the town near the clock tower and the monumental triple arch of Hadrian, built in honour of Hadrian's visit in AD 130.

A Walk Around Antalya

Descending from the steep road leading down from the clock tower on the main street and turning immediately right, you arrive first at the **Yivli Minare** (the Fluted Minaret), conspicuous from many parts of the town. It was built in the early 13th C by the Seljuk Sultan Alaeddin Keykubad, founder of Alanya. The building next to it, its six cupolas supported by columns with Ionic and Corinthian capitals, was originally a church, then converted to a mosque. In the upper courtyard of the mosque is an 18th C *tekke* (monastery) which once housed a community of Mevlevi dervishes. Any one of the winding lanes downhill from here will lead eventually to the old harbour area at the foot of the cliff. Along this walk are **Ottoman houses** with elaborately painted woodwork, gradually falling into decay, though many of them are still lived in.

(margin: Fluted Minaret)

Climbing up the hillside on the far side, you may find among the maze of streets, more by accident than design, the **Kesik Minare** (the Truncated Minaret). Originally a 5th C Byzantine basilica, was converted to a mosque during the Seljuk period and a minaret was added. In a later fire the minaret lost its pointed top and consequently it came to be known as the Kesik (incomplete) Minaret. It is now a derelict ruin. At the summit of the hill by the entrance to the **Keraali Park** are the remains of a tower called the **Hídírlík Kulesi**. It dates from the 2nd C AD and has been variously described as a defensive tower or a lighthouse, due to its position on the clifftop, but its form, with a round tower on a square base is also characteristic of a type of Roman tomb or mausoleum. It stands about 15 metres high in two storeys, the lower square, the upper round, and resembles Hadrian's mausoleum in Rome. It is on the cliff edge of the Karaali Park, beyond its little zoo, that some of the best restaurants can be found, suitable for lunch or dinner. Their spectacular views towards the mountains of Lycia give the best appreciation of Antalya's setting.

(margin: Truncated Minaret)

(margin: Meal with a view)

The only other place worth visiting in Antalya is the newly opened **Museum**, on the western outskirts of town on the main road (open 8am to noon, 1.30 to 5pm except Mondays). Originally housed in the Yivli Minare till 1971, it moved to its

Antalya: the Fluted Minaret with the mountains of Lycia behind

new building which was then closed for extensive repairs and restoration work from 1982, only reopening in April 1985. Quite what has taken so long to prepare is rather baffling. The building is expensively laid out inside and spacious, but there are scarcely any labels telling the visitor what he is looking at, where the exhibits were found or anything at all about them. Perhaps they are still in the process of the labelling and this will be completed some day. Most of the impressive displays, eg the statues, the highly carved sarcophagi and the mosaics, appear to come from Perge, and some of these, in particular the sarcophagi, are very fine. The bronze of Priapus usually attracts a crowd. The ethnic section showing costume and dress is enjoyable, but the carpet display is very disappointing, most being modern, with only four genuinely old carpets from the famous centres of Gördes, Uşak and Ladik.

No information The Tourist Information Office is not worth calling at for anything other than the most basic information on Antalya itself: the world beyond Antalya is unknown to them.

From Antalya, the Return Route to İzmir via Burdur, Dinar, Denizli and Pamukkale

If you have a fortnight's holiday from a starting point of İzmir or Kuşadasí, and have driven along the coast so far, a good option for the return journey is via Burdur, Dinar and Denizli, for the road is fast and it brings you back via Pamukkale and Aphrodisias.

Detour into the Stone Age The road to Burdur is wide and good, a dual-carriageway in parts. Still on the outskirts of Antalya, before the climb up onto the Anatolian plateau, the white domes of Ottoman cisterns can be seen in the central reservation, and a yellow sign points off right, 14km, to the **Upper Duden Falls**, as spectacular as the lower falls but more of a detour. Just off the main road is the **Karain Cave**, with a small museum devoted to the Stone Age way of life. About 30 km before Burder a fork leads off to **Sagalassos**, one of the major Pisidian cities along with Termessos and Selge. Its setting, like the other Pisidian cities, is striking, but the detour is considerable and the site itself is 1½ hours' walk from the village of Ağlasun. Also there is less to see here than at Termessos or Selge. If you are aiming to reach Pamukkale that evening, it does not leave a great deal of time for detours.

Just before Burdur you pass the remarkable **Iksuyu Caves**, well worth a stop and directly on the main road. Here you can walk round a series of extensive interlinked caves with underwater lakes and stalactites and stalagmites. This is a favourite place for family outings and picnics from Burdur on Sundays.

Picnic On this whole stretch between Antalya and Denizli, the only restaurants are at a petrol station before Dinar and along the roadside just after Dinar. Neither is particularly salubrious. If you can, take a picnic lunch for this route as the scenery is varied and attractive and there are many likely picnic spots.

The road to Pamukkale (14 km) forks off right, immediately before Denizli. The total drive from Antalya to Pamukkale non-stop is about four hours, and from Side about five hours.

TERMESSOS: THE EAGLE'S NEST

A visit to Termessos, known as the Eagle's Nest, 1500 metres high in the mountains behind Antalya, is one of the most exciting excursions in Turkey. To do it justice a whole day should be allowed for it from Antalya, or at least a long afternoon, for to see the site and enjoy it without rushing takes a minimum of four hours. The drive from Antalya takes about 45 minutes, and is on a good road, clearly signposted, following the main road north to Burdur then forking off left towards Korkuteli. From the Korkuteli road the final 9 km is a specially constructed forest track leading up to the site, with turnstile buildings at the bottom charging a small fee for entrance. Before this track was built, the walk up to the site was two hours: now it is 15 minutes by car. The road is a bit bumpy in places, but presents no real problems. There is no restaurant or place for refreshments at the site, so if you are going for the day it is advisable to take provisions, especially of the liquid variety, as the climbing involved is thirsty work. Camping at the site is forbidden.

Aggressive and independent spirit

The atmosphere of **Termessos** belongs in spirit to Lycia. You cannot help feel that anyone who chose to build in such a high remote place, must, like the Lycians, have had a fierce love of independence. Where they differed in character from the Lycians however was in their warlike nature, and in each mention of them in history they are initiating the aggression against neighbouring cities, whereas the Lycians fought only in self-defence.

A History of Autonomy

Termessos was never a Greek city like the cities of Perge and Aspendos on the plain. It was in fact Pisidian, Pisidia being the ancient name given to the mountainous hinterland of the Pamphylian plain reaching back to the lakes at Burdur, Isparta and Beyşehir. the Pisidians themselves were always known as a fierce warlike people living a rough life in their mountain retreats. The inhabitants of Termessos called themselves Solymians, after the ancient Mt Solymus, the mountain under which the city stands. The fierceness of these people must have been legendary in ancient times, for Homer relates that the second seemingly impossible task set for Bellerophon after slaying the Chimaera was to overcome the Solymi.

Alexander meets his match

The foundation date of Termessos is unknown, but the first specific mention of it in history is in 333 BC when Alexander, sweeping eastwards with all cities falling to him, came up against a city here that was so impregnable and well-defended that after camping below it for one night he decided to waste no more time and moved on.

Around 200 BC we learn from an inscription found in Lycia that Termessos was at war with the Lycian League. When the Romans took the region from Persian rule, Lycia was given to Rhodes but Termessos was granted independence with a treaty of friendship. This independence was openly flaunted by printing on all the coins of that period 'Autonomous', and never showing the head or title of a Roman emperor or governor.

The ruins of the city, despite being overgrown, have a grandeur rarely equalled, and Termessos was clearly a wealthy city. The origin of this wealth must have come from domination of nearby trade routes, as olive trees were the only produce the city cultivated itself. George Bean puts forward the theory that the fortification wall with its towers still standing much lower down the hillside from the city itself was built to give them control of the valley, so that they could demand a toll from all who passed that way. Previous writers have postulated that this wall was built by the people of the Pamphylian plain to keep the Termessians in their mountain fortress, but this seems rather far-fetched.

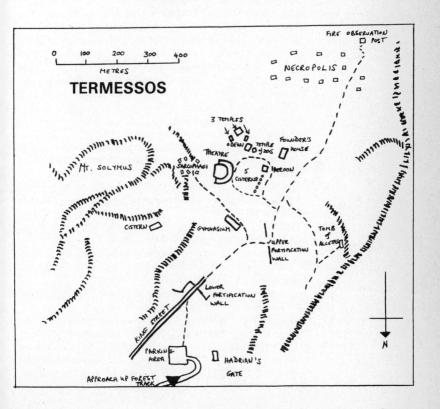

Termessos' major period of prosperity was in the 2nd and 3rd C AD, and most of the ruins date from this period. Towards the end of the 3rd C the population decreased as the city's fortunes declined, and it was abandoned altogether in the 5th C.

Entering the Site

As you approach the site by car, the remnants of the **outer city walls and towers** are signposted but difficult to see. In the grassy open car parking area at the foot of the main site stands the monumental **gate of Hadrian** with a well-preserved doorway and the sunken, now stagnant remains of a spring-house.

Climb to city

It is also from this parking area that a widish path leads off up towards the main buildings of the site. The climb is fairly stiff and takes about 20 minutes up to the first major buildings. On the way up the occasional sign will be passed, several indicating **King Street**, the main street of the ancient city which crosses the path on a number of occasions. Clearly keen to develop the site as a tourist attraction for visitors from Antalya, the authorities have put up neat little signs indicating most of the major buildings. One sign indicates the **aqueduct** and **cistern**: these are situated high in the cliff face to the left of the path, a remarkable feat of engineering. The path then passes the **lower and upper city walls**, both huge constructions which clearly indicate how well the city was defended, and how easily any potential conqueror was daunted.

The first building of the main city is reached off to the left of the path: the **gymnasium**. This is an impressive building standing very high with a **bath complex** alongside. It is in the characteristically dark grey stone blocks of Termessos and the charm of its appearance is enhanced by its overgrown state. No excavation or restoration work has been carried out at Termessos, which adds to the wild feel of the place. Occasional hacking back of the undergrowth is the most that has happened.

The path leads on past the gymnasium, suddenly opening out in a cluster of sarcophagi with splendid views across the mountains. From here the mountain goats among you can scramble up the steep hillside to the right and approach the theatre from the stage entrance. Alternatively, follow the path back past the gymnasium to rejoin the main path, and shortly afterwards a sign points left to the theatre.

Magnificent theatre

The setting of the **theatre** is the most magnificent in Turkey, even exceeding that at Pergamum. The cavea is in Greek style, and could have held about 5000 spectators. The stage building is Roman, with the small doors onto the orchestra from which the wild beasts entered still visible. Just before the theatre is the open grassy agora, at the far end of which stands the high side wall of the **odeon** in beautifually finished stone blocks. Climbing up inside it is something of a disappointment as there is nothing but a heap of rubble with only traces of the top row of seats visible. Immediately next door to the odeon is a small temple. This is thought to be the **Temple of Zeus Solymeus**, guardian of Termessos and god of war. Beyond this are remains of buildings among the undergrowth, one of which, the Founder's House, described in detail by George Bean on his visit here in the 1960s, has now totally collapsed and become a heap of blocks.

Walking round in front of the stage wall side of the odeon through the undergrowth, the remains of a faint path will be found leading across to the remains of **three temples** in unusual proximity to one another. These too are heaps of collapsed stones now. The first still has its door standing with a separate inscription stone in front dedicated to Artemis by one Aurelia Armasta in the 3rd C AD. From here if you cross towards the cliff edge jumping from one stone to another you will see the portal, lintel missing, of an unidentified temple. From here a stone stairway cut into the rock leads up to the collapsed ruins of a third temple, the earlier and main temple to Artemis on the site. It was in Doric style, and two reliefs were found among the stones which confirmed its dedication to Artemis. All the blocks seem to be here, and maybe one day this site will be transformed by the re-erection of many of these buildings.

Following the path round the far side of the agora, it leads past the unusual **Heroon**, cut into the rock, with a flight of steps leading up to a six-metre square platform at the back of which is a grave pit sunk into the rock. It is not known whose tomb this was, but he was clearly a man of great standing to have the honour of his tomb set up in the market place in this way, rather than in the necropolis.

The Necropolis
The path leads next past five interlinked **cisterns**, each with a hole in the ground and not to be fallen down at dusk. Shortly after returning to the main path there is a major fork, left off to the necropolis, right to the tomb of Alcetas. If you want to get all the climbing over with and know it is all downhill from then on, it is best to climb on up to the necropolis first.

Hillside littered with sarcophagi

This path winds up through a remarkable hillside littered in sarcophagi dating from the first three centuries AD. The sheer profusion and extent of the tombs defies description. Suffice to say that it would take at least two days to see each one. Some of the particularly fine sarcophagi with carvings have secondary paths leading off to them. Many carry inscriptions, over 650 of which have been read and published, consisting largely of threats against violation.

If you have the energy it is worth climbing beyond the

tombs up to the hut at the top which you can see from below. This is a fire observation post, and the views from the top over the mountain ranges in all directions are staggering: this really is the Eagle's Nest.

Suicide of Alexander's General

Descending the hill again and forking off left to the **tomb of Alcetas**, the path leads off for about 10 minutes climbing a little in places but mainly on the flat. The path then turns suddenly and ends in a cave-like tomb with extraordinary carvings on the rock face. The tomb is unusual; the carvings have unfortunately suffered from defacement in recent years, but still clearly visible is a mounted soldier, with a suit of armour, a helmet, a shield and a sword. It is thought to belong to Alcetas, one of Alexander's generals, who is associated with Termessos.

After Alexander's death, Antigonus, another of Alexander's generals, was trying to take control of Asia. Alcetas was among those who opposed him, and after Antigonus defeated him totally, Alcetas fled to Termessos to take refuge. Antigonus followed and demanded his surrender. The Termessians were divided, with the elders wanting to give him up and the young men wanting to fight for him. Through trickery, however, the elders had their way, and Alcetas, seeing what was about to happen, killed himself. The young men of Termessos were furious and gave Alcetas a splendid burial in atonement. In the carvings Alcetas is wearing armour identical to that worn by Alexander in the famous mosaic of the Battle of Issus in Naples. This tomb is by far the earliest at Termessos, dating from the end of the 4th C BC.

If you are fortunate enough to visit Termessos when no one else is there, the remoteness and wildness of the setting will make a deep impression, and can even be quite frightening at the onset of dusk. Mountain goats graze wild in the hills and can be seen with binoculars at dusk, and rare butterflies like the White Admiral can be seen at certain times of the year.

Calling at a Caravanserai

If it is not yet dark on your return from Termessos you could make a short detour to **Evdir Hani**, one of the finest examples of a Seljuk caravanserai.

Resting place between the coast and the Taurus mountains

Before the village of Yukarikaraman (about 7 km before the Korkuteli road rejoins the main Burdur-Antalya road), and just after crossing a bridge over a stream, there is a coffee house with a track leading off left. This track is driveable with care and leads direct to Evdir Hani. Built between 1213 and 1219 by Sultan Keykavus, it is one of a series he built linking his capital at Konya with the Pamphylian ports as resting places for trading caravans travelling over the Taurus mountains. This one is larger than most, with a particularly

The apocalyptic necropolis at Termessos

handsome entrance on the south side, with the traditional beehive domed carving.

Before reading the caravanserai, the track leads through the scattered ruins of an ancient town, with several sarcophagi, a small temple with some carved blocks, and many water channels, the main one passing close by the caravanserai still in use. Inscriptions confirm that this was a dependancy of Termessos.

PERGE

The site of **Perge** lies just 5 km east of Antalya, 2 km north of the main coastal road. The flatness of Perge could not contrast more sharply with mountainous Termessos, but the site does have other distinguishing features, notably its round Hellenistic gates and well made main street. Having impressive ruins and being easy to visit, it is a common stopping place for coach tours. About three hours should be allowed for a tour of the site.

Excavations and History

Perge has been the subject of extensive excavations since 1946 under various Turkish parties, but in spite of this there remains a mystery: the whereabouts of the cult temple of Artemis Pergeia. This goddess, like the more famous Artemis of Ephesus, seems to have been a Hellenised version of the ancient Anatolian mother goddess. The ancient coins of the region show the dominance of the cult of the goddess throughout Pamphylia and Pisidia in her primitive multi-breasted form similar to Artemis Polymastros at Ephesus. Her temple at Perge grew rich with the offerings of her worshippers, provoking Verres, an early Roman governor of Pamphylia, to plunder the contents. The neighbouring hillsides and hilltops have been thoroughly searched, with a party of Turkish archaeologists sinking trenches in to all the likely-looking places on the hill, but finding nothing. Although the temple is still missing, the excavators were successful in discovering a wealth of statues and elaborate reliefs, many of which form an impressive display in the new museum at Antalya.

There is no doubt that Perge was founded by the 'mixed multitude' of Greeks who migrated across Asia Minor after the fall of Troy. Statue bases bearing the names Mopsus and Calchas, two of the main leaders of the migration, have been excavated near the main gate of the city. This original settlement was in fact on the low hill immediately behind the ruins we see today, but nothing of that remains. Perge's first appearance in recorded history, as with several other places along this coast, occurs with the arrival of Alexander the Great in 333 BC. The Pergeans offered Alexander no resistance at all, and even sent guides in advance of his arrival to lead his army from Phaselis over the mountains to the north.

After Alexander's death, Perge came under the Syrian Seleucid kings, and at this point the city was extended to the lower slopes and fortified, and these are the walls and gates we see today. It was at this time that Perge produced its only famous citizen, Apollonius, the mathematician who was the

Missing temple

first to make a study of the properties of ellipses and to conceive the epicyclic system of the universe, later developed by Ptolemy. Perge finally passed under Roman rule in 188 BC, growing in prosperity so that many of the monuments we see today date from the early centuries of the Roman imperium. Like Aspendos and Sillyon, the city went into a slow decline at the beginning of the Seljuk period, and was not resettled to any extent in modern times.

Getting Your Bearings
A tour of the site brings you first to the **theatre**, which is separate from the main city. Entry tickets are bought here. It is well preserved, built originally in the Greek style, then later converted to the Roman style, and would have held about 15,000 spectators. Some fine carved reliefs are still *in situ* in the stage building, principally of Dionysus, god of wine and of the theatre. On the outside wall of the stage building, five niches can be seen where the building later served as a public fountain.

Professional sportsmen

For orientation, it is worth climbing to the top seats of the theatre, as it affords a good view across the plain towards the main city and the stadium. This **stadium** is, after that at Aphrodisias, the best preserved in Asia Minor, with a seating capacity about the same as the theatre. The vaulted chambers under the rows of seats were used as shops, some of them still bearing the name of the owner and his trade. Annual athletics festivals were commonplace in all large cities from Hellenistic times onwards. By Roman times sport had long since become professionalised, and each summer athletes made their way from city to city in search of prize money and of the prestige they could look forward to on return to their home town.

Driving across the main part of the site, about 1 km further on there is a second hut, not for tickets, but selling soft drinks, postcards and booklets: there is no restaurant here. It is the golden-stoned circular **Hellenistic gate towers** which first catch the eye among the ruins of the main city. They are the only monuments surviving from the Hellenistic period; the main street leads off beyond them towards the old acropolis hill where the earlier settlement was. Between the two towers is a low wall forming a horseshoe-shaped courtyard, added in later Roman times for ornamentation. The niches in the wall once held statues of the founders of the city.

Passing through the Gates of the City
Passing through the gates, the extensive remains of **Roman baths** can be seen on the left, recently cleared by the excavators. On the other side of the main street is the **agora**, again recently cleared, surrounded by a **stoa**, its granite columns topped with Corinthian capitals. In many places the walkway round still has its black and white *mosaic paving*. The circular

Colonnaded Street

building in the middle of the agora must have been a *decorative monument* with statues.

You should return now to the **colonnaded main street**, the most pleasing feature of the city. The *ruts of chariot and cart wheels* can still be seen in the paving. The street must have been magnificent, 20 metres wide and with a broad *water channel* running down the centre for its full 300-metre length, fed from the nymphaeum at the acropolis end. The colonnaded porticoes lining each side had numerous shops; in front of one of these the marble slab in the form of a games board was found, now on display in the Antalya museum. Near the top of some of the marble columns, just under the Corinthian capitals, are some unusual *reliefs*, small but lovely. One shows Artemis Pergeia holding a bow, an arrow and a torch; another, less well-preserved, shows Apollo with a crown in a four-horse chariot; and a third shows a man dressed in a toga pouring a libation at an altar: this is possibly the founder of the city, Calchas.

Paul's first converts
Further up the street to the left are the ruins of a **basilica** where St Paul, arriving from Cyprus, met St Banrabus. Paul is said to have delivered his first sermons and won his first converts here. Further into the undergrowth is another baths.

Where the road arrives at a crossroads shortly before the foot of the low escarpment hill, extensive excavations have been conducted and the area has been fenced off to visitors. But if you are able to walk on into this area you will see a **nymphaeum** at the end of the street, built into the foot of the acropolis hill. From here, the water channel down the centre of the main street was fed. Turning left at the crossroads, an open square can be seen just to the right of the road which has been identified as a **palaestra**, the open courtyard usually next to a gymnasium where exercises were done. Its south wall is still quite well preserved with many windows overlooking the street. It is dated to AD 50 by an inscription to the Emperor Claudius found on it, which makes it the earliest dated building at Perge after the Hellenistic gates. The ruins left on the acropolis hilltop are all of a later date, mainly Byzantine.

Street of tombs
The tombs at Perge were laid out, in the normal way, beside the roads leading to the city gates. It was on the road leading out beyond the palaestra that a handsome street of tombs was found in 1946 by the Turkish Historical Society. More than 30 sarcophagi were discovered, elaborately sculptured and decorated. Many of them are on display in the Antalya museum.

The Role of Women

If you have just visited the Antalya museum the many statues on display from Perge will be fresh in your memory, along with the tales of the generosity of Plankia Magna, the city's most eminent citizen. At least 20 texts and inscriptions have

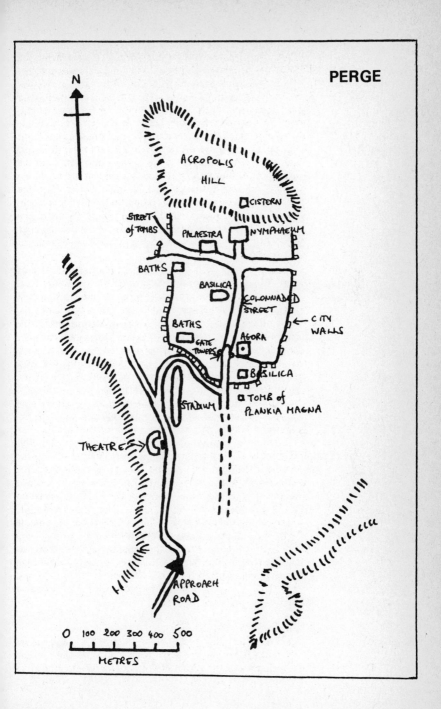

PERGE

N

ACROPOLIS HILL

CISTERN

STREET of TOMBS

PALAESTRA

NYMPHAEUM

BATHS

BASILICA

COLONNADED STREET

BATHS

← CITY WALLS

GATE TOWERS

AGORA

BASILICA

STADIUM

TOMB of PLANKIA MAGNA

THEATRE ←

APPROACH ROAD

0 100 200 300 400 500

METRES

been found on the site recording buildings or statues erected by this lady. She was the priestess of Artemis and the Mother of the Gods, and held the highest office in the city, that of demiurgus. The remains of **Plankia Magna's tomb** can still be seen outside the site fence before the hut at the main entrance to the site, lying in a field carefully cultivated around by the local farmers.

Dominant goddesses

Throughout Anatolia it was the female deity rather than the male that was dominant. Atemis predominated over her brother Apollo, apart from his oracular role. The figure of woman was worshipped in its many-breasted, enlarged-hipped form as representing the fertility through which the sacred seed of the ancestors was propagated. The Artemis figure at Ephesus is the most famous example. Women also played a large part in religious ceremonies and public festivals. The annual festival at the Letoon, the national shrine of Lycia, was presided over by a woman; at Patara and at Termessos, as well as at Perge, dedications still visible show that women ordered their construction.

War-skilled queens

The Lycians carried on the custom of their Cretan ancestors by tracing their lineage from the mother's side. The Carians, too, were thought to have partly Cretan origins, and Herodotus saw similarities in their customs to the Lycians. The Carian women of Miletos never called the man with whom they lived husband. In the 5th C BC the Carian Queen Artemisia earned the admiration of the Persian King Darius in her daring war strategems. A hundred years later the second Queen Artemisia ruled after the death of her brother-husband Mausolus, taking precedence over a younger brother. She too earned fame through her cunning defeat of Rhodes.

For women to actually hold the reins of political power like this was nevertheless rare. More often it was in religious activities as priestesses that they made their contribution. Indeed there is an important distinction to be drawn between a matrilineal society where lineage is traced on the maternal side, and between rule by women, for it does not seem to have followed that the one led to the other. The role of women as fertile perpetuators of the seed can be respected and even worshipped, but the men usually held the political power. As one historian put it: 'Ariadne is the very sacred queen, but Minos is the king'.

TO SILLYON AND ASPENDOS

Severe landslip

Lying between Perge and Aspendos, the acropolis of **Sillyon** rising up out of the flat coastal plain is visible from a long way off regardless of the direction of your approach. Considering how close to the main road and to Perge, Aspendos and Side the site is, it is surprising that it has not been more developed. Clearly not many people visit it, as there is no guardian and no refreshments on offer. Yet a visit is definitely worthwhile, for the city has several special features, mainly as a result of the severe landslip in 1969 that caused half the monuments to fall over the cliff, leaving the other half behind on the edge. For this reason Sillyon can be more interesting to visit than some of the better known sites. You should allow at least three and a half hours.

The distinctive yellow sign points you off inland 8 km and the road is tarmac through the village. As it bends round east in a sort of village ring-road, there is another tarmac road (unsignposted) leading directly towards the acropolis. The tarmac soon peters out, and in summer the last 4 km is perfectly good dirt track: in the wet season there may be flooding. Where there is a fork, follow the more major and that which leads towards the left side of the acropolis. There has long been talk of improving the road, but the villagers are too lazy to do it themselves and are still waiting for the government to do it for them.

At the foot of the ruins is a small hamlet. The traveller may be finding the natives a bit wearing by now, and children proffering flowers and wanting to accompany you round the site may have more nuisance value than charm: reactions will doubtless differ.

Ascending the Acropolis of Sillyon

Approach ramps

Walking up the side of the hill towards the acropolis, there is much evidence of landslip and the side buttresses of supporting walls have all slipped to lie almost horizontally. Looking up at the acropolis, you will first see the **lower gate**, with two towers and a horsehsoe court, similar to those at Perge and Side, but smaller. Higher up you will see the impressive **southern ramp** leading up the side of the hill. Two ramps were constructed for ease of ascent up into the ancient city, the northern and the southern. Of the **northern ramp** only the top section remains, and we will make our descent from that. The southern ramp is remarkably well-preserved on its lower part, consisting of a 6-metre wide roadway, handsomely paved, supported by buttresses. The two ramps originally joined at the top at a small courtyard before the upper city gate.

Now, however, the best route to approach the acropolis is through the lower city gate, then passing the impressive bastions on your left as you climb. To reach the summit takes about 15 to 20 minutes. There is a path of sorts higher up, but initially there is a lot of loose rock underfoot, and the exploration of this site is definitely for the strong-ankled.

A show that will have you on the edge of your seat

Reaching the top, you will have a splendid view over the plain. In front of you is the side retaining wall of the **theatre**, and what you see as you round it makes you gasp: on the edge of the sheer precipice are just the top seven or eight rows of the theatre seats. The rest fell with an almighty crash in a huge land-slide in 1969 down into the plain, and massive blocks of seats are still visible in the rubble below. The odeon disappeared altogether. Before 1969, the sight was also remarkable, for an earthquake long ago had cut a deep chasm between the theatre and the stage building.

Walking on along the cliff top you soon come to a series of attractive rock **foundations of houses** with rock-cut stairways. The setting is dramatic, with some having half disappeared over the edge. A little further on, the handsomely crafted blocks of half a **temple** can be seen on the edge of the cliff. Just near this is a long **underground cistern** with gratings in the roadway.

Those who are feeling energetic can walk right round the edge of the plateau and approach the large buildings on the inland side from the other direction. This is quite a long walk, and you may prefer just to retrace your steps to the theatre and then head across towards these buildings. It is best to stick to a path if you can find one, as otherwise the ground underfoot is pretty uneven. Several underground cisterns can be seen on the way across.

Window fastenings

The first building you come to is of Hellenistic date, with a very long and extremely well-preserved west wall, 55 metres long and 6 metres high in parts, with ten windows. The third window in from the cliff edge shows a good example of the curious fastenings the building would once have had for its wooden shutters. Obviously some kind of public building, it is thought most likely to have been the **portico of a palaestra**.

A little further east behind the wall of the palaestra, and now rather overgrown, is a smaller **Hellenistic building** of unknown purpose, but interesting for the extensive *inscription* carved on the inside of the doorframe. This inscription is the only evidence, apart from the coins, that exists of the Pamphylian language, a dialect of Greek spoken here and at Perge and Aspendos, but different to the strange language spoken at Side.

By far the largest of this cluster of buildings is a huge construction, standing very tall with windows set high up in the walls. This was the **keep of a Seljuk fortress** built in the 13th C within the fortifications of the earlier city. Nearby is another building of similar date which was probably Seljuk living quarters within the fortified city.

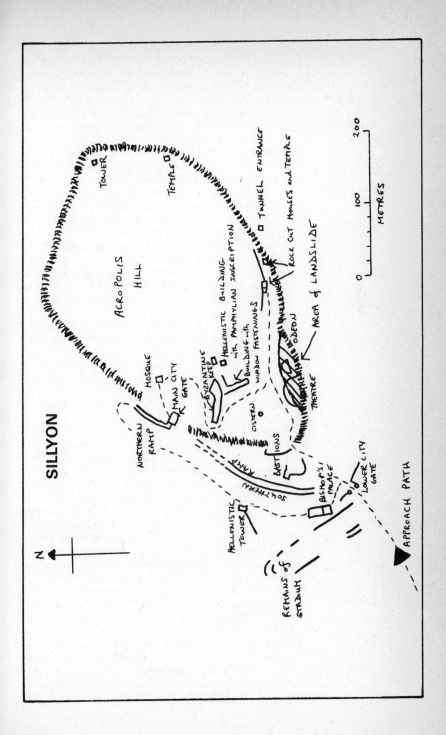

SILLYON

N

ACROPOLIS HILL

TOWER

TEMPLE

TUNNEL ENTRANCE

ROCK CUT HOUSES and TEMPLE

AREA of LANDSLIDE

ODEON

HELLENISTIC BUILDING with PAMPHYLIAN INSCRIPTION

BUILDING with WINDOW FASTENINGS

THEATRE

MOSQUE

MAIN CITY GATE

BYZANTINE KEEP

CISTERN

NORTHERN RAMP

SOUTHERN RAMP

BASTIONS

BISHOP'S PALACE

LOWER CITY GATE

HELLENISTIC TOWER

REMAINS of STADIUM

APPROACH PATH

0   100   200

METRES

233

Getting Down Again

Continuing towards the inland edge of the acropolis, you clamber over the extensive rubble of many collapsed buildings, heading for the small dome of what was once a **Seljuk mosque**, now used as a cowshed. From this point, the northern ramp begins the descent out through the huge **upper city gate**, still well-preserved. The ramp soon deteriorates into a small path further down. As you continue towards the village at the bottom, there is a good view up of the southern ramp and the defence bastions. Further down is an excellently preserved **Hellenistic fortification tower**. It is intact apart from its roof, but a bad crack above the door is the first sign that it may not be for much longer. It was originally joined on to defence walls which have now disappeared.

The descent leads on down through the large building thought to be the **Byzantine palace** from the time when Sillyon was the seat of a local bishop, converted from an earlier gymnasium. The poorly preserved stadium here is difficult to find because it merges with the crops and outlying huts of the village.

A curious tunnel

One final curious feature of Sillyon remains, though it is difficult to visit. It is a **tunnel** running about 30 metres into the hillside from a point about halfway up the slope at the foot of the acropolis cliff under the ruins of the temple above. There is an *outer chamber* from which a small passage less than half a mete wide leads to *three inner rooms*. This was initially thought to be a series of grave chambers, but it is now generally agreed to be the source of a spring, now all but dried up, probably as a result of the serious seismic shocks the hill has endured. Even in the dry season, a strip of green vegetation just below the entrance shows that something of the spring must still survive.

Historical Footnote

Sillyon was founded, like the other Pamphylian cities, by Greeks migrating into Asia Minor after the Trojan War. When Alexander arrived here in 333 BC he took Perge, Aspendos and Side easily, but met resistance at Sillyon. Naturally defended by virtue of its position on the sheer-sided acropolis, historians also record that Sillyon had foreign mercenaries among its fighters, as well as native barbarians. Alexander's first attack was rebuffed and before he could mount a second, news reached him of Aspendos' disobedience, and he immediately returned thence. Sillyon, having no river like Perge or Aspendos, was not a maritime city, so Alexander, whose main aim in Pamphylia was to prevent the Persians from building up a naval base on the southern coast, felt it was not worth the trouble of a siege: he did not return to it after punishing Aspendos for its insurrection.

Aspendos and Its Theatre

Aspendos, boasting the finest example of a Roman theatre, indeed of any ancient theatre, anywhere in the world, lies just 20 minutes' drive east from Perge, 4 km inland from the main coast road. David Hogarth who excavated at Knossos and Ephesus wrote in 1909: 'You may have seen amphitheatres in Italy, France, Dalmatia and Africa; temples in Egypt and Greece; palaces in Crete; you may be sated with antiquity, or scornful of it. But you have not seen the theatre of Aspendos'. It is indeed truly magnificent with quite exceptional acoustics, and is still used for performances.

Lunch on the river
A large recently built carpet house on the fork off from the main road testifies to the number of tourists now visiting the site. On the course of the old road, a lovely 13th C **Seljuk bridge** crosses the river, still in use and perfectly sound. Shortly before the acropolis, near the village of Belkis, an unlikely looking track forks off right to the pretty Belkis restaurant on the edge of the river, with an agreeable terrace on the water's edge. It has unfortunately now been discovered by coach tours, so it is best to eat here outside normal hours to avoid the crowds.

Final battle of the Persian Wars
Situated on the Eurymedon river, 12 km inland from the sea, Aspendos, like the other Pamphylian cities, was founded by Greek migrants after the Trojan War. Aspendos' first

Seljuk bridge over the Eurymedon river at Belkis where the Athenians followed up Salamis and Plataea with another blow to the Persians

mention in history is at the time of the Persian wars, when Darius and Xerxes, the great Persian kings, attempted in 490 BC and 480 BC to invade and subjugate Greece. After the Persian defeats at Salamis and Plataea, Xerxes collected a large army and fleet at Aspendos in preparation for a final battle. The Athenian general Kimon clashed here with Xerxes' fleet at the mouth of the Eurymedon. This sea battle was long and bitter, and ended finally in an Athenian victory. Flushed by his sea victory, Kimon decided to complete his work by defeating the Persian land forces as well. Since his forces were vastly outnumbered by the Persian army he devised a trick whereby he dressed up his soldiers in tiaras and Persian dress taken from his Persian prisoners, put them on captured Persians ships and sent them to land. The Persian land forces were deceived, welcoming the disguised Athenians as friends, and then with the element of surprise on their side the Athenians were able to overcome the Persians against the odds. With this battle the Persians were for a time eliminated from the south coast of Asia Minor. The Pamphylian cities, having supported the Persians, were not particularly pleased at the new Greek domination, despite their own Greek origins, and by 411 BC the Persians were once again using Aspendos as a naval base.

Punishment by Alexander

Like Perge, Aspendos did not oppose Alexander. When he moved on to Sillyon, however, the Aspendians changed their minds and began hastily to prepare for a siege, re-building the weak spots in their town walls. Hearing this news, Alexander immediately abandoned his attack on Sillyon and marched with his full force back to Aspendos. At this, the Aspendians lost their nerve and submitted, and were punished for their disobedience by the imposition of extra taxes.

After this, Aspendos shared Perge's history throughout the Hellenistic period. Under the Roman Empire, Aspendos prospered as a centre of commerce, producing salt from the nearby lake which dries in summer, cultivating vines and corn, and producing coarse Pamphylian wool from its sheep flocks.

Touring Aspendos

Approaching the acropolis, the road forks, and a driveable track leads round the left side of the acropolis for about 1 km straight to the extraordinary **aqueduct**. This is one of the most interesting Roman aqueducts in the world. The Pont du Garde and the aqueduct at Volubilis are better preserved, but this one illustrates very well the grasp the Romans had of the physics of water pressure. It brought the water from the mountains to the north of the city and at the tower about 100 metres from the acropolis hill raised it up again so that it could flow on to the main city on the acropolis. This tower is still intact and one can clamber up the steps inside with suitable care. It dates from the 2nd C AD.

Returning to the fork and continuing on the main road round the other side of the acropolis, you arrive at the **theatre**. No refreshments are sold here, but there is a wash-house with taps in the parking area. Tickets are sold at what was originally the actors' entrance. Spectators would have entered in Roman times from the two sides passages or vomitoria. It was built in the 2nd C AD, and apart from the

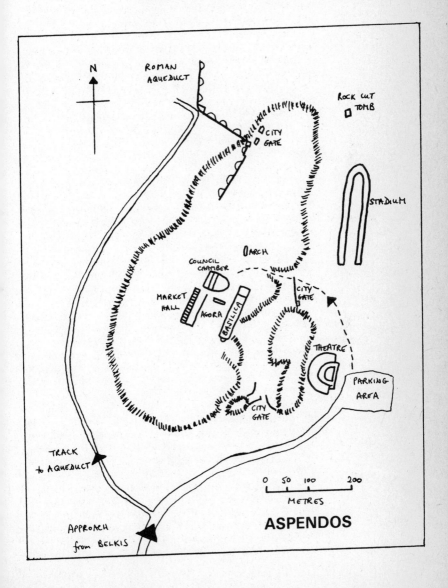

ASPENDOS

N

ROMAN AQUEDUCT

ROCK CUT TOMB

CITY GATE

STADIUM

ARCH

COUNCIL CHAMBER

MARKET HALL

AGORA

BASILICA

CITY GATE

THEATRE

PARKING AREA

CITY GATE

TRACK to AQUEDUCT

APPROACH from BELKIS

0   50   100   200

METRES

237

actual stage which was made of wood, and the statues which adorned the stage wall, it is virtually intact. A few damaged places on the end staircases and the arcade that runs round the top of the cavea have been repaired and restored in recent years, and the new stones used here do not yet match the old ones, though they will weather in time.

Fairy tale

The construction saga of the theatre is like a fairy tale: legend has it the daughter of the king of Aspendos was so beautiful that many suitors pursued her. Her father decreed that he would give her in marriage to the man who built a construction fo the welfare of Aspendos. One suitor declared he would increase Aspendos' water supply by building an aqueduct, while another declared he would improve the city's entertainments by building a theatre. Both embarked on their projects and completed them at the same time, whereupon the king decided the only way to keep his promise to each man was to cut the princes in half and give half to each suitor. On hearing this, the builder of the theatre proclaimed he would rather lose her to his rival than have this unhappy fate befall her; and this unselfishness earned him the hand of the princess.

Roman spectacles

The theatre is still used regularly for wrestling matches and other theatrical performances, especially during the annual Antalya festival in August. Today's performances are of course a far cry from the spectacles that would have taken place in the theatre in Roman times. Greek theatres with their open caveas forming slightly more than a semicircle meant that the seated audience faced out onto the surrounding countryside, and the actors performed on the floor of the semi-circular orchestra. The Romans, however, preferred a totally enclosed theatre, the backdrop provided by the tall stage building and the actors performing on the raised rectangle of the stage. More frequently, however, it was not actors or musicians who performed for the audience in Roman times, but wild animals, let in through small doors at the back of the stage, to provide gladiatorial-style spectacles for the edification of the audience. Today's wrestling matches are pretty tame stuff in comparison.

The *stage building* still stands to its full height, a remarkable feature, and you can even see above and below the top row of windows projecting blocks with holes which would have held upright wooden masts from which a huge awning was suspended over the audience. Above each of the original entrances to the left and right of the stage building, is a 'royal box', accessible from the stage. The stage wall itself would originally have been richly decorated with statues in the now empty niches. The only *relief* that remains shows Bacchus (Dionysos) with scrolls of flowers, presiding over the theatre of which he was patron. High up in the side walls of the stage are grooves slanting downwards towards the back stage wall. These would have held a wooden roof over the stage section, not so much as a protection for the actors, but as a sounding board to help the acoustics.

Seljuk palace The *coating of plaster* still decorating parts of the stage wall with red zig-zag painting dates from later Seljuk times. The Seljuks in fact renovated the theatre, converting the two-storey stage building into a palace, lining it with tiles, fragments of which are still visible. This partly accounts for the unusually good state of preservation of the stage wall today.

Many people, having seen the theatre, now leave feeling they have done Aspendos, unaware of the remainder of the ruins on the acropolis above. This is understandable, as part of the problem is that the ruins are not that accessible; neither are they visible from the theatre below, and reaching them involves either, via the direct route, a scramble out above the theatre and onto the hillside, or, the longer but easier route, by turning left northwards on coming out of the theatre and up through the east gate about 200 metres away. Reaching the ruins by either method is quite time-consuming, as the distances are longer than they appear. A visit to Aspendos including these ruins takes about three hours, whereas without them no more than one and a half hours.

For those who do however have the tiame and energy, a visit to the **acropolis ruins** at Aspendos is worthwhile, for though unexcavated they are nevertheless considerable. The main ruins are those of a **basilica cum market building** standing to a height of 16 metres, and a huge **nymphaeum**, also standing 16 metres high. This bears a striking resemblance to the nymphaeum at Side, and a dolphin's head with throat carved to form a water spout was found next to it. Other ruins include a market-hall, an agora, a council chamber, and a well-preserved ornamental arch. If the approach by the east gate is taken, the ruins of a **stadium** will also be seen to the right at the foot of the acropolis hill. For those willing to walk a little further round the acropolis hill to the north, a large rock-cut tomb with a vaulted entrance can be seen.

SIDE: RESORT AND RUINS

**Charming
resort and
sandy beaches**

Side, the ruins of the ancient city closely mingling with the modern town, is the most charming resort on the southern coast. It offers a host of hotels, motels, pensions, campsites and restaurants, many of them along the excellent sandy swimming beaches, and yet despite all this development it retains an identity of its own. It is also an excellent base for combining a few days' rest with visits to the sites of Aspendos, Sillyon, Selge, Seleuceia and the Manavgat waterfalls, while still being less than an hour's drive from Antalya and its airport.

There is only a very small fishing harbour, hardly noticeable from the beach, and not having a marina it is free from yachts and caiques. Small boats for waterskiing are the only craft to be seen apart from the occasional fishing boat. Side has long been a favourite resort for Turks as well as for foreigners, and so its atmosphere is that of a lively, genuinely Turkish resort, less spoilt and more authentic than Bodrum or Marmaris, or certainly than Kuşadasí. It derives great charm from the mix of the ruins with the town right up to the beach. Colourful shops abound in Side, and strolling among these in the evening before or after dinner is an excellent way to buy souvenirs or presents, as there is a varied selection, especially of jewellery, onyx and carpets.

Side lies on a promontory just 3 km south of the main coastal road from where the remains of the fine Roman aqueduct herald the outskirts of the town. The aqueduct carried water to the ancient city from the mountains, a distance of over 32 km. The approach road, just by a petrol station, snakes off towards the sea, passing a bewildering array of adverts for hotels and campsites, and then winds round a sharp bend under an arch just past the museum and the theatre. Just after this arch there is usually a barrier across the road and cars are made to stop in the parking area, thereby making the whole of the town a largely pedestrian precinct.

A visit to the ruins can easily be combined with a day on the beach, and in fact the route to one of the beaches leads right through the main area of ruins.

City of the Pomegranate
Of all the ancient cities on Turkey's southern shore, Side is the only one to have been systematically excavated, the task undertaken by the Archaeology Department at İstanbul University from 1947 to 1966. The effect has been to transform the site, for the British traveller Fellows, visiting Side in 1838, thought the ruins among the least interesting he had

seen, a view he would certainly change if he could see them today.

Side is a pre-Greek place name meaning pomegranate, a familiar symbol of fertility. Unlike the other Pamphylian cities, Side was not founded by Greeks migrating after the fall of Troy, but according to the historians Strabo and Arrian was founded by Greeks from Cyme, an Aeolian city on the Turkish coast north of İzmir. They worshipped Athena Nike, goddess of victory, and their coins, minted from 500 BC onwards, show a helmeted figure of Athena on one side and a pomegranate on the other. It is these coins which also illustrate the strange language of Side, quite different to the Pamphylian dialect of Greek spoken at Sillyon, Perge and Aspendos, and as yet undeciphered. It may have been the original Anatolian language of the region; it died out in Side after Alexander's arrival and his conquest of the Persian Empire. After this Greek became the official language all over the east and the indigenous local languages gradually disappeared.

Slave auctions Of Side's early history little is known, though Sideans were evidently not held in high esteem. Stratonicus, famous for his sharp tongue (see Caunus), when asked who was the most rascally of mankind is said to have answered: 'In Pamphylia, the men of Phaselis, in the whole world, the men of Side'. This may be connected to Side's fame in the 2nd C BC as a slave market. Strabo tells us that Cilician pirates used the harbour of Side as a dockyard where prisoners from their forays were sold as slaves at auctions. When in 67 BC Pompey cleared the coast of the pirates, the people of Side were quick to build a monument and statue in his honour to exonerate themselves, and we certainly know of no punishment that the Roman Senate imposed on them.

Moslem immigrants from Crete Under the Roman Empire Side flourished and most of the extant monuments date from this period. In early Byzantine times Side was the tenth metropolis under the Patriarchate of Constantinople and had 15 bishoprics under it. But with the Arab forays of the 7th C along the coast from their base in Syria the decline of the city set in; in the 10th C it was deserted totally after a fire. The present village on the site dates only from the beginning of this century when it was founded by a group of Greek-speaking Moslem exiles from Crete. After the earlier abandonment of the town sand began to drift in, blocking the old harbour and covering many of the ruins. It is likely that somewhere under this sand is the stadium which Side is known to have possessed but of which no trace has yet been found.

Approach to the On-site Museum
A complete tour of the site takes four hours, including the museum, or two hours if only the museum and the area round

the theatre are visited.

Fortifications As you approach from the main road, the **main city gate** is so ruined that you easily pass by it without noticing. The Hellenistic defence **walls**, however, inset with towers at intervals, especially to the left of the gate, are still impressive, and Side's flat position made these fortifications essential. Just outside the gate is a monumental fountain or **nymphaeum**, similar to that on the acropolis hill of Aspendos, its facade originally faced in marble, and in the Corinthian order, with a basin in front of it, erected in the 2nd C AD. Enthusiasts can walk along outside the defence walls on the left and enter through the **east gate**, a massive construction with two towers. Passing the ruins of a large 5th or 6th C basilica near a group of buildings identified as the Bishop's palace, you now return to the main gate along an **ancient street** of the city with column drums lying scattered from the original arcades and traces of *mosaic paving*. Foundations of *houses* can be seen alongside these streets, with marble paved courtyards and a cistern in each courtyard.

Museum in the bath house The main tarmac road now leads on to the heart of the city by the massive theatre, and to the museum just to the right of the road. The **museum** (9am to 12, 1.30 to 3pm) has been converted from the Roman baths of the 5th C and still retains the original room plan: the apodyterium (changing room), frigidarium (cold room with dip pool), tepidarium (warm room), sudatorium (steam room) and caldarium (hot bath room). It contains all the significant finds of the site including some of the finest Roman statues, carvings and reliefs found anywhere in Asia Minor. Many of these statues have unfortunately lost their heads, decapitated by over-zealous Christians soon after St Paul converted them to Christianity.

Downtown

Directly opposite the museum is the open square **agora**, in the centre of which is a circular base believed to be the foundations of a *temple to Tyche*, goddess of Fortune. A covered portico originally ran round all four sides of the agora with shops set off it. Here the prisoners of the pirates may well have been sold into slavery. In the west corner, backed up against the theatre, were the public latrines, consisting of a semi-circular arched passage lined with marble, originally containing 24 seats with a water channel beneath. One's daily achievements in classical times were not, as they are today, private affairs to be performed in solitary confinement, but rather an excuse for a social gathering. Since in all ancient sites there only ever seems to have been one set of latrines, not two, you wonder whether they were mixed, or whether the women were expected to confine themselves to the home facilities.

A social occasion Backed against the theatre near the road is an elegant monument in white marble, a **public fountain** with two water basins in front, built in AD 74 in honour of the Emperor Vespasian. Immediately to the right of this the road leads on through the **Roman archway**, a later gate to the city, which then winds round the back of the supporting wall of the theatre into the present-day village.

From the agora you can ascend into the 2nd C AD Roman **theatre**, easily the largest in all Pamphylia and one of the largest in Asia Minor, with 58 rows of seats and a capacity of about 17,000. There is a beautiful view from the top seats over the site and out to sea, especially at sunset. This theatre differs from most in Asia Minor in having a vast cavea, not set into a hillside but, due to the flatness of the site, supported on

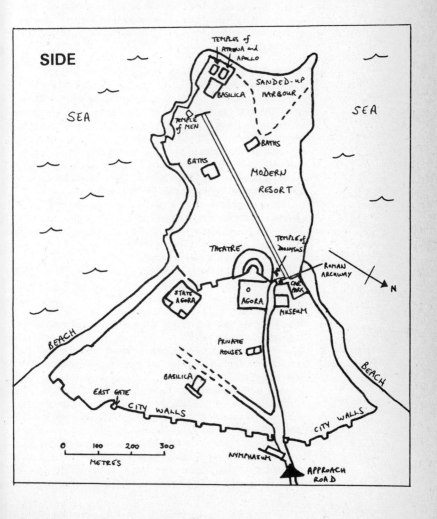

massive piers. The stage building was badly collapsed before restoration work began, but has now regained some of its past glory. The 2-metre high wall surrounding the orchestra was built to protect the audience from the animals during wild gladiatorial spectacles. At a later date the theatre seems to have had two small *chapels* installed, one at each corner of the auditorium, where traces of fresco can still be seen.

Returning to the agora and continuing eastwards away from the main road you arrive at a building whose identity is still uncertain. It was here that many of the finest statues now on display in the museum were found. It consists of a large courtyard, and on its far side a tall building with three large rooms. The favoured verdict is that it was the **state agora**, with public buildings off it, such as a library or hall; other suggestions are that it was an imperial palace, or even a gymnasium, with the adjoining open palaestra for outdoor exercise.

Towards the Promontory

From the museum and passing through the arch of the later city gate you pass the ruins of a **temple of Dionysus** just to the left of the road under the back of the theatre. The final group of ruins are to be found by the sea near the edge of the promontory. Just south of the harbour are the remains of the two **principal temples** of Side, to Athena and Apollo, dating from the 2nd C AD. Two hundred metres inland from here stands a large ruined **baths with vaulted porticoes**; further baths are on the opposite side of the promontory.

The **necropolis** lay, as usual, outside the city walls and covered a wide area, now largely covered by cultivated fields. There is a grand **mausoleum** by the shore to the west of the city, near the new hotels. It was in the form of a temple raised on a base surrounded by a courtyard and is still impressive, despite its ruined state, by virtue of its size and its arches gaping out to sea.

A Short Excursion

Lunch at the waterfall

If you are staying in Side for a few days, or even if passing through, a very pleasant lunch excursion can be made to **Manavgat**, only 20 minutes away. This involves returning to the main coast road and continuing eastwards for about 2 km to arrive at the town of Manavgat, from where a yellow sign marked Şelale points off inland. Following this road for a further 3 km or so, you will see an open parking area on the right of the road. There is a nominal admission to see the **waterfall**, and you then walk through the crass souvenir shops (for Turks as much as for foreigners) arriving at an extensive restaurant area with tables scattered under trees, some perched up on individual platforms built out on the edge of the rushing river. It is a lovely cool spot, even in the height of summer, and next to the water there is always a welcome breeze. The waterfalls are more like rushing rapids, but are nevertheless very attractive. The compulsory eating here is excellent fresh trout, helped down with refreshing Turkish white wine.

LONGER EXCURSIONS FROM SIDE: SELGE AND SELEUCEIA

A visit up into the remote mountains behind Beşkonak to visit the ruined city of **Selge** is a full day's excursion from Side, or even Antalya, and is not to be undertaken lightly. The journey is gruelling and the road is terrible, but for those who persevere it amply repays the effort.

Jeep expedition

The last part of the journey, from the Roman Köprü Kanyon bridge, is really only suitable for a jeep. As a hotelier in Side said when asked whether it was possible in a private car: 'If you have a hired car, it is possible; but if it is your car, no'. Unless you thrive on the excitement of never quite knowing whether you are going to make it, for peace of mind you should hire a jeep for the day via your hotel or an agency. Be sure to take provisions and water for the day.

Selge is reached by turning off the main coast road about 6 km east of the Aspendos turn, to Beşkonak, also signposted as Köprülükanyon Millipark. The drive from Side to Beşkonak (meaning Five Houses) takes about 1¼ hours (c60 km) and is all on good tarmac road. The stretch from the main road up to Beşkonak is very pretty, winding through forests with glimpses of the wide Eurymedon river to the left. Hardly a car is to be seen on the road, though herds of goats are abundant.

Tree house restaurant

At Beşkonak the tarmac stops, and a track continues on inland for about 6 km to reach the much-photographed **Roman bridge** over the canyon. The road up to this point is not too bad at all, and so the timid or the cautious could come this far just to stop at the charming restaurant and coffee house with tables up on tree house platforms overhanging the river. The restaurant, situated just before the bridge, is not visible from the road but there is a sign advertising its kebabs. Unfortunately the restaurant does not have a view of the bridge. This is also a very welcome place to stop on the return journey for a cool beer and to enjoy the river setting. Shortly after the restaurant there is a fork in the road and you take the left one marked Altínkaya 14 km. Altínkaya (meaning golden rock) is the new name given to the small settlements on the plateau at the top where Selge and the modern village of Zerk lie.

The fun of it

The fork leads you down to cross the remarkable Roman bridge, a superb construction across the canyon, as sound now as the day it was built, and here the fun starts in earnest. After the bridge, take the right hand fork leading up the hillside, which starts off being solid rock. From this point on the road is very rough indeed as it climbs 700 metres steeply up the hillside to Selge. A car has to be in first gear for most of the journey. This section is strenuous driving, with only the next 100 metres of the track visible before it snakes round the next steep hairpin bend.

Snow-mountain setting   Near the top of the ascent weird rock formations can be seen at the side of the road, called 'fairy chimneys', and there are fabulous precipitous views across the mountains and valleys. It was these deep gullies and precipices, according to Strabo, that 'protected the town from ever, even once, becoming subject to another people'. There is no sign of habitation anywhere on this stretch. Once the main ascent has been made, the road becomes less rocky and more earthy with high ruts. The sight of cultivated fields at the top gives warning of imminent arrival in the village of Zerk, and then you finally see the plateau ringed with snow-covered mountains behind. The theatre is instantly very impressive, standing amidst the village with the hills as a backdrop. It is best to drive on right through the village, following the track round in front of the theatre, on up the hill behind it, and then to leave your car or jeep on a flatter area up behind the theatre where there is turning space. The air temperature up here (altitude 1000 metres) is noticeably cooler than on the coast, and there is always a breeze. In the winter it is perishingly cold, with snow up to a metre high, and most of the villagers go down into the valleys until spring.

Culture Gap

Sitting on the top seats of the theatre looking out over the ruins and the village in their midst, it is difficult not to wonder at the contrast between the splendour that was ancient Selge and the poverty that is today's Zerk. Selge, Strabo records, had highly fertile soil with abundant pasture, vines and olives. Its population rose to 20,000 at its peak, and indeed the capacity of the theatre must be at least 10,000. The soil is still fertile, but the difference today is lack of water. With only one meagre spring the village is now largely dependent on rainfall, which is unpredictable. Ancient Selge overcame this problem by building an aqueduct which brought water down from the mountains, and the clay pipes of its water system can still be seen in many parts of the city.

Warlike and independent   According to tradition Selge was founded by Calchas, one of the leaders of the Greek migration into Asia Minor after the fall of Troy, and later re-settled by Spartans. It is surprising that the 'mixed multitude' of Greeks should have sought out such a remote and mountainous location when they had seemed by and large content to settle on the plains below, as at Perge and Aspendos. Selge, from its location, is generally placed in Pisidia along with Termessos, Pisidia being the mountainous region behind the plain up to the lakes on the Anatolian plateau at Burdur, Isparta and Beyşehir. In practice, however, Selge was constantly warring with its

Pisidian neighbours and preferred to associate itself with the Pamphylian cities of the plain. From the 5th C BC the city was minting coins virtually indistinguishable from those of Aspendos, with a pair of wrestlers on one side and a slinger on the other. These early coins carry the city's name as Stlegiys or Estlegiys, similar to the early name of Aspendos, Estwediiys. These names are pre-Greek and must relate to early Anatolian place-names.

Alexander had no designs on Selge, being interested only in securing the coastal cities against possible use as Persian naval bases. When the Romans first arrived the Selgians negotiated a treaty that allowed them to keep their territory and their independence, and only later during the empire did they come loosely under Roman domination. The city was clearly prosperous throughout, as evidenced by the abundant coins it minted right through till the 3rd C AD.

The Selge Site

The **theatre** has a Greek-style cavea in slightly more than a semi-circle, but is joined to the now collapsed stage building in the Roman fashion. Many of the seats just below the diazoma still retain their curved backs. There are 12 stairways, and unusually they lead all the way up to the top, crossing the diazoma. Ordinarily the number of stairways is doubled in the upper part. Here in the theatre you will be surrounded by village children for whom you are the local entertainment. The small number of visitors means that the children are still unspoilt, and they want nothing more than to hold your hand, help you over rocks and accompany you round the site. If at the end of the tour you are pressed to return to their house to eat with them it is difficult to refuse without causing offence.

From the top of the theatre a path leads off to the right towards a hill where the **Temples of Artemis** (the higher of the two) **and Zeus** have been located but are now largely heaps of stones. In a dip on the far side of this hill to the north towards the mountains lie the ruins of a building claimed by the locals to be a hospital, quite why is unknown: no excavation has ever been carried out on the site.

Walking in an easterly direction along the ridge of the hill is a mass of ruins, with foundations, blocks carved with friezes and columns protruding above the ground. The area is crying out for extensive excavation to reveal what buildings are here. The vague path continues along the course of what seems to be the **main street**, with evidence of the *drainage system* underneath. A great many of the carved blocks have been carried off by the villagers over the years and put to modern use. A fine block with a carved eagle, wings spread, has been incorporated into a stone wall to pen livestock near the Temple of Zeus, for example. The main street path leads

The visitor
as travelling
player

An offer you
should refuse

248

eventually into a paved courtyard, likely to have been the
agora, near the arch of the main gate. Lying on the flagstones
here was a very fine *carved bull's head* in marble and several
other blocks with flower motifs. The villagers may suggest
you take it away as a souvenir, and by now it may no longer
there but on display in the home of some less then scrupulous
person. Be warned of the severe laws in Turkey governing the
sale or export of antiquities. If you are found in possession of
any antiquity you are liable to be arrested and imprisoned.

The building in a dip below towards the village looks likely
from its position to have been a **baths**. Ancient Selge used to
grow a kind of iris from which an exotic oil was made and
used for massages. From here you climb a short way up onto

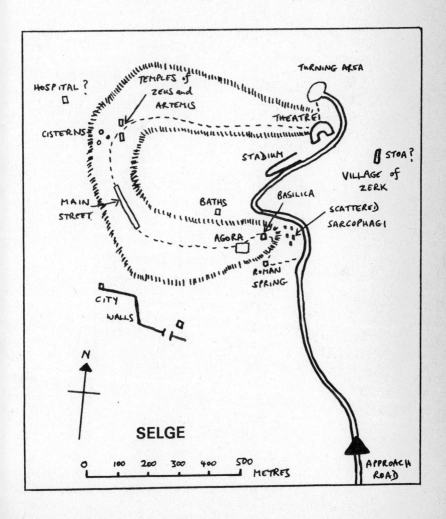

SELGE

the second hill with the scant remains of a **Christian basilica** on top. Selge was in Byzantine times the seat of a bishop, ranking above Aspendos but after Side. A climb down the back of this hill gives good views over the extensive walls which once enclosed the whole city. Along the way there is a **Roman spring** from which a small amount of clear drinkable water still trickles.

Rejoining the road and returning in the direction of the theatre, you will notice to your left on the hillside a few scattered *sarcophagi*, some with the distinctive Selgian circular decoration on their sides that looks like two eyes in a face. Columns and a portico are visible in a field in the lowest part of the valley below the theatre; these may mark a stoa. The road also takes you past the **stadium**, to the left, which has all but disappeared beneath the tillage; apart from four or five rows of seats on the northern side, not much else can be seen. The southern row of seats would have been exactly where the road now runs alongside it, so the blocks must have been carried away and used elsewhere. As you walk through the village, you will in fact see everywhere pieces of the old Roman city in use: marble carved basins are used as animal troughs, segments of carved pillars or column drums are used as seats or tables in the gardens. The contrast between the splendours of Selge's past and the simplicity of its present could not be more sharply juxtaposed.

An Easier Outing

An attractive excursion, more for those staying at Side than for those passing through, is the half-day trip to the site of **Seleuceia**. It is rarely visited, surprisingly so, given its proximity to Side and the good state of preservation of its ruins. To reach it you follow the same route as to the waterfalls at Manavgat, but then continuing on about 4 km to the village of Şíhlar. From here you can either walk to the site (about one hour) or drive carefully most of the remaining distance.

The site is on a hill with vertical cliffs on three sides and is approachable only from the south side. At the entrance to the site is a narrow col, inside which, in a hollow to the left, is a cave with a fine spring of water. Just above this is a building still standing to a fair height and visible from a long way off south. It was clearly a **baths**, with its five vaulted rooms and traces of the water system still visible. Further on you will see the ruins of the **city gate**, flanked with two rectangular towers, leading into the agora. This **agora** is surrounded with remarkably well-preserved buildings; a few columns of the original Doric portico have been re-erected. On the side of the agora, directly opposite the gate you have entered, is the **market-hall**, the most impressive of the buildings on the site, its lower storey virtually complete, while the upper storey still

Is it still there? (see Selge, the agora)

has its facade and fine large windows. In one of the eight chambers of the lower storey a mosaic was found of Orpheus charming the animals. Adjoining this building is a semi-circular construction, thought from its form to have been an **odeon or a buleuterion**, though no seats now remain.

A little north of the agora is a **small temple**, also well-preserved. Towards the western edge of the hill is the **necropolis** with masonry built tombs.

There are many towns all over Asia Minor called Seleuceia, after the Syrian dynasty of Seleucius. The best known of these is further east on the Cilician coast, at Silifke.

PRACTICAL INFORMATION

ANTALYA

Antalya Oteli (4-star), 150 rooms, enroute to Lara. Pool, private beach. Good restaurant.

Perge (2-star), 25 rooms, in a good setting overlooking the cliff, near the Karaali Park.

Motel Antalya (1-star), open April through October, enroute to Lara, 12 rooms, beach.

Villa Park (1-star), 11 rooms, in the Karaali Park.

The best **restaurants** are grouped above the marina on the cliff, and at the cliff edge of the Karaali Park.

Annual **festival** with theatre, music and cinema, with some performances held in the Roman theatre at Aspendos. Held end of September, beginning of October.

SIDE

There are over 20 motels and 40 pensions in Side. Many of these are charmingly situated on the sea with beachside open-air restaurants. The best thing is to explore and ask prices till you find the one you like best. Service tends to be very good in the smaller places. The more luxurious motels tend also to be the bigger and most are situated 1

or 2 km from the town. Of these, the following are the best:

Defne (3-star), 92 rooms, 20 minutes' walk west of town. Very modern style, only hotel with air-conditioning in Side. Pool and beach. Water sports.

Turtel (2-star), open April through November, 66 rooms, 2 km from town. Attractive gardens, good restaurant.

Cennet (2-star), open April through October, 55 rooms, close to Turtel, on the beach.

Athena (1-star), open April through November, 63 rooms, on beach.

Dolmuş taxis link the outlying hotels with the town centre.

There is an endless choice of **restaurants** in the town, many with nightlife too. Take B&B at your hotel if possible, so that you get a chance to try a few.

MANAVGAT

Tusan Akdeniz (2-star), open March through October, 40 rooms, pool.

Restaurant by the waterfalls, 4 km inland from Manavgat town, fresh trout from the river.

ALANYA TO MERSIN (ANCIENT CILICIA)

ENTERING CILICIA AT ALANYA

As you continue eastwards beyond Manavgat the road soon comes in closer to the sea passing numerous sandy coves, all deserted. The scenery begins to change, leaving behind the flat plain of Pamphylia, for you are now approaching the borders of Cilicia. This the name given in antiquity to the region extending from Alanya, on the edge of Pamphylia, eastwards to the borders of Syria. It is a very large region and divides naturally into two distinct geographical districts: the mountainous 'Rugged Cilicia', from Alanya to Silifke; and the flat Cilician Plain, from Mersin to Iskenderun.

Magnificent drive

Rugged Cilicia is one of the poorest and most sparsely populated regions along the southern coast, though it is also the most beautiful. It has been opened up to easy traffic relatively recently, with the completion of the new coast road in 1967. The drive is magnificent if tiring, winding endlessly over a succession of wooded headlands and round deep bays, with the cliffs dropping away dramatically. The vegetation is semi-tropical with lush orange groves and banana plantations lining the thin stretch of land beside the road.

Around Alarahan

After about half an hour's drive from Manavgat, a sign points off left to **Alarahan**. Following this turn for a few kilometres you arrive at the remains of another Seljuk **caravanserai** just to the right of the road, quite overgrown, but with a richly decorated main door. Unusually, lions' heads are carved on the lower ends of the arch and on candlesticks inside. On the summit of the hill north of it is perched the breathtaking **fortress** built at the same time by the Seljuks in the 13th C, its fortification walls clinging to the hillside. It is reached by a tunnel and was used as a place of refuge for travelling merchants if they were in danger of attack by bandits. It takes at least an hour to climb up to the summit. A further 20 minutes' drive on from here takes you past another Seljuk **caravanserai** on the side of the road, built between 1236 and 1246 in the reign of Sultan Keyhusrev, and was one of several built along the main route from the Seljuk capital at Konya to their principal port at Aloanya.

Seljuk monuments

Alanya: Modern Resort and Seljuk City

A drive of a further 20 minutes along the scenically beautiful coast road brings you in sight of the mighty rock of Alanya with its crenellated red fortress dominating the coast for miles around.

By virtue of its impressive site and good beaches **Alanya** has become in recent years the most developed resort along the

254

southern coast of Turkey. Hotels have mushroomed, most of them larger and more western-looking than those at Side, and certainly the feel of these two resorts is quite different, for whereas in Side the old is mingled in with the new, in Alanya there is a divide between the old town perched in and around the fortress up on the rock and the modern sprawl of recent development on the two beaches beneath it.

A red Gibraltar   If you concentrate on the rock, however, a visit to Alanya can be very enjoyable, and the mighty red fortified town with its 146 towers is certainly unlike anything else to be seen along this coast and is a fine example of Seljuk architecture. The general appearance of the rock jutting out into the sea has been likened to Gibraltar.

In classical times Alanya, the ancient Coracesium, was an insignificant place, only achieving notoriety during the 2nd C BC as a headquarters for Cilician pirates who dominated the whole of Pamphylia and Cilicia at that time. The pirate leader, Diodotus Tryphon the Voluptuary, at one stage became so confident with his raids that he even tried to seize the Seleucid throne in Syria but was finally killed by Seleucus VII around 130 BC. The Romans finally put an end to the piracy that was rife along this coast by sending Pompey to deal with the pirates for once and for all, and this swift three-month campaign culminated in 67 BC in a battle off Coracesium with the total destruction of the pirate fleet.

Gift to Cleopatra   When, after Brutus' murder of Caesar in 44 BC, Mark Antony was in command of eastern Asia Minor, he presented Coracesium and the surrounding territory as a gift to Cleopatra. His purpose was to give her a region that was not only scenically beautiful, but also rich in timber, so scarce in Egypt, which she could use to construct ships for her navy. But afterwards the town slipped into obscurity, remaining a minor place till the Seljuks under Keykubad I arrived in 1221, changed its name to Alanya and turned it into the magnificent fortified city seen today. It became Keykubad's winter quarters and naval base, and he also developed it as a cultural centre.

The Seljuks

Seljuk rule in Anatolia in the 12th and 13th C saw the first flowering of Turkish civilisation; many of the loveliest build-**Flowering of** ings in Turkey today are the legacy of the Seljuks. They were **Turkish** originally nomads from the region of Samarkand and **Civilisation** Bukhara descended from the Tu-Kin people in the steppes of Mongolia, and this Chinese name evolved to give us the modern name Turk. They worshipped their own weather gods and were renowned for their physical prowess. In the 11th C a wave of Seljuks surged out from their homeland, through Persia, Iraq, Syria and Palestine. Here they were converted to Islam and brought their new religion with them when, in 1067, under the leadership of Alp Arslan, they pushed up from Antioch (modern Antakya) into Anatolia to Konya.

Although the Seljuks were effective fighters, once they had established themselves and the fighting was over, their greatest sultans, notably Alp Arslan, Malik Shah, Keykavus I and Keykubad I (Alaeddin), were enlightened rulers, laying down the foundations for commercial prosperity, education and the arts. Alp Arslan introduced the appointment of vizirs (ministers or advisors), and his first vizir, Nizam Al-Mulk, was responsible for founding universities, observatories, hospitals and mosques. Over the two centuries of their rule, the Seljuks evolved a remarkable welfare state where medical schools were linked with hospitals, orphanages, poor-houses, mental homes, baths and religious schools, all offering their services to the needy free of charge. Many of these institutions are still in existence.

Caravanserais along the trade routes

The system of caravanserais they built facilitated trade and concentrated the trade routes; they were usually built a day's journey apart. The services they offered for the travelling merchants were remarkable for their time, with the central mosque and ablution fountain, the range of sleeping quarters, the baths to revive aching limbs, the cafés for refreshment, the blacksmith and leatherworker ready to do repairs, and musicians to relax and entertain. Stabling was offered for donkeys, horses and camels, with the doors varying in height to suit the height of each animal. Most remarkable of all, however, was that these services were offered free by the state, which funded the system through taxation.

In Seljuk architecture the elaborate tiles and carving distantly reflect Persian influence, and in the strength and power of their castles and minarets there are traces of Syrian Arab influence. But the Seljuks also developed their own distinctive forms, such as the cylindrical mausoleum (türbe) on a square base with a conical roof (the most famous example being the Mevlana Tomb in Konya). It has been suggested that this shape was meant to recall the pointed tents of the Seljuks' nomadic origins. The double-headed eagle, symbol of the Seljuk state, can be seen on many of their buildings, which were usually constructed in red brick with plain high walls contrasting with the very elaborate decorations and carving in niches and doorways. The main entrance was always highly elaborate with honeycomb (or stalactite) carving, as can be seen in the extant caravanserais and madrasas.

Madrasas for body, mind and spirit

Madrasas were generally charitable foundations and taught, besides the Koran, Islamic jurisprudence, languages, mathematics, geometry, astronomy, medicine and music. Sports were also practised, and famous wrestlers often came from these schools. In many ways, madrasas were the Islamic version of the gymnasiums of the ancient world, as gymnasiums were as much for teaching as for sport, and frequently had schools and libraries attached. Their layouts too were similar, with buildings arranged round a courtyard.

Tiles and carpets
Tilework was something the Greeks and Romans never learnt, but the Seljuks brought this exquisite art with them from Persia. They evolved the Persian style into their own form of tile mosaics in plain colours and geometric designs, which so often embellish their mosques, tombs and madrasas. The best examples of tilework in Turkey are on display in the Karatay Madrasa museum in Konya. Carpet weaving was the other great Seljuk art. Their colours are rich: blues, brick red, soft green, with sand and earth backgrounds. The motifs are geometric often with stylised animal, bird or tree forms. Like the türbe's roof, this art recalled their nomadic background, for the carpet is the essential piece of tent furniture.

The Seljuks' most important contribution to religion was the foundation of the Mevlana order of Whirling Dervishes at Konya, the Seljuk capital. This form of Islamic mysticism continues today despite Atatürk's dissolution of the order in 1925 in his attempts to secularise modern Turkey.

A Tour of Old Alanya

The visitor should head first of all up to the summit of the rock to gauge the extent of the fortifications and to admire the wonderful view. The outer wall is 7 km long and took 12 years to build. You can drive all the way to the top on a tarmac road, though if you have the time and the energy you will get a better feel for the site if you leave your car before reaching the top and walk through the old section of the town.

Climbing up to the old town
As the road winds up from the modern town, it passes first through an arch, recently constructed to allow cars through, beside which is the original **main gate of the outer fortification wall**. It is a double gate with two entrances at right angles to each other, a typical Seljuk feature. The road continues upwards towards the tip of the promontory for about 500 metres then turns back and winds up to the gate of the **Inner Fortress**. It is near here that the car can be left and the journey continued on foot on the narrow paths and lanes among the houses and trees.

Near the first bend after entering the gate the Seljuk wall can be seen built up on the original **Hellenistic wall** of ancient Coracesium. Over the ruins of a tower in this wall a tiny **Byzantine chapel** was built. The path leads on into the castellated area called the Ehmedek, or **residential quarter** of the fortress. Still inhabited and with its quiet air of dilapidation, it could not contrast more strongly with the modern town below. The approach leads through a door in the outer wall to a gatehouse with the usual right angle turn. Inside the gate a courtyard opens out with cisterns, and a stepped path leads up on the left to the ruins of three towers, and ahead and to the right are three more towers.

The heart of the Seljuk City

From the Ehmedek a path leads south to a group of buildings which form the centre of the Seljuk city: the Süleymaniye Mosque, a simple square building, and a bedestan (bazaar) and a caravanserai, both overgrown. The rooms off the caravanserai courtyard were accommodation for the travelling traders and the large vaulted extension at the back was stabling for the animals.

Death on the rocks

From here a little path leads up to the west to a curious building, quite overgrown, a mosque called **Akşebe Türbesi**. Inside are tombs, but a little apart stands a bricked minaret. Continuing on up the path you now reach the highest point of the hill, the **citadel** proper, where Keykubad's palace stood. It consists of a large open space strongly defended by walls and towers. The main features are the large cisterns, about seven of them, and the pretty little Byzantine church, still with traces of wall painting, dating from the 6thC. The other buildings here were shops and soldiers' barracks. At the northwest corner, where a platform has now been built out at the edge of the cliff, a magnificent if windy view can be had over the sea and town. This was the spot from which condemned prisoners or women convicted of adultery were hurled down on to the rocks below. From the other outer corner of the citadel you look down onto a rocky promontory reaching 300 metres out beyond the wall. On it are the ruins of three buildings: the closest and most conspicuous is the Red Tower, the next one, largely destroyed, has been identified as a mint, though the location is intriguing, and the furthest is a monastery with its associated buildings. Between the monastery and the mint is a great cleft in the rock, making the monastery accessible only from the sea, and that with difficulty. The descent to the buildings from the citadel is very dangerous and should not be attempted.

The boss

The most prominent monument of the lower town is the **Red Tower**, Kízíl Kule, built by Keykubad to defend the port. It was skilfully restored in 1951–53 by the Turkish authorities. Octagonal in shape, it has five stories inside. At the third storey there are archery slits and holes for pouring hot oil on attackers. High on the exterior to the west the inscription testified to the might of the Sultan Keykubad: 'This sacred tower was built by order of Keykubad, Prince of the Believers, greatest of all Sultans, Master of the fate of all nations, King of the Kings of the world, Guardian of God's regions and Protector of his worshippers, Greatest leader of Religion, Supporter of Islam and the Moslems, Maintainer of Justice in both worlds, Protector of the tyrannised from Tyrants, Shadow of the Almighty on earth, Living embodiment of the powerful State, Origin of the vitality of the nation, Creator of Justice and Righteousness, King of the Land and the two Seas, Mightiest King and Crown of the Sons of Seljuk,

The walls of Alanya are seven kilometres long

Greatest Conqueror and son of Keyhusrev, grandson of Kilic Arslan. May God prolong his reign for ever. Year of the Hegira 623'.

Near the tower is a fountain which supplies the only running water on the promontory. The population was generally dependent on rainwater cisterns, of which there were about 400, 100 of which are still in use today. About 200 metres further along the harbour towards the promontory is the old **Seljuk dockyard**, the only one of its type in Turkey today. It was designed for the construction of ships and is still in use, with five vaulted galleries, one for each ship, linked by arched openings. This is guarded by the **arsenal tower** just beyond it.

Cave to cure diseases

Round on the other, western, side of the promontory, a road leads to the **stalactite grotto of Damlataş** at the foot of the hill adjoining the beach. It was discovered by chance in 1948 when workmen were blasting rock for the new jetty. Apart from the stalactites, the cave has a constant temperature of 23°C and very high humidity which is thought to be beneficial to sufferers from asthma and bronchial diseases, and consequently many visitors come, some of them from great distances, to spend time lying in the atmosphere of the cave. Mainly men, they can be seen prostrate in various parts of the cave where they think it is doing them most good. The cure is meant to take 20 days, four hours per day. Near the

259

entrance to the cave is a small **archaeological and ethnographical museum**, its most notable exhibit a bronze statue of Hercules dating from the 2nd C AD in perfect condition.

From the port you can, if you have the time, hire a boat to visit the many grottoes which honeycomb the foot of the rocky promontory. There is the pirates cave, the lovers cave and the phosphorous cave, to say nothing of Cleopatra's beach, where the Egyptian queen is reputed to have bathed in the sea.

TO ANAMUR AND ANEMURIUM

Beyond Alanya, eastwards to Silifke, the mountains come down closer to the sea, the coast is more precipitous, and the road extremely winding. This rugged coastline of Cilicia was notorious for piracy and brigandage. The heavily wooded land made the robbers safe from pursuit and the numerous tiny inlets and coves made perfect hiding places from which to launch attacks. The important trading route from Syria to the Aegean passed along this coast, and the attacks of the pirates on this shipping had a gradual weakening effect on the Seleucid Empire in Syria. Alexander the Great made no attempt on Rugged Cilicia, clearly deciding it did not warrant the effort.

Crumbling cities and fortresses

Despite its sparseness of population today, this region must have been heavily inhabited in ancient times to judge from the large number of ruined Hellenistic and Roman cities and Byzantine, Crusader and Seljuk fortresses littering the coast. Most are in a poor state of preservation, set up on remote hilltops and not easily accessible, though a few are within reach of the road. The Greek cities in this region were all founded by the 'mixed multitude' of Greeks who moved southwards after the fall of Troy, settling first in Pamphylia, some of them then moving eastwards to Cilicia.

At the southernmost beach in Turkey

The first ruin is **Iotape**, about 35 km east of Alanya, a city founded by the Seleucid King Antiochus IV. Nothing of it remains except a few scattered column drums and some defence walls on a promontory overlooking the sea. Passing the growing town of Gazipaşa with its good beach, the road leaves the sea for a while and lush green banana plantations are much in evidence, growing well on this warm sheltered coast. Tomato growing is also becoming popular, the unfortunate plastic roofing that accompanies it disfiguring the landscape. Further on, to the right of the road on a promontory jutting out into the sea, are the crumbling ruins of **Antiochia ad Cragum** (on a crag, literally), another town founded by Antiochus IV to defend his shipping route from Syria along this pirate-ridden coast. Entering a river valley, the village of **Kaladiran** is dominated by the remains of a Byzantine fortress, but none of these ruins are of any great note compared to Anamur, the site of ancient Anemurium, as well as of the largest and best preserved Crusader castle on the southern coast of Turkey with all its walls and 36 towers still standing.

The Crusader Castle of Anamur

The road crosses the flat fertile plain of Anamur and leads straight alongside the **castle** near the far end of the bay, standing right on the shore with the waves lapping on its outer walls. Just beyond it is a motel of reasonable standard, the first likely accommodation since Alanya, set on the sandy beach next to the castle. There are also a handful of simple restaurants in the immediate vicinity of the castle. The modern town of **Anamur** is set a few kilometres away slightly inland. The guardian of the castle sits by the moat and sells tickets and postcards.

The castle, known locally as Marmure Kalesi, dominates the plain and was the foothold of the Lusignan Kings of Cyprus in Cilicia, this point being the closest on the southern shore of Turkey to Cyprus. They withdrew and returned to Cyprus in the face of Ottoman expansion in the mid-15th C. The Ottomans restored the castle in 1840 and continued using it as a fortress till the last few days of the empire in 1921.

It is extremely well-defended, with the sea on one side and a stream on the other from which a moat was dug all round its land sides. The crenellated outer wall is virtually intact, though the buildings inside, which were later Turkish additions consisting of a mosque, barracks, fountain and baths, are not so well-preserved. On the left as you enter the open grassy interior, a stairway leads to the huge **14-sided tower** which defended the exterior enclosure. From the top of this tower you can overlook the whole fortress. Many other stairways leading up to towers at various points can also be climbed, and the sentry wall-walk is intact in many places.

The Crusades

The Christians take Jerusalem...

The Byzantine Empire and its capital Constantinople was on the wane in the 11th C, with the Moslem Seljuks masters of the whole of southwestern Anatolia. This was the scene when the army of the First Crusade gathered from all over Europe outside Constantinople. The religious motive of the Crusaders to free Jerusalem from the Moslem infedels was the slogan, but in practice many of the leaders had ambitions to grab and plunder rich oriental lands. The French Baldwin of Boulogne established himself in Edessa and abandoned the Crusade, while Bohemond of Tarantum took over Antioch and went no further. Jerusalem was taken in 1099 and a series of feudal states established in the Holy Land.

The Second Crusade began in 1147 in the same disreputable way as the first, with a trail of rape and pillage across Europe to Constantinople, then fizzling out in quarrels between the French and the Germans. The Great Saladin's recapture of Jerusalem in 1187 inspired the Third Crusade, with Frederick Barbarossa and Richard Lionheart as its leading players. This ended with the drowning of Barbarossa in the Göksu river near Silifke, and the French and English squabbling. The only achievement was the capture Cyprus, destined to become the last refuge of the Crusaders driven from the mainland.

The Fourth Crusade was directed by the cynical Venetian Doge Dandolo against Christian Constantinople itself. When the city fell in 1204 its wealth and treasure was greedily seized and the lands of the Byzantine Empire were for a while ruled over by Venetians and Frankish knights.

The Byzantines, though threatened by the Moslems, respected their eastern neighbours; the Western European (mostly French) Crusaders came to the Holy Land with the notion that they were vastly superior to the infidel, whereas in fact the Moslems were generally more civilised than the Franks whom they in turn regarded as 'animals possessing the virtues of courage and fighting, but nothing else'. They made a strange alliance then, the Byzantines regarding the Frankish Crusaders as rough-mannered barbarians, and the Franks for their part despising the refinements and formalities of the Byzantine court and coveting its wealth. This antagonism between the ill-matched allies continued to fester till the Fourth Crusade, when the Frankish armies turned on their fellow Christians in Constantinople, delivering a blow to eastern Christendom from which Byzantium never really recovered, succumbing finally to the Ottomans when they conquered Constantinople in 1453 and made it the capital of their Moslem empire.

The Crusades were a failure as a counter-attack against Islam. As Sir Steven Runciman has put it: 'The Crusades were launched to save Eastern Christendom from the Moslems. When they ended the whole of Eastern Christendom was under Moslem rule'.

Ancient Anemurium

The ruins of the city of ancient **Anemurium** cover the hillside of the rocky promontory on the western side of the plain of Anamur, and the road leads off to it shortly before the modern town of Anamur. This is the southernmost tip of Turkey.

The ruins are interesting for the traces of mosaic and painting still remaining, but most impressive is that so much of the town survives, including many private houses, giving the impression of a ghost town deserted just a few years ago, not in the 7th C when the Arab incursions began.

After the Arabs, surging northwards from the Arabian Peninsula following Mohammed's death, had conquered Syria in 660, they established the Umayyad Caliphate, with Damascus as its capital. From this base the Arab armies raided northwards into Asia Minor against the Byzantines. The main object of these raids was booty, and gradually they became a regular summer activity to keep the bored armies fit and well-trained. Though these raids ravaged the cities of southern Turkey, the Arabs were never seeking to gain a permanent foothold and no part of Asia Minor ever became Arabic-speaking. The Bedouin, from whom the Arab armies were mostly recruited, were driven not just by religious zeal but also by economic necessity, the desire for tribute and the luxuries of the civilised regions to the north. A verse of a later Arab poet puts it well:

'No, not for Paradise didst thou the nomad life forsake;
Rather, I believe, it was thy yearning after bread and dates.'

Exploring the Site

Anemurium was originally a Phoenician colony, reaching the height of its prosperity in the 3rd C AD, and most of the buildings date from this period or later. The whole town was walled and much of this **defence wall** can be seen leading up the hillsides to the citadel on the summit of the hill. Following the access road, you reach the **theatre** on the right, very ruined, but with an identifiable cavea. Among the numerous buildings to the left and right of the road are several **Byzantine churches**.

Ghost town   Immediately after the theatre you reach the southern and most powerful rampart, and behind the theatre are various ruins, notably those of **two aqueducts** following a course nearly parallel to that of the current access route to the site. Between the two aqueducts a ramp climbs gently up towards the citadel on which stand clusters of **houses**, many with vaulted roofs, some cut into the rock.

Beyond the theatre to the right of the road stands the most impressive and best-preserved building of Anemurium, the **baths**. It still has two storeys with many of the vaulted chambers having traces of wall decorations and even some tiles in place.

Mosaics and   Opposite the theatre on the other side of the road are the
frescoes   ruins of a **buleuterion**, beyond which steps lead down into a small courtyard with various shops and glassmakers' workshops. Although heavily overgrown, a certain amount of paving and decoration survives. Walking towards the sea beyond the buleuterion, you will see a **vaulted apse** with three niches which belonged to a vast building dating from the beginning of the 3rd C whose function is still cause for speculation. In the rooms of this building are many *mosaics* showing abstracts and animals, some with strong colours remaining. It may be difficult to find these mosaics as they are often covered over with sand or gravel, but if the site guardian is in attendance you may be able to get him to reveal them for you.

A little further on are the ruins of a **nymphaeum**, a complex building with several rooms closed off by an apse, with cisterns and basins. Returning to the road to turn right opposite the theatre, you will reach the ruins of another **baths** (on the right of the road, ie the sea side) with various pools, joined on to a vast **palaestra** (open space for exercises). There is much good paving left here, with *mosaics* in many of the rooms. Beyond the palaestra towards the sea are the remains of three **churches** and a small baths dating from the 5th C with more mosaics.

Returning along the access road near the beginning of the site, about 50 metres left of the road is the church of the necropolis. All around this stand **tombs**, some of which still have the remains of murals on the walls, restored in 1974 and 1975 by a Canadian archaeological mission from the Universities of British Columbia and Toronto. The most interesting is a good 100 metres after the aqueduct towards the right, beyond the bed of a small stream. Built in the 3rd C AD, it was given an additional alcove and extra storey a century later. In the older structure are *paintings* in the antichamber and funeral chamber (allergorical figures of the Seasons, a winged Eros, Hermes and the conductor of souls, and pictures of the dead). The paintings in the alcove date from the later period, as does the mosaic in the funeral chamber of the upper storey, which shows a cupid attacking a panther with a lance.

East to Silifke

Continuing eastwards beyond Anamur, the road winds on round a succession of rocky promontories and sandy bays, passing the remains of more mediaeval fortresses perched up on hills overlooking the sea, till you round the final promontory of Rugged Cilicia, called **Cape Cavaliere**, which opens up onto a fine sandy beach. Just offshore from the bay is a strange islet covered in broken sarcophagi, tombstones and ruins of mediaeval buildings with a small Crusader church. It is called **Provençal Isle**, after the Knights of St John of Provence who had a stronghold here in the 13th C.

On the far side of the bay you pass a small octagonal 14th C Turkish fortress commanding the port of **Ağa Liman**, the landing place of Silifke, once a notorious pirate haven. Continuing on past the remains of two mediaeval chapels, you are now approaching Silifke, on the eastern edge of Rugged Cilicia.

Knights of Provence

SILIFKE AND EXCURSIONS

Persian palace

From either Anamur or Silifke, an interesting and unusual excursion can be made inland to the rock citadel known as **Meydancík Kalesi**, near the town of **Gülnar**. The route to Gülnar (about $1\frac{1}{2}$ hours' drive from either start point) is extremely picturesque, taking you through some remarkable limestone landscapes. The impressive rock citadel has been occupied from Hittite through to Byzantine times, a commonplace in Turkey, but the unusual aspect here is the discovery following excavations in 1971 of a palace thought to date from the Persian Achaemenid period (546–334 BC as opposed to the later Persian Sassanid dynasty), in which sculptures were found resembling those at Persepolis, Persia's chief city at that time.

Each new occupant of the citadel, unusually, cleared the site of the debris of earlier occupants by throwing it over the edge of the mountain, which has made the study of the rubble at the foot of the citadel a priority. Among the remains on the summit, a royal Hittite cartouche from the time of Mouwattali (c1300 BC) enables us to date a bastion entered by a monumental gateway. Near the southern (roadside) edge of the citadel the ruins of the unusual palace were discovered, belonging perhaps to the satraps installed by the Persians to govern Cilicia, and it was here that the Persepolitan style relifs were found. An inscription in Aramaic found near the entrance of the Hittite fortress seems to confirm this theory.

Arriving at Silifke

First female martyr

Just before Silifke, a sign points off up left to the Byzantine **Church of Aghia Thekla**, impressively situated by itself on a hill. Only the tall apse remains of the once huge basilica, and you can still go down into the crypt to see the tomb of the saint if the guardian with the key is to hand. The church was built by the Emperor Zeno around 480, leader of the wild tribesmen from the mountains above the Cilician plain (Isauria), who had been converted to Christianity. St Thekla was Paul's first convert and the first female Christian martyr. She broke off her engagement to be married after her conversion to Christianity, declaring she wished to keep her virginity. Her fiancé was furious and she was punished by being stripped naked in the amphitheatre on his orders. The lions which were meant to devour her merely crouched docilely at her feet and the fire her tormentors lit beneath her failed to burn her. She died finally a natural death in ripe old age in her retreat in Isauria.

You now approach **Silifke**, the ancient Seleucia, founded by Seleucus I in the 3rd C BC. The town is the largest on the coast since Alanya, and has a pleasant open feel, situated on the banks of the wide Göksu river overlooked by the Crusader castle on the summit of the acropolis. It was further up this river that Frederick Barbarossa drowned while bathing in 1190, thereby bringing the Third Crusade to an abrupt end.

Vast fortress   Of the ancient town nothing remains except the **Roman bridge** over the river and the scant remains of a Roman temple. The best thing is to head straight up to the **castle** where there are several restaurants offering wonderful panoramas. Vast, overgrown and crumbling in parts, the castle is not maintained and there is no ticket office or official entrance. Entry therefore is by a narrow path round the east side of the castle where a breach in the walls can be crossed. Once inside you can clamber all round the edge of the fortress, taking care to avoid the crumbling sections. Originally Byzantine and built in the 7th C as a defence against the Arab raids, it was rebuilt by the Crusader Knights of Rhodes into this colossal structure with 23 towers and bastions. In the cellars was a cistern whose waters were reputed never to dry up. The Ottoman Beyazit I later built a mosque inside.

Diocaesarea Detour

From Silifke a signposted road leads north 38 km to **Uzuncaburç**, the site of ancient **Diocaesarea**. Although this involves a considerable detour along a winding road, it is worth it if you have the time, for the drive itself is attractive and the site is one of the most impressive on the Cilician coast.

From about 8 km outside Silifke, the road through the mountains and pine forests is dotted about with **Roman tombs** often in the form of temples, some of which are remarkably well-preserved. On the right at the entrance to Uzuncaburç, a road leads to Ura, a village identified with the ancient city of **Olba**. Here are remains of a nymphaeum, an aqueduct and several Byzantine churches.

Oldest Corinthian temple   Uzuncaburç itself is a pretty village, isolated in the mountains. Leaving your car in the village square, to the left before the square is a **theatre** dating from the 2nd C AD. Passing through a monumental Roman **arch** which crossed a colonnaded street, you come to the **Temple of Zeus Olbius**. Built at the beginning of the 3rd C BC by Seleucus I, it is the oldest known temple in the Corinthian order. It was later transformed into a Christian church at the beginning of the Byzantine era. Most of its columns are still standing.

Beyond the wall of the temple enclosure you see on the right another colonnaded street leading to a Roman gate, and beyond this the remains of the **Temple of Tyche** of the 1st C BC: a vast foundation with five Corinthian columns on high bases. Returning to the arch near the village square, turn left, and after passing the school you find a small restaurant where you can eat before or after your visit. Immediately after this a path leads to a powerful **Hellenistic tower** nearly 25 metres high which has given the village its name (Uzuncaburç meaning tallish tower).

The Three Graces

Crossing the marshy delta of the Göksu river east of Silifke, you come after about 15 minutes to the village of **Narlí Kuyu**, the Pomegranate Well, where you can eat a good if expensive fish meal at one of the pretty restuarants suspended on stilts overlooking the sea. On the village square before the restuarants are the remains of a Roman baths of the 4th C AD. It is known locally as the **Baths of the Maidens** from the lovely *mosaic* flooring inside depicting the Three Graces. The fountain of the baths was reputed to endow its bathers with beauty, intelligence and long life.

Heaven and Hell

From this village also a road leads off 5 km inland to the legendary but disappointing Heaven and Hell (Cennet and Cehennem), two caves which were regarded as so different in character from each other that they earned these epithets. The **Vale of Heaven**, Cennet Deresi, is a huge natural chasm at the edge of a field of Roman and Byzantine ruins of ancient Paperon. The ruins are indifferent, the only striking one being right on the edge of the chasm, a high-walled basilica. The descent is by an easy path to the bottom of the chasm, and from here a less easy, somewhat slippery path continues down 200 metres to the cave mouth where you will see a pretty little early Christian **church**, dedicated to the Virgin in the 5th C. Bathed in a strange bluish light, the church appears to have been built from older stones from the 2nd and 3rd C BC. In the apse are traces of murals. Inside the cave you will hear the roar of an underground river, which according to tradition is the Stream of Paradise which flows out at the Fountain of Knowledge at the Roman baths at Narlí Kuyu below. The ascent is less easy, and about an hour should be allowed for the total visit. The general atmosphere of the place, with rags tied in bushes and the rubbish of picnics littering the area, is far removed from heaven.

From the parking place a second path leads off right to the **Vale of Hell**, Cehennem Deresi, a frightening narrow pit, accessible only with a guide for those with experience of potholing. According to both Christian and Moslem tradition, this was one of the entrances to Hell. Rags of clothing and pennants are tied in the trees and bushes around it by superstitious locals to ward off evil spirits who might escape from below.

Disappointing heaven

A damn good hell

The Maiden's Castle from Korykos

Kíz Kalesi

Another 5 km east beyond Narlí Kuyu brings you to the famous **Maiden's Castle**, Kíz Kalesi, in fact two castles, one on the sandy beach and the other in the sea. The beach here is not well endowed with hotels, but is a very popular camping area with a BP Mocamp nearby. The castle on the shore was built in the 12th C by Armenian kings and was originally linked by a causeway to the Maiden's Castle itself, now apparently floating in the sea about 100 metres from the shore. Its name derives from local legend that the king built the castle to protect his beautiful daughter after it was predicted that she would die of a snakebite. One of her admirers unwittingly sent her a basket of fruit in which a snake had hidden, and on reaching in she was bitten and died. The castle can be reached with difficulty on a small boat or air-mattress, but most locals leave it well alone, as the fatal snake is reputed to live on in the castle.

The snake and the maiden

The **land castle** can be explored though it is heavily overgrown inside. On the other side of the road from the castle lie the extensive scattered remains of the city of **Korykos**, which was a pirate refuge before Pompey's campaign of elimination in 67 BC. Cicero lived here when he was governor of Cilicia from 52 to 50 BC.

East to Mersin

Continuing east between Korykos and Mersin the remains of many ancient cities can be seen, again indicating how much more populous this part of Cilicia was in antiquity than it is now. None of the ruins are particularly spectacular or impressive and do not require a visit as such, but can simply be peered at from the car in passing. As so often, it is the tombs which have survived the best, and along several stretches of the road rock tombs and sarcophagi can be seen lining the sides.

Solecism

The first of these sites is **Ayaş**, only 3 km beyond Kíz Kalesi, noteworthy for its temple which has survived well. Further on, a road leads off 3 km to the village of Kanlidivane, the site of ancient **Kanytelis**, where you can see a vast Roman necropolis. At about 10 km before Mersin a road leads off one kilometre to the sea at Viranşehir, site of ancient **Soli**, occupied since the end of the 3rd C BC, later destroyed by the Armenians and rebuilt in the 1st C BC by Pompey, and thereafter named Pompeopolis in his honour. The people of Soli spoke such poor Greek that the term solecism was coined, meaning a grammatical offence. The principal remains of the city are the splendid columns of a **street** nearly 500 metres long running down to the ancient harbour. Only about 20 of the original 200 columns, with Corinthian capitals, are still standing, leading to the sandy beach. Inhabitants of Mersin come out to swim here, and reasonable accommodation is available for the traveller.

RETURN ROUTE VIA KONYA AND THE LAKES

If you are on a three-week holiday from a starting point of İzmir or Kuşadasí, it can have taken you about two weeks to reach Silifke. An interesting return route which makes a contrast in scenery and affords you the chance to get a feel for the Anatolian plateau and the staggering variety of Turkey is via Konya and the lakes, then joining up at Burdur with the return route already described from Antalya, via Pamukkale and Aphrodisias.

Barbarossa takes a dip

The road leads north from Silifke, following the gorge of the Göksu river up into the Taurus mountains. You will see here some of the most spectacularly beautiful mountain scenery in Turkey. About 7 km out of Silifke you will notice a parking area on the right of the road from where there is a magnificent view of the **Göksu gorge**. A nearby plaque commemorates the drowning of the German Emperor Frederick Barbarossa in the river below here in 1190, on his way to Palestine, thereby washing out the Third Crusade.

Mut is the first sizable town, down in a valley surrounded by mountains. A brief stop can be made here to see the sturdy 14th C Turkish fortress built on the edge of the town. More interesting, however, is the striking contrast in atmosphere between this mountain town and the towns of the coast. The feel is wild and remote in a way that the southern coastline has not been since Lycia and Termessos. The local children are particularly charming.

Mountain Monastery

At 20 km beyond Mut, just opposite a little café, a sign points off right to **Alahan**, a further 2 km up a reasonable dirt track. This is a detour not to be missed, as Alahan is the remote site of a ruined Byzantine monastery complex, the like of which is rarely to be seen. The setting is magnificent, on a terrace overlooking the lovely Göksu gorge and wild mountains all around. The only other form of life you may encounter here is goats, or sometimes a site guardian.

Christian victory over pagan gods

You arrive first at the great **western basilica**, built at the end of the 5th C, with elaborate relief sculptures on its beautiful doorway of the four Evangelists. On the insides of the pillars of the main door are reliefs of the archangels Gabriel and Michael, trampling underfoot figures which represent Cybele (the Anatolian mother goddess), a bull and a priest of Isis, representing the triumph of early Christianity over paganism. From here you pass the stark **baptistry** to the **eastern church**, built some 50 years later in the early 6th C, with a simple but beautiful facade, remarkably well-preserved. Inside, the arches and slender columns give a marvellous impression of grace. The buildings backing into the cliff, some of them cut into the rock, are the refectory, kitchen, bakery and guest rows. Many carvings of animals and abstract motifs are to be seen in the complex on blocks of the softly coloured stone.

At the entrance to the complex you will notice a series of caves cut into the cliff. These were **cells** for the early monks, with little nooks carved out for cupboards.

Onto the Plateau

After Alahan the road crosses a pass, then descends onto a barren plain, your first glimpse of the central Anatolian plateau, a bleak and pitiless landscape. Most of this plateau lies at 1000 metres above sea level.

Pitiless landscape

You now reach Karaman, a surprisingly green oasis in the barren colourlessness of the plateau. If you feel you have time, you could detour to the town centre and drive past the Seljuk citadel near which is the **Ak Tekke** (1371), a former monastery of Mevlevi dervishes, and the **Yunus Emre Mosque** (1349). The Karaman region was for a long time inhabited by Turkish-speaking Orthodox Greeks who wrote Turkish in Greek script. The town is now somewhat unappealing and there is a dearth of places to stay and eat. Konya lies about 1½ hours' drive further on across the plateau, and on the way there are two excursions you can make if you have the time and inclination.

The first excursion is some 40 km north of Karaman, to a region called Binbir Kilise, a **Thousand and One Churches**, an important monastic centre from the 9th to 11th C. The route is fine until the nearest village of Maden Şehir, then rough dirt track for the last 8 km leads to the most impressive group of ruined churches and monasteries near the hamlet of Değler. Sir William Ramsey and Gertrude Bell made a study of these Byzantine buildings in 1905.

The world's first city?

The other detour is about an hour's drive north from Karaman where a road forks off right 26 km to **Çatal Hüyük**, the most ancient and important Neolithic and Bronze Age site in Turkey, and thought to be the oldest known city in the world. Discovered in 1958 by James Mellaart, the finds date back as early as 6800 BC and reveal a remarkably advanced Anatolian culture with sophisticated tools, jewellery, sculpture and above all extraordinary wall paintings which decorated their shrines. Despite the importance of the site it is, like most Neolithic and Bronze Age sites, uninspiring to look at today, not least because all the finds have been removed to the Ankara Museum of Anatolian Cultures.

Konya

If you have been driving along the coast, turning inland at Silifke, then **Konya** will be the first proper city you have visited since Antalya. It is something of a shock to see traffic lights and roundabouts and the hubbub of people. The best thing to do is to find a central hotel or pension where you can leave the car, and then explore the city on foot. Fortunately, the major sights are concentrated within a square kilometre of the city centre, the main square, Hükumet Maydaní. It takes

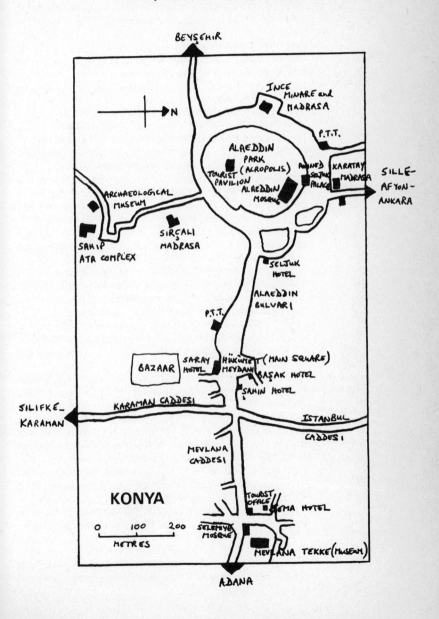

273

the best part of a day to see them, so that two nights here is generally the minimum. Avoid Mondays as the major monuments close on that day. The prices of accommodation in a city always seem outrageous after those of the more rural areas, so be prepared.

Konya is Turkey's most religious city, and so in Ramadan it is one of the few places where restaurants and cafés close during the day, which can make life difficult when you have been walking in the heat and are desperate for a cold beer. Konya is also the centre of Turkey's carpet trade: you will not have to go in search of them, however, but will doubtless be invited to view.

Holy Seljuk City

According to Phrygian tradition, Konya was the first city to emerge after the Flood: at any rate there were prehistoric, Hittite and later Roman settlements here, though none of this remains today. Rather it is the Seljuk monuments of the 13th C that have earnt Konya its fame. It owed its importance throughout its history to its location on the junction of major trade and communication routes. The Romans built ancient roads which were followed by the Seljuks and then by the Ottomans, and today's main roads follow the same course, as can be seen from the number of Seljuk caravanserais still standing at the sides of the roads.

Mevlana and the Whirling Dervishes

The most famous and striking monument in Konya is the conical, turquoise-tiled fluted dome of the **Mevlana Tekke**, where Celaleddin Rumi, known as Mevlana, is buried (died 1273). Mevlana, a Sufi and the founder of the Whirling Dervishes, was also a poet and philosopher, believing in ecstatic universal love, a state which he induced by the practice of whirling round and round. This ritual can now be seen only once a year in December during the Mevlana Festival. A sacred Islamic shrine and object of pilgrimage from all over Turkey, it is this tekke (monastery) which gives Konya its special status as a religious city. The tekke was the centre of mystic Sufi culture for more than six centuries till the dervish sects were banned and dissolved by Atatürk in 1925. The following year it was opened as a museum, for it is crammed full of precious works of art and opulent furnishings, even housing what purports to be a remnant of the Prophet Mohammed's beard.

Next to the Mevlana Tekke is the huge **Selimiye Mosque**, severe in its early Ottoman style.

The other monuments of Konya are mainly grouped around the Alaeddin Park, the former acropolis of Roman Iconium. The most major is the **Alaeddin Mosque**, the largest Seljuk mosque in Konya. It took 70 years to build; the sequence of construction is uncertain and the plan is irregular. Eight Seljuk sultans are buried here. Opposite is the **Karatay**

The Mevlana Tekke in Konya

Madrasa, a theological college built in 1251, whose elaborately carved entrance *portal* is considered to be one of the best examples of Seljuk stonework. Recently refurbished, it is now a museum of Turkish tiles from the Seljuk and Ottoman periods.

On the far side of the Alaeddin Park are the **Ince Minare** (Slender Minaret) **and Madrasa** with an elaborate, almost Baroque Seljuk portal, and the **Sírçalí** (Glazed) **Madrasa**, now partially ruined. If you have the time you can also visit the **Sahip Ata** complex of Seljuk mosque, türbe and oratory, and the **Archaeological Museum**, where the only evidence of Konya's pre-Seljuk history is to be found. The most notable exhibit is a Roman sarcophagus with a bas relief showing the 12 Labours of Hercules.

Escape

Northwest of Konya is the little village of **Sille** (8 km), in a valley with an interesting series of **hermit caves** in the cliffs and some **Byzantine church ruins**. It is a pleasant place to escape from the bustle of the city. The Turkish military is in evidence here, but tends to keep itself to itself.

The Lakes

Leaving Konya and driving west towards Burdur and Isparta, you first cross the bleak Anatolian plateau on good fast road with very little sign of life, till you reach **Beyşehir** on the first of the Pisidian lakes. Here you can stop to visit the mosque and türbe built in 1298 on the lakeside. The town was founded by Alaeddin in 1230 on the caravan route linking his capital Konya with Antalya and Alanya, his winter quarters.

Most beautiful lake

You now drive on to **Eǧridir**, the most beautiful of the Pisidian lakes, whose trees and vegetation are a welcome change from the bleak plateau, and where you can spend a very peaceful couple of days to recoup from the bustle of Konya. As the altitude is 1000 metres the lake water is cold except in the height of summer, but its clarity and blueness is so inviting that the desire to immerse yourself in it is likely to overcome any hesitation. The mountain setting is exquisite, and the little town of Eǧridir itself offers reasonable accommodation and restaurants, with a lake speciality being baby crayfish.

The **town** is situated on a little promontory forming a peninsula on the lake. The remains of a **Seljuk castle** with a minaret on this promontory enclose an extraordinary series of **old Turkish houses** perched in precarious positions on the edge. A pebble-built causeway now links this promontory with two little islands. Apart from being a pleasant stroll, it is interesting in particular to see the Turkish houses, mixed in with **old Greek houses**, most of which are now derelict. A Greek basilica on the far island with its roof still intact testifies to the size of the Greek community which lived here till the exchange of populations in 1923.

At **Barla** on the lake shore to the north, the mosque has an attractive tiled minaret, and the drive there takes you past some of the best swimming areas of the shore. One particularly impressive lakeshore complex just on the outskirts of Eğridir on the Barla road is in fact the officers' mess of the local army camp. The military base here in no way intrudes on the peacefulness of the spot, but in some ways just adds to the interest.

From Eğridir the road continues on to Isparta and Burdur, where it links up with the return route to İzmir from Antalya via Pamukkale and Aphrodisias, described earlier.

PRACTICAL INFORMATION

ALANYA
Two hours' drive from Antalya **airport**.

Two good public **beaches** either side of the rock.

Alantur (3-star), open April through October, 100 rooms, 6 km beyond town towards Adana. Private beach and pool.

Hotal Alara (3-star), 100 rooms, 24 km before Alanya. Excellent setting and well furnished rooms. Extensive gardens. Seawater pool. Watersports.

Aspendos (2-star), open April through October, 84 rooms, 23 km on Antalya side, before Alanya. Private beach, pool.

Banana (2-star), 116 rooms, 2 km towards Adana. Popular with English. Pool and beach.

Motel Incekum (2-star), open April through November, 53 rooms, 25 km before Alanya on Antalya side. Beach.

Selam (2-star), open April through November, 20 rooms, beach.

Motel Merhaba (2-star), open April through October, 62 rooms, 1 km towards Adana. Seawater pool, beach.

Yalıhan Motel (2-star), open April through November, 48 rooms, 25 km before Alanya on Antalya side. Beach.

Hotel Gunes (1-star). Small hotel right on beach under a kilometre from Alanya town centre. Beach terrace.

Hotel Bayirli (1-star). Newly built, in quiet position overlooking Alanya harbour. Roof terrace restaurant.

Kaptan (1-star), in town, 45 rooms, pool, roof restaurant, short walk to beach.

A selection of fish **restaurants** along the front, but most people eat in hotels on a half-board arrangement.

ANAMUR
Karan Motel (1-star), 16 rooms, near the castle, on the beach. This is the only motel here.

SILIFKE
There is no **accommodation** in Silifke itself, but there are hotels on the beach east and west of the town.

Motel Lades (2-star), open April through November, 20 rooms, in Taşucu, 8 km west of town. Well-maintained and situated on the sea. Pool.

Motel Boğsak (1-star), open April through October, 27 rooms, 18 km west of Silifke, Modern and comfortable on good beach.

Aile Motel, 60 rooms. On beach at Korigos near Kíz Kalesi, east of Silifke.

Mocamp, near Kíz Kalesi, a few simple chalets for non-campers available. Communal facilities shared with campers. Rocky beach.

Car ferry boats from Taşucu (west of Silifke) to Kyrenia in Turkish Cyprus on Tuesdays, Thursdays and Saturdays (return journey on Mondays, Wednesdays and Fridays). Hydrofoil service also available.

Restaurants are grouped up on the citadel under the castle, with a good panorama.

Music and folklore festival, 20–26 May.

KONYA

All hotels are fairly old-fashioned, and all are 1-star.

Sema, 48 rooms, traditional hotel off a side street near the Mevlana Tekke. There is a Turkish bath a few yards away in the same street.

Başak, 40 rooms, off main square, Hükumet Maydaní.

Şahin, 45 rooms, off main square.

Saray, 54 rooms, off main square.

Seljuk, 52 rooms, towards the Alaeddin Park, the only more modern hotel in Konya.

Whirling Dervish Festival, 9–17 December, to commemorate the death of Mevlana, the Islamic mystic poet and philosopher. This internationally famous festival consists of dancing dervishes in costume in the Sema ceremony, accompanied by mystical music played on the *ney* (a kind of reed flute).

Konya Cookery Competition, 24 September. Open to everyone, with several categories for main courses, desserts, etc.

EĞRIDIR

Çinar Pansiyon, 19 rooms, overlooking the lake.

Eğridir Hotel, balconies overlooking the lake where breakfast can be taken, 20 rooms.

Restaurants on the lakeshore, where the speciality is baby crayfish.

ISPARTA

Pansiyon Bayram, 16 rooms, in town.

MERSIN TO ANTAKYA (THE CILICIAN PLAIN, CAPPADOCIA AND THE HATAY)

ACROSS THE CILICIAN PLAIN

Once east of Pompeopolis, you have left behind the rocky coastline and mountains of Rugged Cilicia and have entered the flat and fertile plain of Cilicia. This plain in some ways resembles the Pamphylian plain, but is larger and far less attractive. The magnificent ruins of Perge, Aspendos and Side on the Pamphylian coast have no equivalent here, as most of the plain is now covered in rice fields and cotton plantations, with all signs of antiquity long since buried. Its climate is hotter in summer than Pamphylia, and can be unpleasantly so, while it is colder in winter. The scenery is monotonous, as the area from Mersin to Adana is a huge alluvium created by three large rivers. It was settled however far earlier than the Pamphylian plain, chiefly because it lay on the main route between the Middle East and the Anatolian plateau.

After the Arab invasions the population decreased markedly and the plain became a winter home for the Turcoman nomad tribes who spent the summer on the Anatolian plateau. Hence in the 7th and 8th C AD it was largely devoid of permanent settlers, and there was still buffalo hunting in the marshes of the delta. The cultivation of cotton dates back to the 1840s when both the crop and the peasants to grow it imported from Egypt. It is now Turkey's chief export earner.

Among the Oldest of Cities

Mersin, the first city we come to on the plain, is the largest port on the southern coast of Turkey. Its history stretches back to the Hittite Empire, but in the modern city of today nothing remains of interest to warrant a detour and you might as well use the Mersin bypass to continue on to Tarsus.

The original town was built on a mound about 2 km inland where excavations have revealed Neolithic dwellings and evidence of Hittite settlements, demonstrating that Mersin is one of the oldest continuously inhabited places in the world.

Mystery of the Hittites

Three thousand five hundred years ago the Hittites rivalled the Egyptians as the greatest power on earth. Yet until a century ago the Hittites were a mystery race, our only documentary evidence of their existence being in the Old Testament: King David married Bathsheba, widow of Uriah the Hittite. When Egyptian hieroglyphs were deciphered in the early 19th C an inscription on the wall of the Karnak temple at Luxor was found to set out the terms of a mutual defence treaty between Ramses II and the king of the Hittites, Hattusilis. Ramses II later married the Hittite king's daughter to cement the treaty. No further clues were found in the

Hittite warriors cut in relief from their mountain rock

mystery of the lost Hittite Empire until a Frenchman, Charles Texier, discovered in 1834 at Boğazkale in central Anatolia the ruins of extraordinary and puzzling rock palaces and monumental rock sculptures which he was unable to identify. Later excavations in 1906 under a German revealed thousands of cuniform tablets; when finally deciphered in the 1940s they revealed the full history of the Hittite Kingdom which ruled Anatolia from the 19th to the 13th C BC

Mountain Culture Their most memorable relics are the simple but powerful sculptures cut into the rock, often depicting their ceremonies and their weather god whose sacred animal was the bull. The figures are broad, squat and heavy, with none of the grace and subtlety associated with Egyptian or Babylonian art. They represent a tough mountain people, accustomed to a harsh climate and conditions, constantly prepared for war and attack, contrasting strongly with the valley cultures of Mesopotamia and Egypt where man had lived and peacefully pastured his flocks on the sides of great rivers, with no need for defence fortifications. The Hittites were the only prehistoric civilisation to exist and develop in inhospitable mountainous country.

There is an important Hittite site at **Karatepe**, about 1½ hours' drive northeast from Adana, where a lot of the reliefs are still *in situ*. Otherwise, there is nothing to see of the Hittite past within reach of the coast, and at Mersin only the slightest traces of its Hittite connection.

Romance at Tarsus

Half an hour's flat uneventful drive brings you to **Tarsus**, famous as the birthplace of Paul (Saul) and for the meeting between Antony and Cleopatra so vividly described by Plutarch and Shakespeare. Tarsus' history stretches back as far as Mersin's, but again very little of its past is in evidence today. Despite this, the town, built on a mound with old houses and gardens of great charm, has the feel of an ancient and historic place. The river Tarsus, the ancient Cydnus, is particularly cold and turbulent, and even Alexander the Great, bathing in the Cydnus in 333 BC, caught a severe chill. In Hellenistic times, Tarsus became a great and prosperous city, rivalling Pergamum and Alexandria both commercially and culturally.

Cleopatra conquers Antony It was to Tarsus in 41 BC that Antony summoned Cleopatra from Egypt to discuss his strategy for the East and, as he discovered, to embark upon one of the great love affairs of history. Plutarch sets the scene: 'She came sailing up the Cydnus on a galley whose stern was golden; the sails were purple, and the oars were silver. These, in their motion, kept tune to the music of flutes and pipes and harps. The Queen, in the dress and character of Aphrodite, lay on a couch of gold brocade, as though in a picture, while about her were pretty boys, bedight like cupids, who fanned her, and maidens habited as nereids and graces, and some made as though they were rowing, while others busied themselves about with the sails. All manner of sweet perfumes were wafted ashore from the ship, and on the shore thousands were gathered to behold her'.

Cleopatra was able to sail right up to the city of Tarsus as there was a large lake between it and the sea that has since silted up. Nor have the sweet perfumes of history lingered: today there is only an old **Roman gate** at the entrance to the town from Mersin, variously called St Paul's Gate, Cleopatra's Gate or the Gate of the Bitch.

Agricultural Heartland

If you are continuing on into Syria, rather than turning up north from Tarsus into Cappadocia, a short drive east from Tarsus brings you to **Adana**, Turkey's fourth largest city, set in the heart of the Cilician Plain on the banks of the Seyhan river. As the centre of a rich agricultural region and of the prosperous cotton industry, its population is increasing rapidly.

Roman bridge Its history reaches back to the first millenium BC, but as with Mersin and Tarsus, very little remains today. The only ancient monument of note is the fine long **bridge**, Taş Köprü (Stone Bridge), across the river. It was built by Hadrian and restored by Justinian, then repaired on several occasions under the Ottomans: of its original 21 arches, 14 have survived. The only Turkish building of note in Adana is the **Ulu Cami** (Great Mosque) built in 1507 by Halil Bey, Emir of the Ramazanoğlu Turks who ruled Cilicia before the Ottoman conquest in 1516. It is built of black and white marble and the tiles in the mosque and in Halil Bey's türbe (mausoleum) are among the finest in Turkey. The **covered bazaars** are also worth a visit. The city has an interesting small **museum**, housing many of the ancient Hittite finds from the region, and a good ethnographic section showing the homes and costumes of the Turcoman nomads who came to the plain in the winter.

Inland from Adana is the **Ceyhan Dam and lake**, a popular spot for boating and picnics, and towards the sea about 30 minutes' drive away at **Karataş** is the nearest beach.

About 20 minutes' drive east from Adana, a short turn-off from the main road leads you to Misis, identified as the ancient **Mopsuestia**, after its founder Mopsus, one of the three legendary leaders of the Greek migration of 'mixed multitudes' into Cilicia after the fall of Troy. The main point of this short detour is to see the beautiful Roman **mosaics**, notably that of Noah's Ark and the animals. The other ruins include the Temple of Apollo and a baths and a 4th C bridge built by Justinian.

Continuing eastwards, the remains of a 13thC fortress, Yílanlikale (**Castle of the Snakes**) stand on a rocky mountain overlooking the Ceyhan river, its eight towers dominating the plain. It is thought to have been built by an Armenian king known as the King of the Snakes. A detour can be made to the ruins of **Anazarbus** 30 km north of Ceyhan, a Roman-Byzantine city. It is a lovely spot, right on the edge of the Cilician Plain at the foot of a mountain near the village of Anavarza. The principal ruins include a stadium, tombs, an aqueduct, a theatre and several basilicas. A visit to Anazarbus can also be combined with a trip to **Karatepe** (see above, under Mersin), lying 77 km from Ceyhan, one of the major Hittite sites.

INLAND TO CAPPADOCIA

Shortly after Tarsus, the main Ankara road leads north up through the Cilician Gates, the mountain pass of Gulek. The drive is spectacular and leads to the remarkable region known as Cappadocia.

Eroded volcanic landscape

As a result of pre-historic volcanic eruptions here, the countryside was covered in a thick layer of volcanic ash which eventually became a soft porous rock, 'tufa'. Over thousands of centuries the soft tufa was eroded by wind and water into valleys and gorges of weird rock formations. The softness of the rock suited it ideally to carving out cave dwellings, and when hostile invaders crossed Cappadocia the Cappadocians used the environment to their advantage and literally went underground, carving out multi-storey cities and venturing out only for essentials and to tend their fields.

When Christianity arrived in Cappadocia the landscape again came into its own for Christians seeking refuge from persecution. Large communities settled here, retreating into their caves and underground cities when the Arab armies poured through in the 7th C. Today tourists too pour through in their thousands to marvel at the landscape and at the rock churches built by the Cappadocian Christians, for by mediaeval times Cappadocia had become one of the most important monastic centres of the Byzantine Empire.

Byzantine cave frescoes

This weird landscape, fashioned by nature and embroidered by man, is unlike anything else in the world. Rock cones, many standing 50 metres or more high have been carved out to make houses, churches and monasteries. Many of the rock-cut monasteries have 9th to 12th C frescoes, provincial and crude compared to the imperial art of Constantinople, but also free of classical restraint, aiming directly at the emotions and achieving sometimes a great and moving beauty. Look for these in the triangle between **Ürgüp, Göreme** and **Avanos**, but most of all at Göreme, for here are the greatest number of accessible rock churches.

Though barren at first sight, the volcanic tufa is in fact extremely fertile. Far from the usual harsh blacks and greys of volcanic landscapes, the rocks here are soft shades of light grey, yellow, mauve, pink and umber. Vineyards are common; Cappadocia is famous for its distinctive wines, and a wine festival is celebrated each harvest time in Nevşehir from 21 to 25 September. Unfortunately the food available in restaurants in Cappadocia is frequently disappointing.

Exploring the Underground World of Cappadocian Christianity

Ürgüp is the best base, 10 minutes' drive from the Göreme

valley, a small town far more attractive than Nevşehir, the modern provincial capital. The region's Tourist Information Office is in Ürgüp where you can pick up a map. Two days in Cappadocia is the minimum for a proper tour: the first day, a circuit of Ortahisar, Göreme and Üçhisar in the morning, returning to Ürgüp or Zilve for lunch, and in the afternoon a circuit of Avanos, Zilve and Çavuş In; the second day you can make an excursion to the valley of Soğanlí, returning to Ürgüp for lunch, and in the afternoon, pay a visit to the underground cities of Kaymaklí and Derinkuyu, returning to Ürgüp via Avanos and the valley of the rose-coloured fairy chimneys (Peribacalari Vadisi). There are also a number of fine Seljuk caravanserais which you will pass at the side of the road, notably the lovely Sarí Han, the Yellow Han.

The **Göreme valley** is rightly the most famous of all the Cappadocian valleys. Now designated a National Park, it is protected from development and UNESCO also has an active preservation campaign here. Hours of fun can be spent following the paths in the valley, climbing narrow rock stairways and clambering through tunnels to reach the carved-out churches, hermit refuges and monasteries

In the cluster below the car park are about 20 churches, the most notable of which are the **Church of St Barbara**, the **Church of the Apple**, the **Church of the Sandal** and the **Dark Church**, all with 11th C frescoes. Beyond the car park is the **New Church of Tokalí**, decorated with some of the finest 10th C frescoes.

Üçhisar and **Ortahisar** are both picturesque Cappadocian villages, perched on large rocky outcrops pitted and honeycombed with endless cave dwellings. South of Ortahisar are several rock churches with 10th and 11th C frescoes.

Avanos is a town on the banks of the Red River, famous for its red clay used from antiquity to the present day for pottery which is exported throughout the eastern Mediterranean. Alabaster is the other product, and workshops in the town abound with pottery and alabaster souvenirs.

Rare Pre-Iconoclastic paintings

Zilve has one of the most spectacular landscapes in Cappadocia, almost more fantastical than Göreme, but on a smaller scale. The troglodyte village of Zilve was abandoned a few years ago because of the danger of rock falls, but you can still see here the **rock-carved mosque**, the only Moslem sanctuary in Cappadocia. In the cliff face is a cluster of ten or so churches from the 9th and 10th C and also three earlier chapels with Pre-Iconoclastic paintings. There is a small restaurant here suitable for lunch.

Çavuş In is another troglodyte village built into a cliff face, on top of which stands the impressive **Church of John the Baptist**, a three-aisled basilica dating from the 5th C, and hence the earliest known church in Cappadocia. Five hundred metres north of the village is the Pigeon House or **Çavuş In church**, dating from the 10th C. A constant battle is waged between the tourist authorities and the local farmers, who like to block up the cave entrances and use the churches as pigeon cotes. The pigeons are highly prized for their droppings which are used as fertiliser, perhaps accounting for the local wine's distinctive taste and aroma.

In the **Soğanlí valley** there are more than 30 rock churches and monasteries decorated with frescoes from the 9th to the 13th C.

Kaymaklí and **Derinkuyu** are just two of the 20 or so underground cities in the region, but are the only ones prepared and open to the public. Built on eight to ten storeys, the upper levels were living areas while the lower levels were storerooms and places of refuge. They are probably pre-Christian in date, and were used as a place of retreat as recently as 1839 to hide from the invading Egyptian army under Ibrahim Pasha.

Monasticism flourished in Cappadocia for over 1000 years, reaching its peak in the 11th and 12th C. During this period wealthy Byzantine officials commissioned some of the best artists of the day to decorate a large number of Cappadocian churches and monasteries. The flowering of Byzantine art here was brought to an abrupt end by the Mongol invasions

Homes, chapels and monasteries are carved out of the weird rock formations of Cappadocia

and the subsequent takeover of Cappadocia by the Seljuk Turks. Many of the churches continued to be used however till as late as 1923 when the Greek Christians were forced out after the Turkish revolution.

The western world was largely ignorant of the existence of the rock churches of Cappadocia till a French priest visited the region in 1907 and decided to devote the rest of his life to their study, finally publishing his vast research in the 1930s and 1940s. Since then their fame has spread rapidly and Cappadocia is now one of the most visited and most photographed regions of Turkey.

THE HATAY

At the point where the road turns south towards İskenderun, you leave the Cilician Plain behind and enter the region called the Hatay or the Sanjak of Alexandretta. This is a region with a very mixed population, as one might expect from its geographical location, with large communities of Arabs, Moslems and Christians mixed in together. With the collapse of the Ottoman Empire after the First World War it was incorporated into Syria under the French Mandate, but the French gave it to Turkey in 1939 to buy Turkish support in anticipation of a new war against Germany. The Syrians have never accepted the transfer. Pleasantly hilly, it is a welcome contrast with the flat plain of Cilicia.

Towards İskenderun

On turning south towards İskenderun, you come first to the **plain of Issus**, the scene of Alexander the Great's famous

The battle of Issus

defeat of the Persians under Darius III in 333 BC, after which he was able to penetrate southwards to Syria. An impressive **Crusader castle** at **Toprakkale** marks the entrance to the plain. A little further on, at the sign to Yeşilkent, are the remains of a fine **Roman aqueduct** beside the road. Dörytol, near the coast, is the terminal of the oil pipeline from the Kirkuk oilfields in Iraq.

About 20 km before İskenderun is a short turning off to **Yakacík**, the former Payas, where you will see a huge 16thC Ottoman **caravanserai**, including a mosque, a madrasa (Koranic school), a baths and a covered bazaar with spacious courtyards, leading to a bridge over a moat to a fortress on the sea, known as the Tower of the Jinns. The complex was built at the order of Selim II with the advice of the great architect Sinan, famous for his many mosques, including the Süleymaniye, in İstanbul.

You now reach **İskenderun**, the former Alexandretta, founded by Alexander the Great after his defeat of the Persians. It is a busy port and commercial centre, and is a pleasant town with good hotels and restaurants along the front. In atmosphere it is an attractive combination of Mediterranean, Anatolian and Syrian. Nothing remains to be seen of its past monuments.

Antioch: Turkish Antakya

Leaving İskenderun for Antakya, the road heads inland winding its way up steeply through the mountains to the Belen pass. Sometimes regarded as the Gates to Syria, **Belen** is an attractive place, becoming increasingly popular as a summer resort and famous for its spa waters which are meant

289

to aid stomach and digestive problems. The views from the top and during the descent are spectacular over the Orontes valley and Lake Amik, an artificial lake created by blocking the Orontes river lower down. On the descent, a short detour of 4 km can be made to see the **castle at Bagras**, one of the main strongholds of the Mamluks in the defence of northern Syria. Set up on a peak, it was built by Byzantines and Mamluks rather than Crusaders, who captured it in 1097 during their siege of Antioch. It was abandoned after the Ottoman conquest in the 16th C.

Licentious Antioch   You now reach **Antakya**, pleasantly situated on the Orontes river, the site of ancient Antioch, the prosperous and ostentatious capital of the Seleucids. The town today is only a shadow of its former self, but is still very picturesque with its narrow lanes leading down to the Orontes and its segregated districts where the various religious communities held themselves apart in Ottoman times. The outline of the ancient **city walls**, 30 km long in total, give an indication of the extent of the city in its heyday. In Roman times the city was a great centre for cultural, artistic and commercial activities, becoming notorious for its depravity and love of life's pleasures. As such, it was chosen by Peter for his first mission to the gentiles, and here his converts were the first to be called Christians. St Barnabus and St Paul later stayed here, and from the end of the 11th C it was held for 171 years as a Frankish principality by the Crusaders.

Remnants of Antioch's colourful history are few, amounting to the old **Roman bridge**, a picturesque **bazaar** quarter and the **Mosque of Habib Haccar**, originally a church. A little outside the town on the Aleppo road is the **Grotto of St Peter**, where Peter preached for the first time and founded the first Christian community. It had a secret tunnel which enabled the Christians who met there to escape in the event of a surprise raid. The church was erected here in the 13th C by the Crusaders, and has a fine situation under a cliff overlooking Antakya with a gorge to the south.

Splendid mosaics   The main reason, however, for a visit to modern Antakya is to see the **Hatay Museum** (8.30am to 12, 1.30 to 5pm, except Mondays), the main exhibits of which are the finest collection of Roman mosaics in the world, all discovered in the region of Antakya. These mosaics formed the floors of private houses in Roman Antioch, and in nearby Daphne, the finest ones dating from the 2nd and 3rd C AD.

Marriage of Antony and Cleopatra   South of Antakya, 7 km, an excursion can be made to the crumbling **fortress** of Antioch, more for the magnificent view from the top than to see the building itself. Also south of Antakya lies Harbiye, the ancient **Daphne**, city of pleasures. Apollo's pursuit of the nymph Daphne is reputed to have taken place here and the laurel (*daphne* in Greek) into which she was turned still grows all around. A sanctuary of Apollo

Antioch during Ottoman times, showing the Byzantine walls

was established here which became celebrated throughout the ancient world. It was in Daphne that Mark Antony married Cleopatra in 40 BC, and that the Olympic Games of Antioch, successor to the games of ancient Olympia, were held. Nothing remains of the buildings, but the gardens with their cypress and laurel trees and little waterfalls produced by the abundant springs are the favourite picnic and strolling place of the residents of modern Antakya.

If you continue on to the coast south of Antakya, a 30-minute drive brings you to the beautiful beach of Samandağ, near which are the ruins of **Seleucia ad Pieria**, the ancient port of Antioch and once one of the greatest ports on the Mediterranean. Little remains now except some ruined walls and gates, with some fine underground water tunnels and canals.

Crossing to Syria

Returning to Antakya and forking east, the Syrian border post is reached after about 50 km, from where it is a further 50 km to **Aleppo** (Haleb).

PRACTICAL INFORMATION

MERSIN

Mersin (2-star), 120 rooms, in town.
Neptun (1-star), on beach 10 km west of
Mersin. Good restaurant.
Toros (1-star), 62 rooms, in town but
overlooking the sea. Pool. No restaurant.

From Mersin port, **car ferries** run to
Famagusta in Turkish Cyprus on Mondays,
Wednesdays and Fridays in summer.

ÜRGÜP

Büyük Otel (2-star), 49 rooms.
Tusan Kízíl-Irmak (2-star), at Avanos,
13 km from Ürgüp. Open March through
November, pool.
Tepe (1-star), 36 rooms, pool.
Çimenlitepe Motel, open April through
October, 6 rooms.
Turist Pensiyon, 7 modest rooms.

ÜÇHISAR

Kaya (2-star), run by the Club Mediterranée, 35 rooms cut into the rock. Pool.

ORTAHISAR

Motel Paris (1-star), 24 rooms. Pool.

NEVŞEHIR

Göreme (3-star), open March through
November, 72 rooms, 11 storeys high on
the main street.
Orsan Cappadocia (3-star), 80 rooms, pool.
Viva (1-star), 24 rooms with bath, near the
Orsan.

Several **camping sites**, including a BP
Mocamp (no chalets) between Nevşehir
and Göreme.

Cappadocia Festival, late September.
Held at the same time as the grape harvest,
it amounts largely to wine tasting. Cappadocian wine is justly renowned.

ADANA

Büyük Sürmeli (4-star), 80 rooms, luxury
class.
Ener Motel (2-star), 16 rooms, on the road
2 km east of Adana. Pool.
Ağba (1-star), 76 rooms.
Ipek Palas (1-star), 84 rooms.

Open air **restaurants** in Atatürk Caddesi.

İSKENDERUN

Güney Palas (2-star), 27 rooms, old-
fashioned but very clean and well-run.
Good restaurant.
Hitit (1-star), 40 rooms
Kavakli (1-star), 17 rooms.
Arsuz Hotel (1-star), 45 rooms, open April
through November, on the beach at
Uluçínar, south of İskenderun. Very simple
but clean.

Plaj **restaurant**, on the beach. Specialities
are fresh fish and giant prawns.

ANTAKYA

Atahan (1-star), 28 rooms.
Divan (1-star), 22 rooms.

Restaurants: Atahan and Zumrut, with
Arab specialities, notably meze (varied hors
d'oevres) and hummas (chich-pea dip).

INDEX

(P indicates an entry in the Practical Information section.)

Maps and Plans